Taking It
Personally

In the series
Teaching/Learning Social Justice
edited by Lee Anne Bell

Taking It Personally

Racism in the Classroom from
Kindergarten to College

Ann Berlak and Sekani Moyenda

Temple University Press   *Philadelphia*

Temple University Press, Philadelphia 19122
Copyright © 2001 by Temple University
All rights reserved
Published 2001
Printed in the United States of America

Library of Congress Cataloguing-in-Publication Data

Berlak, Ann.
    Taking it personally : racism in the classroom from kindergarten to college / Ann
Berlak and Sekani Moyenda.
        p. cm. — (Teaching/learning social justice)
    Includes bibliographical references (p.) and index.
    ISBN 1-56639-875-4 (cloth : alk. paper) — ISBN 1-56639-876-2 (pbk. : alk. paper)
    1. Discrimination in education—United States.   2. Racism—Study and
teaching—United States.   I. Moyenda, Sekani, 1960-   II. Title.   III. Series.

    LC212.2.B47 2001
    306.43—dc21
                                                                    00-053213

Quid Pro Quo or Since You Never Scratched My Back (p. 171), words and music
by Wilcia Smith Moore. © 1994 by Wilcia Smith Moore. Reprinted by kind
permission of Wilcia Smith Moore and Blue Wayne Publishing, P.O. Box 2121,
Berkeley, CA 94702, (510) 237-5895.

Ann:

To Eamonn, Lev, Mariam, and Rachel,
my links to the future.

To Sekani, who helped me learn to see

Sekani:

To the most powerful force and influence in my life—
Mom, Wilcia Moore—who taught me to fight for what
is right, despite the consequences.

To Ann Berlak, who at first I thought was simply
indulging one of her students. Instead she turned out
to be a peer who actually thought I had something
important to share with others.

Contents

Series Foreword   ix

Acknowledgments   xi

Introduction   1

Part 1. Our Racial Autobiographies

1 Sekani:
How I Got My "Black Attitude" Problem   17

2 Ann:
How I Developed an "Obduracy of Tone"   34

Part 2. All Right, Who Started It?

The Classroom Encounter and Its Aftermath

3 Sekani: The Bootcamp Presentation:
Classrooms in Crisis   51

4 Ann: Picking Up the Pieces:
Processing Is Everything   65

Part 3. What's Going on Here?

Analysis

5 Ann:
What Makes You Think She's Not an Expert?   89

6 Ann:
Fantasy and Feeling in the Classroom   106

7 Sekani:
The Love Letter   131

Contents

8   Conclusion   156

    Notes   173
    Bibliography   191
    Index   201

Series Foreword

Thirty-five years after the Civil Rights movement, racism remains among the most pressing social issues of our time. Despite busing, desegregation plans, affirmative action, and other remedies, our schools and neighborhoods largely remain racially segregated, poverty endures especially for women and children and disproportionately for people of color, and public education is under attack from proponents of vouchers for private schools and other privatization plans. Today we face a situation wherein the majority of teachers are white and middle class, while an increasing majority of students are from other racial groups and the poor. Multicultural education, which arose from the Civil Rights movement and envisioned an integrated and diverse public school system providing the basis for a racial democracy, is often co-opted and softened to avoid challenging the sensibilities of a white population weary of discussing racism. It is easy to feel discouraged. This book helps us think carefully about the depth and resiliency of racism and reexamines what is needed for a powerful antiracist approach to teaching about this most urgent social problem.

Taking It Personally is about the struggles and promises of antiracist teaching as told through one explosive classroom incident and its aftermath. The incident, a role-playing activity in a required multicultural education course for pre-service teachers, opened up and brought to the fore deeply held beliefs and prejudices not previously voiced by students in this classroom. The in-depth description of this incident brings to life the currents that are always at play when racism is the topic. The authors, a white Jewish woman and an African American woman, explore these currents through their own autobiographical writings, reflective discussions about the incident, and student reactions, journals, and essays. This well-conceptualized and beautifully written exploration takes us deep into the dynamics of racism in the classroom.

Most, if not all, who teach about racism have had such explosive moments in their classrooms. Usually, this is not what we choose to write about, focusing instead on classes that go well, that confirm our skills and abilities and demonstrate effective antiracist pedagogy. This book illustrates how much more instructive it can be to focus on what doesn't work out as planned. The authors, skilled and experienced antiracist educators, dare to expose the problematic, messy, and unresolved aspects of antiracist teaching. What a gift! By taking this courageous step, Ann and Sekani open up important questions and areas for exploration: How do our own biographies as teachers influence our goals and expectations in the classroom and in relation to racism? How do we understand and honor the emotions that swirl through classes on racism? How can we understand the unconscious, the "ubiquitous and uninvited guest" that enters and influences learning? How do we know what our effect on students has been? How do we ensure that students, especially white students, are truly prepared to teach in diverse classrooms? And what do we do when we suspect that they are not?

The authors take us on the journey they and their students traveled in probing their own feelings, reactions, and understanding about this role play and the issues it unearthed. As readers, we are invited into an extended conversation about the challenges, fears, impasses, and breakthroughs experienced in this particular classroom. We are challenged to reflect upon how we might engage students more authentically and honestly in exploring the dimensions of racism in their own psyches and in society at large.

This book offers welcome and necessary tools for thinking through our own practices as educators. It will be a valuable resource for educators, social workers, and others who must balance the urgency of addressing racism with an awareness of the complexity of educating in a domain so psychologically and socially loaded. Amilcar Cabral advised, "Tell no lies. Claim no easy victories." Telling the truth about what we have learned is crucial to working out where we must go next. This book moves us forward on that path.

Lee Anne Bell
Series Editor

Acknowledgments

Ann

From my university students' willingness over the past three decades to acknowledge and confront apathy, hopelessness, and injustices, often for the first time, I learned more about teaching and learning than they will ever know.

Conversations over the years with Roberta Ahlquist, Karen Balos, Jean Barr, Janet Eigner, Elsa Johnson, Patty Lather, Janet Miller, Richard Shapiro, Marcy McMurphy, Celia Oyler, Susan Waugh, my children and my husband, and members of the Sunday night reading group were essential to the growth of my understanding of teaching and social justice, and my desire to write about them.

I want to thank Richard Shapiro for insisting that I experience the Unlearning Oppression model formulated by Ricky Sherover-Marcuse and the folks at New Bridges (now Todos) before I had any idea that the model was precisely what I was looking for at the time, and Hugh, Isoke, Lakota, Nell, Victor, and Yeshi, who with intelligence and grace helped me learn the practice.

Finally, without the enthusiasm of Lee Bell, Lois Patton, and Micah Kleit at Temple University Press and the encouragement of Harold Berlak, *Taking It Personally* might never have come to be.

Sekani

My thanks:

To my friends who helped me write this book, whether they wanted to or not. Thanks for letting me poke and prod you and your families, shaking up your tree of life and having the audacity to argue with you about what fell out. That would be: Jeanina Davis and all her children and friends; Marion E. Bothe, who also has a story to tell; Nancy Moore, who always kept the faith; Jeff Munroe,

Robert Koenig, Karen Aziz, Anne Laurent, Eduardo Almeyda, and Mark Desautel, who put up with my constant conflicts with "white folks"; and Garrett Murphy, another fellow writer and idealist.

To the staff of Rosa Parks Elementary School over the last seven years, especially Ruth Alsandor, our principal: It wasn't easy turning a torn, worn, and forlorn building into a school.

To Garland Grizelle, fellow writer who believed I was worth spending his last days on earth with. I miss you.

I also want to thank Temple University Press for giving this angry voice a chance to be heard. It takes courage and consciousness to know that rage and intelligence are not always mutually exclusive.

Introduction

Ann: How We Came to Write This Book

One July day toward the end of the millennium I asked the students in my Cultural and Linguistic Diversity course—pre-service and experienced teachers—to finish writing their responses to a video we had just seen and then to take a break. They knew that when we reconvened, Sekani Moyenda, an African American woman who teaches in an elementary school that serves predominantly poor Chinese immigrant and African American families, would make a presentation to the class.[1]

We were a little more than halfway through a three-week summer school version of the course I usually teach over a fifteen-week semester. I had been teaching this course, required of all new elementary school teachers in California, four times a year for the past six years.

Sekani had been a student in the course the previous semester. I invited her to speak because, after completing the course, she told me it was her opinion that graduates of our teacher education program hadn't been adequately prepared for the realities they would face as teachers of African American, Latino, Asian heritage, or poor white children. She added that, based on her observations of teachers at her school, other teacher credential programs weren't doing any better. She was convinced that many of the teachers who successfully completed a credential program, if they remained in teaching,[2] were more likely to contribute to the destruction of these children over decades-long careers than to their academic and personal growth and power.[3]

I believed there was far too much truth in what Sekani said and that my course was not exempt from her criticism, so I asked her if she'd like to take two and a half hours of class time to address the students in any way she chose. The day before her presentation Sekani had informed me that she planned to engage the class in a simulation she had created for the occasion to provoke thinking about discipline in classrooms where many of the children are African American and poor. She planned to call the presentation "Boot Camp for Teachers." I really had no idea what was going to happen in the class. The only thing I knew for sure was that we would not be bored.

By the time the Boot Camp presentation was over and the students had gathered up their papers and left the room, I was reeling from the classroom trauma that the students' encounter with Sekani had provoked. During the session two of the white women in the class shed tears, one of them fled the room before the presentation was over, and a heated argument erupted between Sekani and Jim,[4] a white man who had volunteered to play the role of teacher in the simulation. Their voices had reverberated down the hall.

That evening, Jennifer, a white student, would write: "It was one of the most valuable classes I have ever had." Another white student, Denise, wrote: "I am upset and enraged by the message I heard from today's guest speaker." Isiah, the only African American: "Sekani touched a nerve in our classmates. . . . She gave them more in two hours than they will get from any course or class at the university." The day after the presentation, Wong Wan Shan, an immigrant from Hong Kong, wrote: "Teachers . . . must never at any one time while inside a classroom be carried away by our emotions. Yesterday, for that short period of time, the guest speaker let her emotions take over. . . . We are all eye witnesses to the result. . . . The original good intentions of the guest speaker got totally washed down."

Sekani's presentation challenged and disrupted the ways most of the students and I saw ourselves as present and future teachers. It also provided the opportunity for the students, Sekani, and me to explore the depth, dimensions, and significance of racism to a degree that was unprecedented for all of us.

The race and ethnicity of the students in the class were typical of teachers in California.[5] Three quarters were of European descent. The other quarter identified themselves as Chinese or Chinese American (a group that included recent immigrants from Hong Kong, Taiwan, and China), African American, Filipino, Latino/Latina (Mexican American or Chicana/Chicano), or of mixed or biracial heritage.

These students would be teaching young children whose racial and ethnic heritages are as diverse as any in the world.

My primary objective for the entire course was to encourage the students to rethink their assumptions about race, class, gender, culture, language, and sexual orientation that predispose them, like most teachers, to reproduce rather than challenge injustice as they teach. I wanted the students to learn to recognize forms of injustice, including those that are least visible. I wanted them to become aware that as teachers they will have endless opportunities to choose between collaborating with or challenging individuals and institutions that encourage indifference to victimization. I wanted them to refuse to take injustice and exploitation as inevitable, and to act on that awareness.

Sekani had made her presentation toward the end of the course, after students had explored in some depth their racial autobiographies—what and how they had learned, particularly as children and young adults, about race and the racial hierarchy into which they had been inducted. We had already studied personal and institutional racism, internalized racism, and white privilege, investigations that have become legion among many teachers of cultural diversity courses.[6] Thus, the layers and permutations of the various forms of racism that surfaced during Sekani's presentation were both disturbing and surprising to Sekani and to me, and to the students as well. The encounter between Sekani and the class challenged our views of ourselves and the kind of society we live in, and our presumptions of our racial innocence as well.

The idea to write about the encounter came to me a few weeks after the course was over, while, as a result of a three-week house exchange with some Italian teachers, I was sitting on the patio of a seventeenth-century house in a medieval village perched high above the terraced hills of Tuscany. Why was I, thousands of miles from where the event had happened, still thinking about it? Because it was as puzzling as any event that had occurred in any course I had ever taught or taken, and I had a hunch that looking closely at it would move my understanding of my teaching into a different realm.

I also thought that understanding what had happened and writing about it might be useful to others—teachers of diverse racial and ethnic heritages, and teachers of these teachers—who, with or without their awareness, grapple daily with race and racism in their classrooms. And because for a long time I have been aware that people outside the field of education understand far more about racism in the criminal justice and health care systems than they do about how it is played out in schools, I also wanted to write for them, in the hope that they would gain a better understanding of how racism operates in schools, which, after all, belong to all of us.

It was important to me to find a way to write about the encounter and its aftermath that did not portray it solely from *my* point of view, so that both I and my readers would be challenged to look critically at *my* "take" on what had happened. It occurred to me that Sekani, who had formerly experienced the course as a student and whose economic background and racial/ethnic experience differed so greatly from my own, might be willing to share with me the telling of the story. I wanted to write some form of narrative because years of teaching had convinced me that abstract textbook expositions, no matter how wise, rarely penetrated deeply either the hearts or minds of student readers.[7]

As I sat on that terrace in Tuscany, I was aware of some of the problems Sekani and I would face if we were to tell the story together. One would be figuring out how to capture our collaboration in a way that both preserved the differences in our perspectives and conveyed our influences on one another's views as these would surely evolve over time.

Of even greater concern to me was the power differential inherent in a collaboration between an African American teacher of children and a white university teacher. Could we tell the story in a way that did not privilege my use of the languages and theories valued by those who selected books to use in the diversity courses that were proliferating around the globe over Sekani's powerful but academically marginalized ways of expressing her understanding?[8] Could we structure what we would write in a way that encouraged our readers to be aware that in this situation a white academic is in danger of having the last word?

When I returned to California, I proposed the project to Sekani. She seemed as fascinated as I was with the encounter, and we agreed to try to make sense of it together. (Though she seemed to be quite eager, months later she confessed she had had serious doubts about whether I would really follow through on the project.) That fall I pieced together excerpts from students' journal responses to the encounter and its aftermath, and Sekani and I began a conversation that was to continue over several years.[9]

My interest in understanding what had happened in the class was neither idle nor academic. Stark realities spurred me on. Poor children and Black and brown children *of every social class*, by many indicators—academic achievement, suspension, dropout, attendance, and college attendance rates—were continuing to fall further behind white middle-class students with each additional year of schooling.[10] The underachievement of African American students in particular remained both persistent and pervasive.[11] These patterns paralleled and were not unrelated to many extra-schooling demographic facts: the lower life expectancy of African American men;[12] higher imprisonment rates and, in the juvenile "justice" system, stunning disparities in treatment of Blacks and Latinos;[13] and increasing discrimination against Black and brown home buyers,[14] to name just a few. The flip side of those "disadvantages"—white, social, economic, and political privilege of which the recipients are almost entirely unaware—remained a cornerstone supporting this racial status quo.[15]

As we were writing, a flurry of reports appeared in the national news documenting race and class differences in school success, and these disparities became, at least temporarily, of national concern. There was no dearth of proposals for addressing the problem: more standardized and centralized testing, national standards, an end to social promotion, zero-tolerance discipline policies, prescribed curricula, vouchers, and charter schools. At the same time, the State of California had begun to organize the way schools' academic performance was reported, so that schools with high proportions of poor children could be compared to one another. This way of reporting suggested that the ubiquitous race and class disparities were simply facts of life. Nowhere in the mainstream conversation was it suggested that institutional racism might contribute significantly to the disparities.[16]

I do not think schools can be transformed into institutions that promote social justice by requiring teachers to take diversity courses;

research suggests that the effects of most of these courses are neither profound nor lasting.[17] But I do think that if teachers gain an emotional as well as an intellectual understanding of how racism and the other "isms" work, the chances that they will continue to pass on to future generations the systems of inequality that structure the society they live in can be reduced. This applies not only to white teachers but also to teachers of color, who, like their white counterparts, often bring with them blindness to racism and unexamined and dangerous notions about members of their own group, as well as groups of people who are different from themselves.[18]

Diversity courses often focus on racial/cultural differences in learning and communication styles. Though I think an understanding of such differences is important, I am convinced it is of little value if teachers do not understand how institutional racism has powerfully shaped both their views of and aspirations for the children they teach and their attitudes toward their students' parents. I am certain that any teacher who sees Black and brown and poor children and their parents as "less than" cannot possibly teach these children successfully.[19]

I am not claiming that changing what happens in schools will eliminate social injustice. Black male high school and College graduates will continue for the foreseeable future to earn less on average than their white counterparts,[20] and middle-class Blacks and Latinos will still encounter racism at every turn no matter how equitable their schooling might be.[21] But I believe it is within the power of self-reflective teachers and teacher educators to contribute to the creation of a more just and joyful world.

I hope the stories we tell illuminate how and why schooling continues to contribute to the reproduction of inequality and suggest what teachers, parents, and other citizens can do to interrupt this process. I also hope our stories of one group of individuals working through their views of race will serve as mirrors that help readers reflect upon themselves.

Finally, I intend by telling these stories to honor and share with others the insights of the students in the diversity class, the youngest of whom was twenty, the oldest of whom was in his fifties, who brought vast and varied experience from far corners of the globe. I also hope *Taking It Personally* will convey how looking closely at teaching can bring about new ways of seeing and understanding, and encourage readers who are teachers to become teacher researchers themselves.[22]

Sekani: Why Should You Read this Book?

It's 2:00 A.M. Occasionally, I wander around the house. I've been without focus or purpose for the last four hours. If you were in this room with me right now, you might say I was enjoying a much needed rest; I'm relaxing. But in fact, I am having one of my chronic free-floating anxiety attacks. Emotional chaos and confusion have gripped me to the point of inactivity. The only feelings I can identify are fear and grief. But I cannot understand the root of these feelings. I can't sort, focus, or identify them enough to do something with them. Although my body needs to move and get some exercise, all my energy is being consumed by these anxieties. I feel like a car that I've revved up but can't get moving. I am fatigued.

I'm thinking all these disjointed thoughts:

"At least my left leg doesn't hurt right now. Hope I hear some good news Monday when I get the results of the MRI. I don't know if I want a nerve graft if I am found to be a candidate. That will mean I will be out of work and school in the spring. Shit, I just had surgery in June.

"I don't have any money again. I wonder how long it will take me to get my transcripts at the end of this semester? How long will it take once I take them to the district to get my salary adjusted? I love my new computer, but between paying for the loan and my medical expenses—this sucks. I need to find a house I can afford; paying all this rent is killing me. How am I going to get the new modem since this one doesn't work? I have to cancel my massage. I don't have enough money to pay for it.

"I need to learn how to use Filemaker Pro. What happened to the Timeliner? They said it would arrive in a week. Why can't I get the color orange in Microsoft Draw—what's the deal with that?

"God, Mom's gonna drive me crazy with her worrying when she sees me in this leg brace. I'm just glad I don't see her on Thanksgiving. That is entirely too depressing and terrifying. I'll spend the holidays at work, as usual. I need a life. I gotta lose weight. Will I ever have sex again? I have to start wearing my glasses when I use the computer."

On and on this goes until I get so fed up with myself, I shut down. I go numb. If I have learned anything about these times, it's to stay away from people. I know, isolation is not a good thing, but what can anyone do for me right now? Assure me that I'm paranoid?

Eventually these feelings become unbearable. I start turning to different ways to deal with them. I've tried sleeping. But I am not waking up feeling any better. I've tried working. Somehow feeling like I'm doing something important gives me some sense of self and meaning. But, except for mundane tasks, I can't think of anything to do that could effectively distract me. I'm single, pushing forty, have no man or family—and, oh yes, I am now going through the "change of life." Why the fuck do they call it that? My life hasn't changed because I'm now barren. That's the problem; some part of me always feels barren. Devoid of fertility. Valueless and insignificant. Unable to find any permanence of self.

In an effort to preoccupy myself, I pick up Ann's latest draft of our book. The subject of racism can always get me going, and perhaps in engaging it I can find some inner peace. I read the criticism some of the students made about my presentation to Ann's class, and it stings. The journals cut to the quick, and when I'm in moods like this I believe every negative assessment of myself by these people. Is it true? Am I trippin'? Am I filled with rage, racism, and "insensitivity"?

I was glad to make the presentation to Ann's class. I wanted to bring a dose of reality to these future teachers. I knew who they were and had my own opinions about what they needed, because for the past few years I had been sitting in classes with them. I created a role play that recreated the classroom I had just finished trying to manage. I set the "teacher" up to fail, because teachers entering such worst-case scenario classrooms *are* set up to fail, and these classrooms are teachers' worst nightmares. I wanted these teachers to see what it *felt* like to be in a chaotic classroom environment, and I wanted to initiate conversation and generate questions about how they would actually deal with it. I did not go with the intention of making two white women cry, and one of them walk out, and one white male bluster and blow his stack. I simply wanted the students to get a feel for what would be the results of trying to apply their abstract, liberal, Eurocentric, often unconsciously racist ideologies in the classroom.

I now see that many of my responses to the students during the presentation were rooted in my need to speak my mind. I was unable to do so where I taught. I had already lost one (nonteaching) job because I had used the R-word to name what I knew was happening. I liked teaching at Rosa Parks and wasn't willing to lose my job because I confronted teachers on their assumptions about how to teach Black children. So, as I see it now, I was glad to have the opportunity to—How shall I say it?— share my issues.

Ann and I were initially amazed that the presentation had triggered the racist conditioning with which most of the students had to one degree or another long been infected. It was only through the process of writing this book that I have come to understand how all my life I have triggered the inner defense mechanisms of white people who consciously or not suffered from racism. I have been getting on white people's bad side since elementary school, but I really didn't understand what it had to do with racism, until now.

When Ann suggested we write this book together (I have to admit I did not at the time actually believe it would happen), I saw it as an opportunity to investigate some of the relationships between racism, racists, and my race, and how they all collide. So this book is, for me, both about the effects of my presentations on the college students and about the impact writing this book has had upon me.

I read Ann's introduction and autobiography. It's ironic that her description of herself is not the person I see. Tuscany? I didn't know she went to Tuscany. I listen to her description of her thoughts, feelings, and history, and I feel far removed. Not just from her experiences, but from this person she describes herself to be. Who is this woman who can afford to go to Tuscany? More importantly, why don't I feel or see this person?

I realize after rereading parts of the draft that I have to follow my healthier instinct—to write. I have been writing a journal since I was about twelve years old. I still have my first diary. I need to write. I have no idea how much of it should be in a book for public consumption. But I feel that if I write now to someone—even Ann— who would read this, I could start to sort out my own confusion, pain, and chaos. I realize that, once again, I can do this by self-reflection. By comparing my present state of mind with Ann's.

A friend of mine, who, like Ann, is Jewish, told me that he thought that I was consumed by racism because it gave my life meaning. He said, "What would you do with yourself if racism didn't exist?" He describes a story about a man working on a door. For years he works meticulously going over and over it, redecorating it, carving it, and reshaping it. Finally, one day, someone asks him when he will be finished. He says, "When someone takes it away from me."

White supremacy is my enemy. But an enemy's only real power is your weakness. While I sit here in my isolation, depression, loneliness, and, yes, bitterness and anger, I have to acknowledge two important things. One, a part of me is indeed consumed by this force we call racism. I think it, feel it, look at it, kick it, open it, slam it, or run into it every day. Second, I didn't choose this door. This door has been put before me and for the rest of my life, I will not be able to move it. *This is not my choice.* Racism will not be eradicated in my lifetime. As long as I am Black in America, I will have to deal with it.

Racism has diminished the quality of my life and, more importantly, has damaged me. There is no denying that other issues in my life contributed to my injury, and I need to focus on those as well. But there is a significant difference between those other issues and racism. Racism doesn't stop. Poverty and deprivation cause injury, but for me, these have stopped. Family traumas (not unrelated to racism, however) have caused emotional injury, but I'm an adult now, and with psychotherapy the effects of these have diminished. Even my own bad habits, ingrained as they are, I can stop. But I have been unable in all my life to avoid racism for more than one day, because it is a pathology that white Americans either refuse or are unable to manage. Unless I stay indoors and don't answer the phone, watch TV, listen to the radio, or read the paper, I have no choice but to engage it in my daily life.

Just writing this makes me tired.

To be honest, even after reading her autobiography, I still don't understand why Ann is willing to assist me in fighting against racism. In fact, today, I'm too tired to care. I'm just glad to have the help.

"I don't like white folks!"

Now, if you are white and you are shocked and surprised by this admission, this is the very book you should be reading. If, after you read it, you find yourself able to understand why a Black woman in America *doesn't* like white people, then the time you have spent reading it will have been worthwhile.

You're going to read a book written in part by a Black educator who at various times in her life has declared herself a militant and an intellectual insurrectionist. Others might call me progressive, radical, extremist, or militant (although not often giving the term "militant" the same positive connotation I give to it). This might be a good time, before you read on, to think about what all that means to you. If you are planning to become a teacher, what will it mean to you if you find yourself teaching in a predominately Black school where you will be working with a parent, staff person, teacher, or administrator, like me? If you are a white parent or a parent of color, what does it mean to you to know that someone who shares my views may teach your child?

What is startling to me is that most white readers, and readers of color as well, have probably not yet really come to grips with the ramifications of crossing the great racial divides to teach in schools filled with people of races and ethnic cultures that are different from their own. I surmise this from having been, during the past three years, in classes with people who are probably very much like you. People of color have goals and objectives that have been shaped by experiences very different from one another's and from those of white people. You will have to change some very fundamental ways of thinking if you are to have any chance of becoming successful teachers of children from diverse backgrounds.

Do you want to change? Do you really want to begin to doubt most of what you take for granted to be just, right, and true? Are you ready to learn that much of what those of you who want to teach thought you had to offer may be of little consequence to those you mean to serve? Are you ready to learn that you have to *earn* the trust of parents, children, and teachers whose racial identities are different from yours? Are you ready to listen to and learn from them?

Most white people and many people of color aren't. Every day many young white women and men, and middle-class, assimilated teachers of color as well, march with credential in hand to classrooms where most of the children are poor Blacks, Latinos, and Asian immigrants, only to have their authority mocked and their requests ignored. They are confused and terrified by their treatment, and, although they may give it their best shot, many "burn out" and quit in less than five years. Others become inadequate administrators who retaliate against every Black and Latino student who has ever humiliated them. And some stay on in the classroom to do ongoing psychic damage to these children as punishment for the children's and parents' lack of gratitude without ever realizing it, or worse yet know they are doing it but are never made to account for this abuse.

* * *

In each of the two years before the "encounter," I had been asked to take over what I now call "crisis classrooms." The first time this happened, I was teaching with an emergency credential. That means I had been deemed qualified to teach on the sole basis of passing the California Basic Educational Skills Test and had taken only one education course. Five white teachers had quit en masse the day before school started and gone to work in the suburbs to punish the Black principal for not providing them with the resources to which they felt they were entitled. The fact that lack of resources is part and parcel of working in public schools populated with poor Black and Chinese students was secondary to their professional ambitions and personal needs.

None of the teachers who quit had had any skills for managing our children. Despite their adamant insistence that their students were learning and doing fine, every formal and informal assessment showed that about 80 percent of *their* African American students were not on grade level and were therefore incapable of the performance they had boasted about.

After the start of the academic year it also became clear that a few students had problems attributable to other factors than the troubled and chaotic classrooms to which they had been assigned. Some of them had specific learning disabilities or were experiencing horrendous home lives that by their very nature would preclude them from learning. No one had identified the problems and sought help. Perhaps the teachers had thought this behavior was normal for "these children." None of this was a surprise to me.

Before the principal asked me to take over, sub after sub after sub, each with an emergency credential like mine, had come in and only made matters worse, to the point where the classrooms had become holding pens.

In the three years since I first gave the presentation, I have taken over crisis classrooms two more times. I seem to have developed a reputation as the one to call when a classroom has fallen apart. When the white—or in one case, Chinese—teacher left, I had to take over not only because of a shortage of qualified permanent teachers, but also because, with rare exceptions, the white teachers or substitutes sent by the central office to take over classrooms were ill prepared to teach and completely unconcerned about the welfare of our children. I doubt that many of these substitutes would have been allowed to return a second day to a school with a white or more affluent and parent-involved population.

With each passing day, as they faced a succession of inexperienced, ill-prepared teachers, the children in these crisis classrooms were falling further behind their peers who attended schools where most of the students were middle-class whites and Asians. It was from the despair and legitimate outrage of this situation that I accepted Ann's invitation to make a presentation to her class.

Part 1

Our Racial
Autobiographies

1 Sekani:
How I Got My "Black Attitude" Problem

We wrote our racial autobiographies into *Taking It Personally* for two reasons. First, we wanted to encourage our readers to read the stories we tell critically. We therefore included those parts of our stories that reveal something of how the lenses developed through which we have been acculturated to see and understand our experiences. Second, we tell our stories to provide examples of racial autobiographies that we hope will provoke our readers to explore how *their* life experiences have shaped the ways *they* see themselves and others who, because of accident of birth, have lived lives that are both like and different from their own.

Writing this racial autobiography has been difficult for me. The part of me that particularly resisted writing it was the one that didn't want to look at the painful effects of racism that I have begun to acknowledge only recently. It was much easier for me to focus on what's wrong with white folks than to look at how racism has marked my life.

I also resisted because I feared my story would bore people of color. I assumed most of them already knew more than they wanted to about how racism has affected them. As I began to write, I discovered gaping holes in my understanding and became aware of the depth of my resistance to filling them, and I began to think there were probably many people of color who, like me, had only begun to construct an understanding of their own relationship to racism. It wasn't until I was well into the exploration process that I began to understand how essential it is for people of color to investigate this issue, particularly if they will be working in the so-called helping professions.

I decided to begin chronologically. But I was stalled again. It seemed I had no early memories of racism. I phoned my mother. She, of course, could only recall events she had intervened in. Our earliest common memory was of when I was fourteen years old. Yet I knew that I must have experienced racism well before that. I began asking my friends about their early memories, and most of them also drew a blank.

Why could we not remember? Why didn't we know how we encountered racism and how it felt? I suppose if we had come of age during the period of old-fashioned racism—at a time when segregation was legal and we knew it was against the law to eat at certain restaurants or swim at public pools—I would have found it easier. I remembered many times when I was punished and verbally diminished at school. As a child I either attributed the mistreatment to the "meanness" of teachers or thought I deserved the treatment I received. I did not consider that there might be a connection between the events and my color.

When I got my emergency credential and began teaching, I had not been in an elementary school in more than twenty years. As soon as I entered the doors, I began to witness racism perpetrated daily in a myriad of ways on Black children by white teachers, administrators, and the school district. I began to think more about how I had experienced racism when I was in school. When I gave my first presentation to Ann's class, I found myself telling a story of an interaction I had with a little blond-haired girl when I was in third grade. I had recalled and told the story a number of times before, but that day was the first time I focused my telling entirely through the prism of race.

If you teach me I'm inconsequential, I'll learn to fight back.

I was seven or eight years old. Some of "us Black kids" were bussed up to the Berkeley Hills to attend the better "white" schools. Back then the goal was to integrate the schools and to prove that Berkeley was truly multicultural.

I don't remember much, except what the school and yard looked like. It was a fancy two-story building. Near the school was what I thought of as a real castle. In reality, it was the Claremont Hotel. There were trees everywhere around, and as you looked up the street from the school grounds you could see that we were on a mountain in what seemed like a forest to me. Unlike the Catholic school I went to back in New York where boys and girls played together, at John Muir Elementary School in Berkeley, the students were separated by gender. I recall how we would sneak past the teachers in the yard. Crossing the invisible line in the yard was fun. We students would run across when a teacher wasn't paying attention, pester someone on the other side, then run back to our side, hoping the other kids would chase us so they would get in trouble.

I also remember how all the girls except me—my mother wouldn't allow it—wore shorts under their school clothes, so they could twirl on the monkey bars. I was fascinated at how they could flip around and around and around on those bars. They used their sweaters to wrap around the bar to keep their legs from getting bruised or burned when they twirled. Some girls could only go forward, with one leg over the bar, holding on with both hands. But if you were really good, you could go backwards with both legs in a sitting position, forward on one leg with *no* hands, and leap into the air and land on your feet. I could never complete one turn. That is the only pleasant memory I have of that grade at John Muir School. But neither the view nor the school yard antics made as great an impression on me as the blond-haired girl.

Back then, classroom desks were always placed in rows facing the teacher. I was seated near the back of the classroom—right behind the little blond-haired girl. I cannot tell you anything else about her. No one from that past has a face. They are only adult or child, Black or white. I was sitting behind this girl on the first or second day of school when she decided to flip her hair into my face and on to my desk. I had seen white people do this in movies and on the bus. I was indeed fascinated that her hair was long, but not fascinated enough to want it lying on my desk or whacking me across the face.

The first time she did it, I thought it was an accident. So I just moved it. But she did it again. This time, being that I was new to the school and didn't want to offend, I asked her kindly to remove her hair. She gave me a "so what" look and did it again. This time I told her to move it. "Move your hair," I whispered intensely through gritted teeth. But she just smirked, waited a few moments, and did it again. This time I took a couple of strands between my fingers and yanked. I was startled when she shouted out, all too dramatically, "Owwwch!" as if I'd pulled a fistful out of her head. It definitely got the teacher's attention.

"What's going on back there?"

"She pulled my hair!" the girl pouted, holding the back of her head as if her brains would fall out.

"She won't get it off my desk. I—" The teacher looked at me and said, "Stop it! Stop it right now. I won't have this in my classroom."

"But I—"

Directing her response to me: "I said be quiet and leave her *alone!*" The little blond girl turned to me with a triumphant smirk to gloat at her victory. It pissed me off.

"Wait 'til I get you outside," I said. But she didn't take me seriously. I already had visions of pulling her hair out in clumps.

I had actually gotten distracted with the girls on the bars again, when she made it a point to approach me. She had her friends with her. I was forced to fight her now. She'd made it a public issue—my place in the school yard pecking order.

I only remember the fight itself and how easy it was to beat her up. Though all loved her flowing hair, it made her vulnerable in a fight. When I look back, I realize she was a one-hit, windmill fighter. She didn't know how to fight. I guess she was surprised when I used my fists and grabbed her by the hair, trying to drag her around the yard. I remember thinking of the Flintstones and how girls were dragged by their hair during "cave" times. I recall feeling her hair break at my first big effort to grab it. It wasn't as strong as it was in the cartoons. I remember how that scared me and I realized deep down that I might actually do some permanent damage.

Fortunately, adults came and broke up the fight before I would have to choose between really hurting her or losing face.

I won the fight, of course. I also won a trip to the principal's office for the lecture. I don't recall what was said, but I was terrified at what would happen to me. My mother was going to "beat my butt" when I got home. I had never been suspended before. This wasn't going to be pretty.

I was sent back to class, and I remained quiet and cooperative the rest of the day. I don't remember what happened after that. I do know that my mother said nothing, and that I was not suspended. Only years later did I discover there had been no call home.

Now that I'm grown, I realize no one wanted the incident to be pursued. Not in a community trying to portray itself as committed to "multiculturalism." I now realize, too, that they probably knew my mother would have fought the suspension had she heard my side. (They wanted to avoid the crazy Black mom.)

The next day I got to school and was in my seat when the little blond girl arrived. I still hadn't figured out what I was going to do about her hair. But I didn't have to do anything. When she arrived at school she had a new hairdo. She had put her hair into two long braids and pinned them to the top of her head in Heidi style.

As I look back on that incident now as a Black educator, I see how it contributed to the particular sensitivity I have to questions of classroom justice and fairness. Not just because I often feel abused and mistreated by white people but because I don't like having to defend myself with one form of violence or another. At the time, however, I doubt if I was conscious that racism was involved. I didn't get it that the teacher didn't listen to my side of the story because she saw me as "less than," or that the blond-haired girl took it for granted that because of her coloring she was entitled to my territory. I was just taking care of Number One.

In my class, violence isn't tolerated. But self-defense is. In my class, I am in charge and there is only one way people are to be treated— and that is fairly. In my class, I listen to both sides and students have the right to file a complaint against me, to the principal or their parents. In my class, children can choose to be defiant as long as they can do one of two things: (1) prove to me that they are on the side of "righteousness" and I am wrong, or, (2) gracefully accept the consequences I will impose—first. If I am later found to be wrong, I will give a public apology and make amends. In my class I take "fair" out of the abstract and teach that there is a big difference between "what you want" and "what is right."

This is an important distinction that is often missed by little blond girls who grow up and become teachers at the school where I now teach.

If you teach me I'm worthless, I'll learn to do it by myself.

After I told the story of the little blond girl to Ann's class I began to remember other stories of my elementary school days. One of these was the story of my mother and Sister Ann. I'm not sure who Sister Ann hated most, us or our parents. The feeling was mutual. She was the first adult I remember that we children and our parents all agreed

21

did not deserve our respect. We called her "Turkey Legs" behind her back because her thighs were so big she couldn't close her legs.

As far as I can determine, Sister Ann didn't like anyone in our class. I now realize the only thing we all had in common was that we were Black. She must have been painfully disappointed to be stuck at St. Columbus in Oakland. She made sure we suffered with her.

One day I had been forced to sit next to Kevin, a boy I heartily disliked—which is precisely why she put him next to me. Our assignment was to use a needle and thread to create geometric shapes using the straight lines we created by sewing from one point to another. Kevin kept picking at me. Trying to upset me. (This was probably a not uncommon form of fourth-grade flirting.) When I complained, Sister Ann would chastise me and he would get a laugh.

At one point I dropped my needle. Kevin shouted to Sister Ann, "Sister Ann! Sister Ann! She threw her needle at me!"

"No, I didn't! He's lying!"

"That's it, young lady! Go to the center of the room! Right Now!"

I stood up and went to the center of the room.

"Class, Sekani's mother thinks she's special. Do you think she's special?"

"NOOOOO!"

"Her mother treats her like she's a rose. Do you think she's a rose?"

"NOOOO!"

I don't remember anything else she said at that time but I do remember being given a note to take home to my mother and feeling humiliated and worthless.

When I got home, my mother could see something was wrong. I gave her the note and prepared for my beating. To my surprise she started laughing.

"What is this about?" she asked, still amused.

I told her about the needle and how I had dropped it and what Kevin did. She knew about Kevin, and she found the whole matter trivial. But her mood changed when I told what had happened next.

The next day my mother "clowned." She showed up with me at school. She waited until all the students were seated at their desks, and she made me wait beside her. Whenever Sister Ann tried to talk to her, my mother just stood there and glared at her. I could tell Sister Ann was scared. I didn't blame her. I had been the object of my mother's glares. I waited in fascination to see what would happen next.

My mother was silent until all the children had arrived. When she started speaking to Sister Ann, she made sure she was speaking loud enough for the entire class to hear.

"I understand you asked the class if my daughter was special." I saw Sister Ann blanch. I didn't know white people could get any whiter. When I started reading novels and the character would be described as having "blanched," I always think of that moment.

"Well?"

"Well, your daughter tried to stick a needle—"

"No, according to the note you sent me she 'flicked' a needle at him. How does someone flick a needle? How could anyone do that without hurting herself? Did you see her do this?"

"Well, I—"

"Did you see her flick the needle?"

"Well, no . . . but she—"

"Don't you ever send me another ridiculous note like this ever again, do you *understand me? I have too much to do to come down here to do your job.*" I don't remember the rest. Once my mother hit her stride, what she said was less important than the intensity of her thunderous roar.

Sister Ann finally took a breath when she saw the principal nun come running down the hall. The principal tried to pacify my mother. (I knew from experience that was a mistake. Once she got this outraged, it was always better to shut up and listen 'til the storm died down on its own.)

Finally, I recall the principal saying, "Well, then, I can assume that you would like to take your daughter out of our school?"

To their surprise, my mother said, "Why? She's going to have to deal with asses all her life. She might as well learn all about them now. Sister Ann is the perfect teacher for that."

Then my mother turned around and looked at me. "Go sit down and make sure you behave yourself."

I sat down with a mixture of fear and satisfaction. While the kids may not have liked me, we were all unified in our satisfaction at the verbal whipping my mother had just given Sister Ann.

Her parting words: "Just for the record, so you're very clear on the concept. I do indeed believe my daughter is special and she is a rose. Do you have a problem with that?" She wasn't leaving until she got an answer.

"No, not at all, she is—"

After that, Sister Ann no longer scared us, and our contempt for her grew.

The hardest part was what had happened inside me. While my mother had shouted to the rafters how special she thought I was, she was clearly focused on what I now know to be Sister Ann's racist abuse of her power. She didn't realize how important it was for me to be liked by my peers, and she didn't realize the damage the incident had done to my feelings about myself.

As a teacher I have learned the importance of openly processing such important social events in the class. How could Sister Ann do that if she could not confront her own shame?

Now, in retrospect, I understand that the other kids probably liked me as well as anyone, in spite of their verbalized agreement with Sister Ann that I was not special. But at no time did any of my classmates ever say they were sorry or that they had not meant what they said. After that incident I was left with a quiet disappointment. I believed I wasn't liked but was too terrified to ask or speak about it. The incident had separated me from my peers. I started on a mission that consumed my interpersonal relationships. I used my energy to prove I was worthy of the other children's friendship. In time, with other disappointments totally unrelated to this, I came to believe friendship was about having something of value to offer. I could not possibly be appreciated for who I really was.

I am not saying that I blame my low self-esteem entirely on Sister Ann. But imagine the power she could have had in reverse! I do not believe in empty flattery as a way of lifting children's self-esteem. However, I do know now that at that time I indeed possessed some wonderful qualities and talents Sister Ann could have noticed and respected and taught me to appreciate. But her focus was distorted, bitter, and racist. It prevented her from performing her duties as a teacher. In fact, she dishonored the profession.

My mother had told me when I was younger and in Sister Ann's classroom that the world was full of asses and I might as well learn how to deal with them. But it was only years afterward that I was able to put the label "racist ass" on this experience with Sister Ann.

If you teach me betrayal, I'll learn distrust.

The first experience that I was able to label racist was a memory my mother and I share. It was at my first job. I was fourteen years old and participating in a jobs program for teens. After working at the Berkeley Public Library for three years, I was suddenly fired. Up until the moment I came home and had to tell my mother, I thought my firing was justified and entirely my fault. Ms. Brocklehurst (who I thought was "really nice") had informed me that I was too slow at covering the book jackets with their protective plastic covers. She had expected me to cover thirty an hour and I was only able to cover between fifteen and twenty.

When I told my mother I had been fired, she was livid. I rarely use that word—livid—but that is exactly the look on her face— stone rage. I felt awful. I had failed my mother, disappointed myself and, yes, Ms. Brocklehurst, who had never said a harsh word to me, as well. When I got to my room, which was covered wall to wall and ceiling with cartoons and jokes, I tore them all down. After that day, I put up pictures of cats, wildcats, panthers, lions, cougars, leopards, and bobcats. (By the time I was a teenager, I put up horror movie posters, *Legend of Hell House, The Omen, Audrey Rose,* and *The Exorcist.* Small children were afraid to come into my room.)

My mother went on a rampage. Her response was rapid and to the point. The next day she took me down to the Employment Opportunity Program office and demanded an explanation. She pointed out that I had been volunteering at the same library since I was eleven years old and had been coming to the library since I was nine. The reason Ms. Brocklehurst gave for firing me, if I remember correctly, was that I was "spoiled." I was "limited" in some way, incapable of performing such a basic task. My mother told the EOP director the library had trained me and if I was so incompetent and, therefore, "unemployable," she was going to sue the library for damaging me. And—if all concerned had any good sense—they would not put the firing in my record, and they would place me somewhere else for the rest of the summer and deal with Brocklehurst appropriately. She noted that if Ms. Brocklehurst was really so concerned about my performance, she would have informed her or the program before firing me. She also noted that Ms. Brocklehurst had replaced me with a white child who was the daughter of a friend of hers.

I remember, on that day, my mother sitting me down and for the first time explaining racism to me. She told me that Ms. Brocklehurst was a racist, and that she had suspected as much for many months, based upon the questions and comments I brought home from work. She used as an example my report to her that Ms. Brockelhurst had asked me where I got my clothes. She said she wanted to know because she was impressed by the fashionable way I dressed. My mother knew that I didn't understand sarcasm but she had not made any comment at the time.

During this first talk with me about racism my mother explained what Ms. Brocklehurst's comment on my fashionable dress really meant and that it had not been a compliment. My mother was of the old school and wanted my work experience to be as close to "real life" as possible. So while other students in the program dressed casually for work (jeans and t-shirts and even shorts, depending on the job), my mother had me dress "professionally."

The problem was that we were poor, and all my mother could afford was to have me wear her dresses, which, quite frankly, were very plain and out of style and hung at least four inches below my knees. (I had not started to grow taller than my mother yet.) But to my mother, being neat and clean in the office workplace was far more important than dressing in style. "Never give white people any excuse to accuse you of *not* being professional." (In retrospect I realize my clothes were stylish, just not in style.)

In the same conversation, my mother told me about another clue to Ms. Brocklehurst's bigotry. It was revealed when I came home and asked about my eyes.

"Mom, am I mixed?"

"What do you mean, are you mixed." My mother had that serious look that always scared me. I didn't know what I was saying wrong—again.

"Am I mixed with another race?" I asked tentatively.

"Why are you asking me that?" My mother was getting angry and I didn't understand why.

"Ms. Brocklehurst told me I had such beautiful hazel eyes that she wanted to know if I was mixed." I remember that I had felt excited over the idea that I could possibly be something more exotic than *just Black.*

"What did you tell her?" My mother was getting still angrier.

"I told her I was Black as far as I knew but that I would ask." By now, my mother's face had taken on her stony rage look and I was very sorry I had asked. *Oh God, I'd really pissed her off now.*

"So, what she's saying is that if your eyes are pretty you can't be all Black? Does that make any sense to you?"

"No." I lowered my eyes, waiting for permission to go to my room.

"No, you're not mixed with *anything.*"

A few weeks later, after I had been fired, during the conversation in which my mother began to initiate me into the mysteries of racism, she reminded me of this incident. She told me that Ms. Brockelhurst's suggestion that because my eyes are hazel they are pretty and that because I am pretty I couldn't be all Black is a good example of what she meant by racism. (Comments about my eyes continued to be made by others, both Black and white. I grew to hate *any* compliments about my eyes because of the deceit behind the false or ignorant flattery.)

To be honest, at the time I didn't really understand what she meant by racism. I was just glad she wasn't mad at me for being fired.

* * *

I recently asked my mother about Brocklehurst. Now, twenty-five years later, my mother explained that what had enraged her was the effects racism was having on me. Her rage had been compounded when I went to my room and pulled all my jokes off the wall.

My mother didn't actually say it, but I now realize that it broke her heart. It hurt her to see the joy leave me, and to see that she was powerless to stop it. It was one of life's inevitabilities in America. Taxes and racism. I asked her why she had not talked to me about racism before my firing by Brocklehurst. She said it was because she wanted me to have my childhood as long as possible. She felt I would have to deal with racism all my life. She wasn't going to bring it to my awareness any sooner than she had to.

My mother's rage was always resolute. She may not have been able to end racism, but she sure could punish racists and protect her children with every weapon available. If there is a "race war" going on, my mother's a general.

I know now that her rage was justified. Her daughter had been violated by two teachers that she knew of. At least two teachers—and who knows how many more—had diminished her daughter's sense of who she was and what made her a valuable human being. Ironically, while my mother must have felt powerless as she fought fiercely on so many fronts to protect me (that alone makes me love her), she taught me not to surrender to racism. Though I was not always conscious at the time that she was fighting racism, I now know I watched her confront it continuously to protect me while I was growing up. I also realize that because it was the first one that had been named, my experience at the Berkeley Public Library was my first clear memory of being abused because of my color. And it was my mother who had named it for me. Today, fighting racism is central to my self-esteem and identity. It is what my mother approves of. It affects my life choices. Even down to who I date.

I learned my lessons well.

My understanding of racism really deepened when I began working with Black children and could observe racist behavior as it was acted out on our little ones. Armed with my emergency credential I took a job as a computer teacher at an elementary school. The school population was 45 percent Black and 45 percent Chinese immigrant, and 10 percent "other." The teachers brought their classes to the computer lab once a week. The principal was a Black woman from the old school. The teachers were mostly white and Chinese. Only four, including myself, were Black. One of my first lessons about how racism operates in elementary schools I learned from another white teacher we will call Ms. Crutch.

My mistake from the beginning was that I was too civilized. She took it for weakness and stupidity. I am the computer technology teacher. I run the lab and teach the children how to use the computers. I use these machines/tools primarily to reinforce the curriculum, although there is much to be learned from technology in and of itself. Though I was used to teaching adults, I was new at teaching little kids. However, I figured the same level of professionalism applied. My second mistake was assuming Ms. Crutch was competent and professional.

We did not get along from the first day. She was arrogant and dismissive. I tried to ignore that about her. I asked her to give me a copy of her lesson plans so I could arrange the curriculum in the lab accordingly. She refused. She told me that my job was simply to be ready for her when she came in and that she would let me know when she arrived what she wanted me to do with her class.

I explained that I was a teacher, not a librarian, that the computer was a tool that the children would have to be trained on—by me— that I had to teach them how to use the software, that I gave teachers a choice: They could either provide me with their lesson plans, or turn the children over to me for half an hour. Most teachers took advantage of the latter alternative with gratitude because they understood that I was more competent to teach children to use computers than they were, and because it provided them with a few minutes' peace.

I asked all the teachers for copies of their students' emergency cards in case I had to deal with discipline. Crutch was the only one to refuse, stating that she would deal with discipline if it was necessary. I had to take the matter to our boss before Crutch would comply.

Working with Crutch was hell. She took the simplest of issues and magnified them into problems, while matters of importance she completely brushed aside. If I needed it, she refused. What I asked her not to do, she did. When I tried to teach, she interrupted me. When I established rules, she allowed the children to break them. So I took the path of least resistance. I tried to stay out of her way. No matter. I had another nineteen classes to get through each week. I explained to her that, given our differences, only one of us could teach at a time. If she wanted to be the teacher I would leave, but if I taught, she'd have to support, not contradict, me.

She wouldn't stop. When I walked away, she claimed she needed help with a technical problem. When I offered help, she disputed my offerings. Finally, I decided to take back the classroom. I set the limits. I went to our principal and submitted a form that made it clear that unless Crutch gave me a lesson plan two days ahead, I would go ahead with *my* lesson plans. The principal agreed.

The next week, Crutch came in with her own lesson without warning. Without preamble she brought in a large poster and began taping it to *my* wall. I just watched her. I had had enough. I let her tell the class what they were going to do. I had already set the computers up for my assignment.

I let her talk, and when she was through, instead of instructing them on how to get to a place in the program where they could do her assignment, I simply said, "But before that, you're going to do this." And I proceeded to teach my lesson. By the time we were through, the class was over. She was pissed.

She went to the principal and said she wanted to teach the class. She could do it if I would simply help her find the software choices on the network. I decided to show her. But I knew what this was really about—her goal was to control me. She had to disprove my credibility in order to prove hers. And though she surely would deny it, she assumed I was not credible because I am Black.

Though she claimed she didn't understand the software and that was why she needed me, when I attempted to show her, she contradicted me.

"Okay. First you press F1, then Enter. That will take you to the language arts programs. Then you—"

"But I want them to go to the reading programs," she insisted.

"But you told me that you wanted them to work on blends. That's where they are located."

"Oh, . . . are you sure? Because at the two other schools it was laid out exactly the same way and they had the same system."

I tried to hold my temper. "If you don't believe me, I can show you how to go through the programs yourself. You don't need me—"

"Don't get defensive, I was just telling you how it was at the other schools."

Crutch's level of condescension knew no limits.

What frustrates me most about some "white folks" is how I can't tell if they are stupid, passive-aggressive, or both. I again tried to let it slide. I didn't want to argue. So I continued.

"So, you press 6 to go to Reader Rabbit and—"

"No you don't, you hit 7—"

I knew I had to raise my voice or slap her. "I know how to do my job. You need to either let me finish showing you or let me teach the children. Make up your mind."

She started the drama. "Well! I don't know why you're talking to me like this. All I want to do is learn how to use the computers."

"No. What you want is to control me, and that is not going to happen."

She stood up, red-faced and angry. She walked around the table heading for the door. I don't recall what she said; but it was stupid and petty. So I told her to *get a life.*

That was all she needed to run crying to the principal's office to accuse me of—what else?—hurting her feelings.

Crutch didn't know that I had already spoken to the principal, who is Black, and who recognizes racism when it happens. I had told her about what had happened and that eventually I would have to confront Crutch, and I had put everything in writing. I waited.

By the end of the year, I had filed an official complaint against Crutch. She continued to try to discredit me, but I had a fair boss and for all Crutch's hype I accomplished more in one day than she could in a week.

In one of the many meetings held about our problems, Crutch proclaimed how much she loved her students and that she was "committed for the long haul," and how bright the children were and how much she accomplished with them, and that I interfered with that process. At the end of the school year, her students showed little improvement. The following fall, one day before school started, she and four other white teachers quit and went to teach in Menlo Park, an upper-middle-class, predominantly white community. This left only one white teacher. So much for the long haul.

The one remaining white teacher left after a nervous breakdown, and I had to take over her class after eight subs (all white) could not manage it. The longest-lasting sub was a speed freak who bailed on the students right before we started standardized testing. Thanks to the commitment of all these white teachers, these children knew nothing more than they had the first day they entered school that year, except that they were "stupid" and "bad." These teachers had managed to communicate that without ever saying these words. Why would children doubt them? They were adults and they were white.

I see Ms. Crutch's treatment of me as a quintessential embodiment of white teachers' dismissive attitude toward Black teachers' knowledge and expertise. This attitude is part of a pattern well articulated by Lisa Delpit in *Other People's Children.* Delpit quotes two Black graduate students who were also teachers:

I'm tired of arguing with those white people, because they won't listen. Well, I don't know if they really don't listen or if they just don't believe you.

When you're talking to white people they still want it to be their way. . . . They think they know what's best for *everybody,* for *everybody's* children. . . . They just don't listen well. No, they listen but they don't *hear*—you know how your mama used to say you listen to the radio but you *hear* your mother? Well, they don't *hear* me.[1]

Mrs. Crutch's behavior toward me reflects the hegemonic assumption that Black teachers are inept—at best only good for solving discipline problems. But the stories I have told, about Sister Ann, Ms. Brockelhurst, the teacher who failed to defend me against the taunting by the little blond girl, as well as the Ms. Crutch story, are more than stories about a series of individual white teachers who have seen and treated me as "less than" because I am Black and they are racists. Taken together, they embody a pattern of institutional racism. It is institutional as well as individual racism because teachers and librarians are agents of institutions that shape the way children and adults think and feel about race. These patterns are part of a long history of systematic forms of racism that have been manifest in U.S. schools from their inception.

It is not always easy for me to see the institutional nature of racism, even now. It is often too overwhelming in the moment for me to remember that the assault is deeply embedded in an institution that continues to hire teachers regardless of their racial attitudes, teachers whose only qualifications (at least in California) may be that they have been able to pass a basic math and literacy test that is well known to discriminate against people of color. It is hard, in the heat of the moment, for me to see that it is a *system of schooling* that has allowed and sanctioned a curriculum that has conveyed views of people of color as "less than," through both what it does and what it does not teach, to the teachers who are teaching our children. It is difficult to remember that "something bigger" is going on. And trying to dismantle institutional racism almost always seems too overwhelming, given how limited my internal resources are. I have to get the bees that are crawling on me off my body before I can go looking to find the beehive to destroy it.

The Black staff and teachers frequently discussed, always out of earshot of white people, why discipline problems usually failed to escalate to the same degree for us as when white teachers entered predominantly Black classrooms. We concluded that white people usually created these problems for themselves. We knew that, though being Black made it easier in the beginning, the fundamental problems the children brought with them to white teachers' classrooms were no different than those they brought into the classrooms of teachers of color. We knew that style and race were not the major reasons for our success, and we all bitterly resented the implication. The conclusion we reached was that chaos didn't reign in our classrooms because we knew that the behavior problems were not about "bad" kids, but about community-based problems that were manifesting themselves in the classroom, and we worked hard to apply every possible strategy to address them. We did so because we knew the children were intelligent and could learn.

Each of us had at some point experienced the wasted effort of recommending to white teachers that they try something that worked for us. While there were white teachers who were receptive, they were few. Most of the time the white teachers dismissed our suggestions, though sometimes, politely but condescendingly, they said they would give them a try. We knew many white people were snow-blind and would disregard advice if it came from a Black person, so if getting the idea across was important enough to us we would make a suggestion to a receptive white who would then convey it to the person who was snow-blind.

But despite the reluctance of the white teachers in my school to listen to Black teachers' advice, in every education course I took, the white students froze and listened to me when the issue of classroom management came up. I doubt it was just because I was "so articulate," as whites would say. It was because they thought I could give them the "secret" to classroom discipline in Black classrooms. (Asians were less curious because most, like myself, planned to work within their own culture, but on rare occasions they would admit they too were afraid of Black classrooms.) If I was directly asked, I often answered honestly. But nothing I could tell them could be really useful to them because there was so much more to it than I could explain without taking over the class. So when Ann invited me to speak in her classroom I had more than enough to say.

2 Ann:
How I Developed an "Obduracy of Tone"

Inuka Mwungazi, a former student of mine and one of my most important teachers, once said to me, "I used to wonder how a white woman like you ended up teaching what you're teaching here in this college. And then I thought, that's exactly where you're supposed to be."

I was teaching then—it was the early seventies—in a white-dominated, white-oriented university in St. Louis with a faculty that was 95 percent white, and a student body that was perhaps slightly less so. I hadn't thought about Inuka saying that for over thirty years, until the day Sekani said she thought we should write our autobiographies into our book, and I began to wonder, What *was* I doing there?

Learning to Be White

> In my class and place, I did not recognize myself as a racist because I was taught to see racism only in individual acts of meanness by members of my group, never in invisible systems conferring unsought racial dominance on my group from birth.[1]

The eyes of twenty-one white children look out at me from a fifty-eight-year-old kindergarten photograph. I and the other children are seated at our desks in a spacious sun-filled room. It is 1942. Though we bring money weekly for war stamps and useful things for CARE packages, the war is far away; we are and feel safe and well cared for. We have everything material we need. Dick and Jane and all the children in our readers are white and comfortable, except for George Washington Carver who is dark and comfortable and had invented many uses for the peanut, and Little Black Sambo.

Few of us have chores to do at home, nor do our mothers clean our homes or do much of the cooking. We often eat out on "the cook's" day off. The Black women who do the cooking and cleaning (then, we called them "colored," or was it "Negro"?) arrive at our houses by seven thirty or eight A.M., on buses that (as I now know) have been scheduled for our parents' convenience, and walk ten or fifteen minutes to our graceful, carefully decorated and furnished houses that are surrounded by deep lawns and well-established trees.

For a while a Black couple, Amanda and Green, lived in the room above our garage. Green went off to work each morning, and Amanda cooked and cleaned. Recently I dreamed about my house on Granada Way. I could recall every detail of it except for that room. Is it possible that I never visited it before, during, or after Amanda and Green lived there?

* * *

A succession of Black women, Drucilla, Amanda, and Josephine, "worked for us," and a few white ones. One night Maxine, one of the white women, packed up my mother's jewelry and selected outfits into my mother's luggage and took off. I believed without a doubt that Amanda, Josephine, and Drucilla, whom I recall as having nurtured me more lovingly than both Maxine and my own mother, would never have stolen my mother's things and left us alone at night. My most vivid recollection of Josephine is of tears rolling down her cheeks while she shelled peas for our dinner and explained to me the virtues and accomplishments of President Roosevelt on the day he died.

I loved and felt loved by Amanda, Josephine, and Drucilla (whose last names I never knew). But my exposure to the smiling Aunt Jemima images in *Gone with the Wind* and on cardboard boxes of pancake mix predisposed me to see them as selfless, sexless, and jovial people who were in my world to give me comfort. Now I imagine the complexity of the feelings of these women who, though some undoubtedly had children of their own, saw to it that *my* soiled laundry reappeared weekly as washed and ironed clothes in my closet and dresser drawers and fed *my* appetites with aromatic yeast rolls and apple pies.

On dark and dreary winter Saturdays my parents drove me and my friends to matinees at the Shady Oak, each feature preceded by a newsreel and a cartoon. Rereading Toni Morrison's *Playing in the*

Dark and re-viewing Marlon Riggs's film *Ethnic Notions,* I now consider these cartoons and newsreels, long lost to my conscious memory, in an entirely new light. No doubt some of their renderings of Black people as "coons," "Sambos," and savages imprinted associations of Blackness with animality and inhumanness that still pollute the synapses of my unconscious.

I have found a one-page essay entitled "Cotton" carefully printed in pencil that I wrote in second grade:

> There are many states in which cotton is grown. Some of these states are North Carolina, South Carolina and Georgia. The cotton needs hot weather and moist ground. In the early spring there are pretty flowers. Then there comes a brown boll. The cotton boll bursts, cotton comes out. In the spring cotton choppers come out and chop the cotton. The darkies do most of the work. If you see the cotton field any time of the year you would think it is pretty!

What I failed to know about those "darkies" says it all.

In eighth grade we gave a choral reading that I can still quote verbatim after fifty years. (Because I am unable to locate the piece or its title, copyright laws forbid me to quote the piece in print.) The reading told the history of Black people in the Americas, and I must have spoken the words of a white southern woman who was attending her first slave auction. In my role as southern woman, I asked my husband to bid for "the coffee-colored girl," "the one who looks afraid." When the white woman noticed that the enslaved woman was carrying a baby in her arms, she simply said, "Oh that. We'll just give the child away."

Of all the poems we dutifully memorized in school, I remember this part of this one that portrays the inhumanity of slaveholders, and the humanity of enslaved people (though I don't recall discussing the poem, or race, or slavery, or racism).

During my childhood, "Negroes" were required to sit in different sections of movie theaters and movie houses than whites, eat at different restaurants, swim in different pools, but I do not recall noticing that the world I lived in daily was so overwhelmingly white. I do, however, remember vividly at the age of ten, on a Florida golf course, seeing (or, perhaps, noticing for the first time that I remember), "Colored" and "White" drinking fountains. What were the visible signs of white supremacy in St. Louis that I had been unable to see?

My life began at the close of what Cornel West called the Age of Europe, an era he characterizes as a constant stream of crimes against humanity, beginning in 1492 with the mass destruction of indigenous people of the "New World," and the expulsion of the Jews from Spain, followed soon after by the enslavement of African peoples by Europeans.[2] The intellectual and moral milieu within which I came to consciousness took colonialism and imperialism for granted and had forsaken slavery a mere seventy years before.

The defeat of Hitler ushered in the age of American imperial hegemony. That age began when I was eight years old. It was a time of steady capitalist expansion. The consequences of this "rising tide" for me personally were material well-being and comfort, lunches at fancy air conditioned restaurants served by attentive and smiling Black waiters. I must have taken for granted that my family's prosperity was the result of my father's hard work and intelligence and that any smart hard worker could get a piece of the pie.[3] On those rare occasions when we drove downtown we cruised by crumbling neighborhoods on newly built highways. I knew that the poor people living there were mostly Black. Knowing nothing about how "redevelopment" policies had preserved and accelerated the Black poverty that had its roots in the unpaid labor of enslaved Black people that was then passed on across generations, the racial differences in economic status must have seemed to me to be natural and inevitable.

When I was eight, African American men who had fought in World Was II returned home to continuing segregation and racism, and many Black people, sometimes with the help of whites, accelerated the process of openly challenging segregation. Times were changing. In Harlem, in the first night club that allowed a mixed-race audience to listen to jazz under the same roof, the Black jazz singer Billie Holiday was singing the explicitly antilynching song "Strange Fruit," though Holiday encountered Jim Crow in every place she sang, including St. Louis.[4] I of course knew nothing about this at all.

In 1954, the year before I left for college, the Supreme Court handed down the *Brown v. Board of Education* decision that officially ended school segregation. I don't recall discussing it at home or school. The following year the gruesome lynching of Emmett Till occurred. I must have seen the photograph of Till in his casket, his mottled face and head swollen many times their normal size, an image his mother had insisted be displayed for all the world to see?[5] I have no recollection of pondering the photo and the event it symbolized.

I recall no African American, Asian, Latino, or American Indian classmates at Swarthmore College, nor any mention of racism, race, or segregation in any of my classes. I took a course called "The British Empire." Issues of racial justice and white supremacy were never raised.[6] I graduated with honors without understanding that the history I was learning was told from the perspective of white people and served as an apologia for European domination of the world and the status quo. As I write, I consider the possibility that these ideas were taught but passed me by. But if that were so, how could I have graduated with honors?

Just one year after I graduated from college, the Greensboro sit-ins galvanized students to form support groups at many colleges and universities that had been mired in Fifties apathy, and I suppose Swarthmore was among them. But by then I was at the Harvard Graduate School of Education getting prepared to teach. There too I encountered a vast silence about injustice. The only mention of race in any of my classes was the assignment to read Gordon Allport's *The Nature of Prejudice*. I don't think we ever discussed it, or what it might mean for us as teachers. Perhaps we did, and I simply assimilated it into a mindset that had no place for racism.

We were being trained to teach in white middle-class classrooms and, through silence on the subject, to ignore all forms of inequality. This was 1960. After the Montgomery bus boycott; after Governor Faubus and Little Rock. My first three years of teaching were in the all-white middle-class suburbs Harvard had had in mind for us. I did tutor one summer at a church in an area of Boston—Roxbury—that was poor. What I intended to be doing was to help children, one by one, gain skills so they could move into the middle class. I don't think I knew or wondered why the children we were tutoring were Black. I had no sense of what the Civil Rights movement was all about.

What *Was* a White Woman Like Me Doing There?

> No one was white before s/he came to America. It took generations and a vast amount of coercion. . . . It is probable that it is the Jewish community—or, more accurately, its remnants—that in America has paid the highest . . . price for becoming white. For the Jews came here from countries where they were not white, and they came here in part because they were not white; and, incontestably—in the eyes of the Black American (and not only in those eyes)—American Jews have opted to become white.[7]

As Sekani and I talked about what stories we would tell about ourselves, she asked me to explain to her what being Jewish had to do with my commitment to antiracist teaching, and it dawned on me that she took for granted that my experience as a Jew would be central to my story. As she began to see that I neither saw being Jewish as central to my identity (though, as a consequence of writing my story, this has changed) nor understood that many Black people trusted Jews more than other white people, she was surprised. She told me that many African Americans, particularly of her and her mother's generation, including she herself, believe Jews are significantly less racist than other white people.[8]

What Did Being Jewish Have to Do with It?

When I was twelve, my father began driving me to North St. Louis to work as a junior counselor at a Jewish Community Center, and a few years later I became a counselor there. The director, as I see it now, influenced by the burgeoning Civil Rights movement, was a strong advocate, in the lingo of the white progressive community of the time, of "racial tolerance." Mike taught all of us white Jewish campers and counselors songs that condemned prejudice and celebrated the "fact" that "we are all the same under the skin." We sang, "You can get good milk from a brown-skinned cow; the color of the skin doesn't matter no how." We were being taught to be "color-blind"—not to notice "color." Years later I realize that this ideal of color-blindness obstructed my ability to grasp the significance of racial identity, racism, and the privileges that came with being white.

In 1938, my family moved to Ladue, a quiet suburb of St. Louis. We were the first and only Jews there. It was not until almost a decade later that a few more Jewish families began to trickle in.

I have only snapshot recollections of our yearly spring Passover celebrations. My immediate family was joined by my maternal grandparents and the two great-aunts. We performed the ritual recital of the Exodus from slavery and read from a Haggadah distributed by Maxwell House coffee.

What stands out for me is that Aunt Carrie regularly brought black-bean soup. Somehow I knew we were supposed to have matzo ball soup at Passover. Both my parents were at least several generations from their European roots. My mother's mother had arrived in St. Louis from New Orleans, her ancestors sailing there from Jamaica, and theirs, from Spain via Portugal many generations before. Though their progeny had "forgotten" most Jewish rituals and their meanings, unlike many of the descendants of Sephardic Jews, my mother's mother's ancestors had, evidently, in defiance of the Inquisition, and in danger for their lives, refused to convert to Christianity. My father's forebears were of Western European origin and had not experienced the same degree of anti-Semitism as the vastly more numerous and more recent Eastern European Jewish immigrants. They had been allowed to adopt, or, in my father's family's case, to aspire to, the lifestyle of the modern Christian bourgeoisie.

My most pungent memories of childhood celebration cohere around not Passover but Christmas. We decorated a tree as beautiful as any Christian's and hung up our stockings as faithfully. Clear in my memory are the Christmas cards, mostly from my father's customers and business associates, crowded upon our mantel piece. I loved especially the ones that pictured snow-covered churches from whose windows streamed light that illuminated sparkling snow. Gathering around the tree in the entrance hall at my elementary school to sing the familiar and glorious Christmas carols seemed to me pure bliss.

One year I was chosen to be the angel in the Christmas pageant, where, in the darkened and crowded auditorium, hung with pine boughs and redolent, I spoke the words, "Fear not, for behold I bring you good tidings of great joy which shall be to all men. For unto you is born this day in the city of David a Savior which is Christ the Lord." Grace Paley, in a short story, "The Loudest Voice," tells a similar tale of a Jewish girl taking the lead in the Christmas pageant. But, in contrast to that girl, none of the Jews I knew, including my parents, seem to have given the pros and cons of my speaking those words a second thought. On Christmas morning, I would join in the phone frenzy to share with my friends reports of the gifts each of us had gotten. Lighting candles and getting gifts at Chanuka, even though we did it on eight different nights, never even began to measure up to Christmas.

I went to Camp Shoshoni in Colorado for three summers before I started junior high. I loved the quiet mountains and transparent blue skies, the wildflowers, the peace, the flowing mountain streams, and the hymns to Jesus that we sang at Vespers on Sundays, gathered around a fire as the sun set, dressed in clean white shirts and orange ties. I loved the "Half-Christmas" celebration there on July 25, for which we cut down, hauled to the lodge, and decorated a gigantic pine tree. We brought from home small gifts to exchange with one another.

Throughout my childhood, privileged in so many ways, I always felt I was on the margin and somehow not quite good enough. Susan Thomas, the blond, blue-eyed girl I most wanted to be best friends with, did not invite me to Michigan, where her family vacationed each summer, though she invited Patsy Brown and Judy Hanser. I finally decided that not being among Susan Thomas's favorites meant that somehow I didn't have what it took to be "popular," but I couldn't figure out what it was I lacked.

Once my father and I dressed in our best clothes and, using tickets provided by one of his customers, attended the crowning of the Queen of Love and Beauty at the Veiled Prophet Ball. This yearly event preceded the Veiled Prophet Parade, where the queen and her maids of honor, seated on thrones on the first of many glittering floats that rolled slowly along the downtown streets, waved graciously to the crowd while thousands of people, Black and white, stacked twenty deep along the sidewalks, watched with awe and pleasure.

At the ball, St. Louis debutantes (one year, one of the Shoshoni camp counselors among them) were "introduced" to St. Louis "society." My father and I watched from the balcony, for Jews were not allowed on the "floor." (Later, in the Sixties, a Civil Rights action parodied the ceremony by crowning a Black Veiled Prophet Queen.)

One summer my family went to a resort in Wisconsin where one of my father's customers had made reservations for us. The morning after we arrived, we departed precipitously. It seemed my parents had discovered a prominently displayed sign, "Restricted Clientele." Sekani, upon reading this part of my story, asks, "What did your father say about it?" He simply said without apparent affect that "Restricted Clientele" meant "No Jews allowed."[9]

I don't think I was conscious of the anti-Semitism that lingered in those postwar years. After all, it wasn't Nazi Germany. Christian people were nice to us. What I knew about anti-Semitism was that there had been a war, and many Jews, among others, had been killed. I had read *The Diary of Anne Frank*[10] and seen newsreel images of piled-up skeletons and emaciated people that greeted the liberators of the death camps, but I must have fended off the emotional knowing that it was only by a series of historical accidents that I had not shared Anne's fate. Though Jews of my parents' generation knew enough about anti-Semitism to have written tomes about it, the elders I came into contact with breathed hardly a word about it to us, their children.[11]

I learned little to be proud of about being Jewish. The Reform temple where my family belonged had, in fact, reformed. It had substantially reduced the differences between Christian and Jewish traditions. Our modes of worship had come to resemble more closely the Protestant norm: prayer caps and shawls were forbidden. We went to Sunday, not Saturday, school; confirmation, not bar or bat mitzvas were the coming-of-age ceremonies. We went to temple, not to shul, and singing was accompanied by the organ, as in church. I learned nothing of the languages my forebears spoke, and almost nothing of the Jewish literature, history, or traditions of political action for social justice that reached back for centuries, or of the legacies of struggle and resistance. Perhaps I was taught some of this at Sunday school, but I had no reason to retain it since it was not valued knowledge in the Christmas tree world of Susan Thomases and Patsy Browns to which I wanted to belong. Membership in their community required suppressing resonant feelings toward all types of persons beyond that white community's racial pale.

My desire to look, act, and be like my middle-and upper-middle-class white Protestant classmates was reinforced by my parents and teachers, who, with or without their awareness, valued me more the more closely I approximated the white and upper- or upper-middle-class ideal. My desire to be that sort of white person was then in part a form of self-protection against rejection by the very communities into which I had been born.[12]

In 1963 I found myself teaching third grade in a school outside of Santa Barbara, California, where a third of the children had parents who were University of California Santa Barbara faculty, a third were poor white children living in trailer parks, and a third were native Spanish speakers whose parents worked in the nearby lettuce and tomato fields. I rolled up my sleeves and got to work. First, I identified ten or so "trade" books and made reading guides to go along with them and set the already reading UCSB children down to do their reading independently for the foreseeable future. Then I concentrated my full attention on the others.

I did not consciously decide to do this. It seemed to me the only thing to do. Six weeks later I was called into the principal's office. One of the UCSB mothers, a former teacher, and wife of the chair of the Literature Department, was on to me and had reported to the principal that "the parents" were concerned that I wasn't teaching their children. The principal commanded me not to waste my time on the native Spanish-speaking or the trailer park children.

In the context of the story I am telling now, I see this event as evidence that by 1963 I took for granted that it was my responsibility as a teacher to redress injustice, although I was far from being able to articulate this commitment. How had I come to think about teaching this way, with virtually no support from formal education? Did my actions flow from the contiguity of my observations of the social world and the silences about what I had seen, from the contradictions between the "Colored" and "White" drinking-fountain signs and the promises of democracy that had been fermenting ever since I had with hand upon heart pledged allegiance to the symbol of liberty and justice for all in those sunny classrooms so many years ago? Had my sensibilities to injustice been shaped by a tradition of critical thought and commitment to social justice that is built into Judaism, as Sekani repeatedly suggests?

I moved back to St. Louis with my husband in 1963. This time I was to live in University City, considerably closer to the "inner city" than my St. Louis home in the affluent suburb of Ladue had been. "U City" had been predominantly Jewish when I was growing up, but now many Jews and other whites were moving out—west into Ladue—and lower-middle and middle-class Blacks were moving in. By the time our youngest child was in high school, University City schools would be 90 percent Black.

Now it was I who hired a Black woman to care for my children, to offer them milk and cookies when they came home from school while I was finishing my doctorate and beginning to teach teachers at a university nearby. Elizabeth Collins had come up from Mississippi to St. Louis when she was perhaps thirty and, having rented several rooms, had gone back for her eight children, whom she was to raise alone in as segregated and racist a city as any in the land.

Over the years Elizabeth told me many stories about her life in Mississippi and St. Louis. I can today see her sewing school clothes for her children out of flour bags by the light of the Mississippi moon; I can see her cooking for the train porters who would stop off at St. Louis's Wabash Station in the Fifties and head to Mrs. Collins's, just a few blocks away, for barbequed chicken and sweet-potato pie.

Once during the late Sixties, Elizabeth fell ill with what would later be diagnosed as diabetes, and from which she would eventually die. She was told she would have to wait six months for an appointment at the public clinic. I was outraged and decided I would go to the Homer Phillips Hospital Clinic and get her an appointment right away. I took her to the clinic and requested, then demanded, an earlier appointment. From that experience I learned that neither my race nor my know-how could impact the institutional racism that lay behind the long wait for an appointment. I began to realize how little I knew about racism.

Toward the end of Elizabeth's life I began to get to know one of her daughters, Ruth, born on the exact date that I was, November 21, 1937. Sometimes I tell my students this about Ruth: She would have been standing in my place today, if she had wanted to and had been born to my race and class privileges, or if equal opportunity meant anything at all.

Perhaps in part because of what I was learning from Elizabeth and her family and in part because of a curiosity fed by the deafening silence about the African American presence in my formal education,

I chose a thesis topic that would allow me to learn more. The title was "Conceptions of Authority and Deviance of Fifth-Grade Boys Whom Teachers Label Troublemakers." My data were responses to open-ended questions about race and racism I asked Black and white fifth-grade boys and girls and their teachers, all of whom were white. The setting was a newly desegregated school.

My analysis was unsupported by any writings by Black or white scholars of race. No one of my university teachers suggested I read James Baldwin, Franz Fanon, W.E.B. Du Bois or Lillian Smith, a few of the many who had written on the subject of race and racism. I learned from all the interviews, but especially from those with the Black boys—Anthony, Mark, and Boris. (The internalized sexism implicit in my decision to analyze only the boys' interviews does not escape me now as it did then.) I had a knack for listening, and these boys were eager to talk. They wanted to sort out what was going on, particularly whether the principal and all their white teachers and classmates were racist. They wanted to set me straight about race, and to educate me about the "greatest living soul singer," James Brown. I was listening to Elton John, the Beatles, and Beethoven at the time.

Teaching Is the Best Teacher

I remember my first contact with her like it was yesterday: Inuka, a poor Black woman, a recovering alcoholic, was a student in a course I was teaching for the first time, "Crime and Delinquency." The first night's assignment was to read chapter 1 of the critical Marxist text I had chosen. The reading was hard going for me, and I doubted if any of the students would be able to understand it. Inuka had misunderstood the assignment and returned to the next class two days later having read section—not chapter—1. One hundred pages of dense prose. She had, she said, understood every word of it, and I remember how excited she was at having been required to read a book that "told it like it was." She hadn't known people put such things in books. During that course and others she took from me, she spoke from her experience and greatly expanded my understanding of racism. When Inuka spoke, I listened.

I discover, on the now yellowed paper, notes for a two-day teaching sequence for a sociology of education course I taught sometime in the early Seventies. On the first of the two days, I had planned to say that we hadn't yet had a vigorous conversation about race, in part because there are no students in the class who advocate a militant Black perspective, and that I had therefore invited two militant Black students to join our conversation. The two I had invited were Inuka and someone named Keith. I have a vague recollection of Keith, an African American student who regularly attended classes with a rope noose around his neck. The discovery of these notes suggests that somewhere along the way it had already become important to me that students understand and seriously entertain a militant Black perspective.

It was only in the late Seventies, when I began to teach about the history of racism in the United States to students who had been young children when the Freedom Riders went South, that I began to grasp the enormity of the events of the decade that had just passed. I recall having felt stomach-churning fear and anxiety when I first saw on TV the fire hoses turned against the children of Birmingham, and the headlines and the grainy photographs on the front pages of the *St. Louis Post Dispatch* of the many dead—Medgar Evers, Martin Luther King, the three little girls murdered in the Birmingham church, and the three Civil Rights workers, Schwerner, Chaney and Goodman, in the summer of 1964—and realized that there were white people who would protect the social order of white supremacy at all costs. (This was well-known to members of Black communities and to many other whites, but it was news to me.)

But I began to understand how superficial that awareness had been when I revisited this period with my students in a social movements course I taught and we watched *Eyes on the Prize,* with its extended outtakes of footage that never made it to prime-time TV. Why hadn't I felt the full force of the horror sooner? My commitment to "teaching for outrage and empathy," as I put it in a 1989 paper by that name, grew.[13]

I recall now, for the first time in many years, that I argued incessantly—this was 1974—that Webster College needed to have a student body that was more racially diverse and therefore we needed to diversify the faculty and the curriculum, to add jazz courses to the music department's offerings and to rename and expand the required Western civilization course to include non-Western perspectives. No one on the faculty had come to my support. It was during that time that I was refused promotion. The reason given: "Her colleagues sometimes read in her an obduracy of tone that lessens the desire for interaction and cooperation." I was surprised and devastated. Though a colleague and I challenged the decision and won a reversal, it was only as I tried to understand my "obduracy" that I began to see that it was not only students whose worldviews I was challenging.

By the time I moved to the San Francisco Bay Area in 1990, my commitment to teaching for social justice was well established, but the frame or worldview that structured my teaching was still focused primarily on wealth, poverty, social class, and capitalism.

During my first semester in San Francisco, I taught at a small college. I was asked to coteach a required "humanities" course with Lakota Hardin, a Native American woman, using an "unlearning oppression" model or framework. I taught this course frequently during the next four years, with Lakota, Victor Lewis (who will appear later in this book as a central character in the film *The Color of Fear),* Nell Myhand, and several others. In this way I began to grasp and make my own a way of thinking about teaching and social transformation that gave equal weight to a range of forms of injustice, racism, sexism, heterosexism, anti-Semitism, and ableism as well as class oppression.

The goal of the model was to promote the building of alliances across differences. The hope was that these alliances would make it possible for people of diverse identities to work together to identify various forms of injustice in social institutions, including schools, and to join as allies to change these institutions.[14]

During my years at the college I read dozens of students' journals. Each told a unique story of socialization, primarily through family, schooling, and the media, to value, dismiss, and/or despise one's own and others' multiple identities. Reading the journals helped me build a deeper understanding of how the multitude of incarnations of sexism, racism, anti-Semitism, class injustice, and language oppression affects the ways we feel and see.

It was while teaching this course that I first began to grasp experientially the concept of internalized oppression and to examine my own internalized anti-Semitism and internalized sexism. An exercise that is a keystone of the alliance-building process is the "Power Shuffle." In this exercise students who identify themselves as members of a category of people who are targeted by a given form of oppression (for example, gays and lesbians, women, Native Americans) can choose to walk across the room and then turn and face the others when the facilitator calls the name of a group to which they feel they belong.

As we debriefed the "Power Shuffle" in the second year Lakota and I taught together, Lakota commented that she saw a change in my demeanor between the first and second time I walked across the room in response to the calling of the identity category "Jew." She told me that the first time I had stood facing the others with downcast eyes, but that the second time, only six months later, I had walked proudly. Her reading of this was that in the intervening time I had begun to recognize the depths of the internalized anti-Semitism that I had not previously even known I felt, and as a result I had begun to "unlearn" it. This "unlearning" experience surely helped me grasp more deeply how internalized racism, internalized classism, and internalized heterosexism work in my students' lives.

I began to teach the cultural and linguistic diversity course at a California state university when the course was newly mandated by the state for all prospective teachers. The purpose of the course was to prepare students to teach in racially and ethnically diverse classrooms. I had learned from the building alliances model to think about teaching in terms of the hypothesis that all of us to some extent carry within us, consciously and unconsciously, the attitudes and perspectives of the dominant society that some groups of people are of lesser worth than others, and that these views are deeply embedded in and passed on by all the institutions of the society, including schools.

I had come to believe that in order for students in a one-semester course—in a mere fifteen weeks—to destabilize ideas they had been incorporating throughout their lives (and were continuing to incorporate daily) and to experience any significant changes in their views of and relationships to the children, parents, and teachers they would be working with who have identities different from their own, they needed to engage in deeply personal self-explorations. Though such explorations are somewhat unusual in required courses at universities, I had come to believe that to do anything less was to be part of the problem rather than part of the solution.

Part 2

All Right, Who Started It?

The Classroom Encounter and Its Aftermath

3 Sekani: The Boot Camp Presentation
Classrooms in Crisis

Simulating a Classroom in Crisis

Setting up the Role Play

My goal in planning the presentation was simply to give Ann's students some teaching tips they wouldn't learn in any credential program I know about. My intention as I entered Ann's classroom that morning was to address the students' greatest fear: managing classroom behavior in predominately Black, and especially poor Black, classrooms. I had never seen this issue satisfactorily addressed anywhere in the teacher education program, and I wanted to bring some reality to students unfamiliar with the true scope of the responsibilities and difficulties they would soon be confronting as they began to teach in the district's elementary schools.

I had no idea we would end up dealing with racism. I knew Ann had worked hard with this class and had incorporated a great many discussions and readings about racism. Though I felt certain the students would not have overcome their racist conditioning entirely, I assumed it would at least remain covert, as it almost always had in the classes I had taken in the credential program over the past two years. Like most Black people who had been taught the rules of social conduct around whites, I knew that if I used the R-word to refer to any individuals in the class, the students would latch on to it and disregard anything else I might say. So in planning the presentation I reminded myself not to label anything a student said as racist. As it turned out, however, such precautions didn't matter.

I did not think I could help all of them develop better skills for managing the children I teach. The best I thought I could hope for was that if I broke the code of silence I had held to when I was a student, I might scare those who were incorrigible racists away from teaching in our schools, enlighten some of the naive, and affirm and encourage the righteous. My hope was to improve the teaching of Black children and make life easier for the staff who, like myself, so frequently had to clean up after inadequate predominantly white teachers who had failed and left our classrooms.

Ann respected me enough (which in itself is rare for a white person) to let a Black woman loose in her class to speak her mind. I understood the dangers of my speaking honestly, even if Ann and most of the students in the class did not. I knew I risked the wrath of racists by speaking out. But I had survived far worse than the personal condemnation of a few white individuals—years of experience with institutional and personal racism. The possibility of a few white folks in a college classroom bad-mouthing me did not seem very scary.

If I hadn't been so hungry to be heard, I might have seen the enormity of the coming conflict, particularly since I knew Ann planned to show the film *The Color of Fear* on the same day. Little did we know the film would make it that much harder for the students to suppress their racist conditioning.

I had planned three parts to the presentation: an introductory speech, the role play, and a conversation about the role play. I envisioned the role play illustrating the worst-case scenario of an elementary classroom experience. I therefore based the roles that participants in the role play would act out on children I had taught over several years, including, of course, those whose behavior had deteriorated because they had been in crisis classrooms. I wanted the activity to be different from ones we had done in other classes, where we discussed situations and presented case studies from textbooks but never made them come alive. I thought it would be cool, since we are teachers, to use our kinesthetic intelligence.

I introduced my presentation by telling the students I had planned a role play that would direct their attention to issues related to classroom management that I'd never seen satisfactorily addressed in the teacher education program, but that before we began the role play I wanted to tell them something about who I was.

I told them I had grown up in the Civil Rights generation and, strongly influenced by my mother who had been a Black Panther, was a great proponent of "I'm Black, I'm proud." I told them I thought one of my primary functions as a teacher of Black children was to prepare them to become militant Black adults. I wasn't interested in attacking whites. I simply wanted to do something I could not do at work: tell the truth.

I told them I believed my whole life had led to teaching in a community similar to the one I had been raised in. I wanted them to know I had had to research my own culture's values, not just implement the ones my family taught me, that I had had to broaden my understanding of the strategies we as Africans in America used to succeed and survive, and to decide which aspects of Black culture I, after close examination, still chose to live by and implement in the classroom. I wanted them to realize, if *I* had had to work so hard to learn about my own Black culture, how much more will and effort it would take for them to move beyond a superficial understanding of its diversity and complexity.

I told the students I thought one of the most common sources of problems teachers of poor Black children who did not come from my community faced was confusion about what African American ethnic culture is, and that this confusion often resulted in an inability to tell the difference between traditional Black ethnic culture and drug culture. I told them that racism and poverty can cause such severe dysfunction in families that the families may convey the values rooted in their ethnic culture in fractured and inappropriate ways, and that in communities where drugs and alcohol are epidemic, many parents, some of whom are children themselves, may be completely unable to teach Black cultural values to their children.

I said to them that in my opinion the damage that can be done to a Black child by a Eurocentric teacher who cannot make the distinction between behaviors that flow from the values of the ethnic culture and those that are the result of debilitating experiences inflicted upon them by an institutionally racist society is far more severe than what a child of an addict can inflict upon that teacher.

To convey to the students more about who I was, I told two stories. First, I told the story of my fourth-grade experience that ended with me beating up the little white girl with the swooshing blond hair.[1] After I told the story, I posed a question to the class: "What do you think I learned from that experience?" Several students suggested different possibilities: "You learned the teacher wouldn't listen to you." "You learned not to trust white people."

"That might be what you would have learned," I told them. "But what I learned is that sometimes only violence works. I learned that violence can be an effective deterrent to those who insist on exploiting their white privilege."

Then I told the story of my experience with Ms. Crutch. After I had finished, I asked if there were any questions. A student raised her hand and asked, "How do you know that Ms. Crutch treated you like that because of race?"

Ann reminds me that my response was simply, "It's interesting that you would ask that question." I was eager to get on to what I saw as the focus of the presentation, the role play activity.

I intended the simulation to set the stage for addressing the teacher's *other* responsibilities. I wanted to focus on two issues that the credential program as I experienced it had failed to address. The first was how to navigate the district and state rules, regulations, and bureaucracy that magnify the difficulties of classroom management.

The second was how to manage classrooms of poor Black children, including several who come from severely damaged families. I often heard white teachers complain about the extra duties they aren't paid for, primarily what they consider parenting responsibilities. One of the ongoing complaints, especially from the teachers having difficulty controlling their classes, was having to take the time to teach children how to act, something that in their view children should know before they come to school. I designed the role play to get the students to examine this assumption and to realize that in some cases they will be the ones who must teach the children how to interact with others both in and outside the classroom.

My entire presentation depended upon using the role play to recreate the level of chaos I walked into after a succession of teachers had left me in charge of crisis classrooms. I was going to provide a shortage of supplies, little information on the students, a list of school rules that the teacher would not be able to enforce, and no backup outside the room both because support would not be provided without the necessary paperwork and because the support staff was severely overworked. In addition, I was going to give the teacher only twenty minutes to teach a skill.

I warned them. I told them I had set this up for them to fail and that after the role play we would discuss how to address some of the problems that came up. Though I didn't tell them in advance, I particularly hoped to raise the issues of administrative procedures, laws, and paper work associated with classroom management, and how understanding the children's home culture and experiences is relevant to management strategies.

I had created the role play scripts based on many of the issues that were manifest in my classrooms, over the past few years, from the child who didn't get enough sleep to the one who was obsessed with pleasing the teacher. I included extreme behaviors that teachers were most afraid of: those that were the result not only of parental violence and emotional distress and involvement in drugs or alcohol that many of these children lived with on a daily basis but also of having spent months in crisis classrooms. The scripts were designed to raise the social and ethical issues that my children through their behavior presented to me many times each day.

I hoped that during the discussion after the role play, I could convey that discipline should not be based in blind conformity to rules but in ethics, that we should never ask the children, "What did you do wrong?" unless we had created the broader context of "What was the right thing to do?"

There was no way the "teacher" in the role play could successfully manage these behaviors unless he or she was prepared to help the children manage these issues themselves. And teachers were, in my view, doomed to fail at this if they themselves had not investigated, researched, processed, and analyzed the issues first. Only after they had done so could they begin to create a classroom management system that took into account the children's perspectives. After the role play I hoped to discuss these "other" teaching issues.

I began to assign role play parts to volunteers; each of the twelve who would play one of the "children" was given a sheet on which were written the child's goal (for example, to sleep, to get kicked out of school, to learn), a script (a few lines that described the essence of the child's classroom behavior); the child's tactics for accomplishing the goal (for example, sleeping, hitting, name calling, reading a book); who the child interacts with ("partners in crime"); an academic level; an "escalation level"; and selected aspects of the child's background ("parental drug abuse," "absence of mother or father," "mother is a paraprofessional). There were four escalation levels.

Level 1: Angelic. When distracted returns to work if respectfully asked to do so.

Level 2: Usual. Gets distracted but not disruptive unless provoked.

Level 3: Disruptive. Has little to no awareness of the needs of others. Preoccupied with personal needs.

Level 4: Destructive. Preoccupied with home/family issues, angry, and determined to punish the world because of it. Highly insubordinate as well as disruptive.

Sample Role Play Scripts

Dontrel:

Character overview. Dontrel is a bright African American fourth grader. He will not sit still or follow directions. He cannot remember anything (or so he claims). He may be ADD. He was in special ed. but his mother insisted he be mainstreamed. He is not well liked by children or adults. He is constantly negative, cruel, and preoccupied with his new word—"bisexual."

Goal. To humiliate anyone for a laugh.

Script. Talk and play with Clarence, get distracted from tag game, and eat food Sandra has hidden in her desk. When she won't share a second time, snitch on her for having food in her desk. If you are chastised, become defiant, and escalate until sent to the office. Together with Sandra, verbally defy the teacher. When questioned on your behavior, simply say, "I forgot."

Academic level. F

Escalation level. 3+

Partners in crime. Clarence, Daniel, LaTipha, Sandra

LaTipha:

Character overview. LaTipha is a ten-year-old African American who reads at second-grade level. She is big and loud and capable of getting the entire class's attention. She is smart enough to stop short of physical violence. Her mom is mentally ill, drug addicted, alcoholic, and angry. LaTipha emulates her mom's behavior.

Goal. To get sent out of school and on to the streets so you can be with your friends. To impress upon other students how cool you are and how much control you have over adults.

Script. You do whatever is necessary to pick a fight and get sent home. If the teacher sends you out of the room, you go without protest. You encourage other children to play in the classroom. You play tag with Clarence, Daniel, and Dontrel. If caught, you start an argument with the teacher. Disagree with anything teacher says or asks. Only stop long enough for the teacher to focus her attention back on the lesson and go back to what you were doing. Write nothing.

Escalation level. 4

Academic level. F

Tools. Big, loud, and intimidating.

Partners in crime. Dontrel, Clarence, Daniel and your mother, who will defend your actions no matter what the teacher says.

Peter:

Character overview. Peter's first language is Chinese. He is still learning English. He is impatient to finish assignments. When he doesn't understand, he simply guesses.

Goal. To be praised by the teacher. To complete assignments regardless of correctness.

Script. You constantly check with the teacher after every question to see if the answer is right; you have the wrong answer much of the time.

Academic level. C

Partners in crime. None, because you're isolated by language.

Tamura:

Character overview. Quiet. Unable to complete work and unwilling to ask. She has three sisters and very little stability at home. She has missed a lot of school

Goal. To get some sleep.

Script. Lay your head down and if the teacher calls on you, sit up and pretend to begin working. When the teacher is distracted, go back to sleep.

Academic level. F

Escalation. 1

Lakeisha:

Character overview. Lakeisha is a GATE (gifted and talented) student. Unfortunately, that is not on her academic record. As a matter of fact, no one has taken the time to have her tested or to acknowledge or encourage her. She aims to please and is an overachiever. Because her family moves around a great deal and she is often in classrooms with numerous children with academic and behavioral problems, she falls through the cracks. She thinks this means she's just not good enough. Lakeisha's role is to help anyone who needs it and/or will accept it.

Goal. To please the instructor and peers by performing well academically and helping others to succeed.

Script. You will finish your work, then help the person nearest you finish theirs. You'll offer to help, but if ignored you will just go to your seat and pull a book out of your desk and read or watch the drama in the room and try to think of ways you could fix it.

Academic level. A+

Escalation level. 0 (This is the rare student who not only is angelic but a part of the solution.)

Tamika:

Character overview. Tamika is mature and intelligent and well dressed. She is the student whom teachers place next to second-language learners or children with disabilities. She will take care of them.

Academic level. A+

Escalation level. 2

Script. Get your work done quickly and offer to help Tamura. Get up and go over to her without asking the teacher. If the teacher asks you why you are out of your seat, explain what you're doing and ask if its all right to help. Do whatever the teacher says.

In addition to scripts for six other student roles, there were scripts for a counselor, a principal, a paraprofessional, and two parents of level 4 children.

Parent #1, LaTipha's mom:

Character overview. 100% wacko, paranoid, hostile, loud, disruptive, and drunk.

Goal. To blame everyone else for your problems.

Script. When you show up at school, you will be far more disruptive and vulgar than LaTipha, making her embarrassed and eager for suspension. You will argue with your daughter in front of the class and with the teacher, denying that your daughter did what the teacher says she did.

Academic level. 5th grade

Escalation level. 4+. You even offer to "beat" teacher.

Partner in crime. Colt 45

Finally, I ask for volunteers to play the teacher, and for sixty seconds or so no one seems willing. Then Jim, a tall, blond white man, volunteers. He receives the following script:

Mr/Ms. Prozac:

Script. Your goal is simply to teach a lesson. You will be given a story the children are to read, and the questions they will have to answer about it. Have the children finish the assignment carefully by the end of the class period. Do not accept any papers after twenty minutes. You will try to get the students to

(1) Listen to you and obey the classroom rules I have posted on the wall.
(2) Complete the handout. You will evaluate each student's work. *Do not accept incomplete or inaccurate work.*

You must complete a referral form before you send any child to the counselor, as per school rules. You must try to reach the parents of children who have escalated beyond your control to ask them to pick up their children or to arrange a meeting with them.

You must refuse to accept any further students into your classroom no matter how much the principal or counselor insists.

If a fight breaks out, you will have to deal with it. You will have to contact the parents, fill out a referral form, and suspend the child for this day. Expect the unexpected.

Seven Minutes of Chaos

I was amused and pleased when Jim volunteered to be the teacher. He gave off that arrogant vibe that only a white man (or a Black woman) can give. I was pretty sure he would not get through the lesson, though I had doubts that we would be able to recreate the chaos of a real classroom in crisis. The credential students seemed so—well—tame. While I knew that teachers were frustrated actors, I didn't realize they would inhabit their roles—How shall I say?—so robustly.

I remind Jim he's set up to fail. He asks me if he can try to succeed. I say, "Of course, you can *try.*"

I set the timer for twenty minutes and the play begins. There is immediate chaos as the Level 3 and 4 children become possessed by their disruptive roles. Jim, in his role as teacher, immediately calls a class "meeting" to reiterate the class rules that I have taped up on the wall. None of the "children" pay him any heed. Instead, as directed by their scripts, they send paper airplanes into the air, chase one another around the room, punch and return punches. The Level 1s observe quietly, stare dreamily into space, read, put their heads down on their desks, or raise their hands, unobserved, for help on the work sheets that the teacher has passed out. As the Level 2s observe the escalation rise, they join in, as directed by their scripts.

Jim becomes visibly agitated and red-faced. "Sit down," he yells. "*We're having a class meeting.*" After no more than seven minutes of chaos, the classroom is a virtual madhouse; I call the role play off.

From Simulation to College Classroom Confrontation

What Happened Next

With all players in position, Jim and I begin the "heated argument" almost all the students will refer to later in their journals.

* * *

Jim: This situation is totally unrealistic. I've been teaching for a year and I've never seen it happen.

Sekani: Well, I've seen it happen many times in the school where I teach. Especially in the classrooms of white teachers. It's based on my experience. I don't know where you've been teaching . . .

* * *

Sekani: What could you have done to diffuse the situation? Why didn't you use the "para" to send the Level 3s who were out of control to the counselor?

Jim: I would never throw a child out of my classroom, no matter what. They'd never trust me if I did that.

Sekani: Perhaps knowing you will teach them what the limits are might be just what they need in order to learn to trust you; abused and neglected children can often not be counted on to listen to reason. They may be imitating a parent's drug-induced rage.

* * *

At one point during the dialogue between Jim and me, Jim goes over to the list of classroom rules I have posted and below rule number 8 he writes number 9, "HAVE FUN," in bold letters. He tells the class, "I love being with kids. I'm just a kid, myself."

I respond: "These children don't need an adult kid. They need adult role models, not buddies; they can have fun *after* school. Your job is to teach. If you can't control the classroom, you can't teach. The children are there to learn. You better not sacrifice the learning of my children to what you think might be the needs of an out-of-control child. If you want to play, become a camp counselor." In a more modulated voice I add, "No one should try to heal his conscience by saving poor Black kids."

Now, addressing the entire class, I tell them many white teachers don't understand children who have been abused and have experienced violence. At this, one white woman breaks into tears and, speaking through her sobs, tells me I don't know much about it if I think that there is no alcoholism and violence in white middle-class homes.

"With all due respect," I respond, "I am a total stranger; I don't know you. If what I say doesn't apply to you, it doesn't apply. But I'll say this: If I can make you cry by making an off-the-cuff comment, you're in even bigger trouble when you get into a classroom and school filled with people like me."

I tell the class I can understand that some whites fear Black children and adults and add that I myself fear whites, particularly rednecks. Jim responds, "I don't appreciate your comments about rednecks; some of my best friends are rednecks." I tell him, "Then you may want to reconsider working in a predominantly Black environment. None of us are too keen on *your* friends."

* * *

I reiterate that I want the children in my class to become militant Black Americans and add that this means "activists, breaking into banks with computers—not guns—and depositing money into the school systems' accounts. Just kidding—no I'm not."

* * *

Lois, a white woman, breaks into Jim's and my dialogue to say she wants, in the remaining ten minutes, to hear how I would deal with Level 4 children. We all return to our seats.

"How do you handle children like LaTipha?" she asks.

"Well, in the case of LaTipha, sometimes I could cajole her to do the work, or to sit at her desk and not bother anyone. But mostly on her bad days the only option I saw was to ask the para to escort her to the office. I simply cut her loose."

Ann's Recollections

I recall standing on the periphery watching the process of confrontation unfurl and having absolute confidence that whatever Sekani would say would be important for the class to hear. Perhaps a few years ago I would have been afraid that somehow "the administration" would find out what happened and question my judgment, or that the students would, as a result of the escalating feelings, give me bad teaching evaluations. But what I remember most was my stunned realization of how much further many students still had to go—that though we were nearing the conclusion of the course, we had only begun to scratch the surface in confronting the students' racist conditioning. I think I also realized in that moment that my surprise was a good indication of how much I still had to learn.

A friend of mine, upon her initial reading of this chapter, said she thought I needed to explain in more detail what had happened to provoke all that emotion, the anger, the tears. "That's all that happened," I told her. I could perhaps put in more adjectives, describe more carefully the body language and tones of voice. But that is, in essence, what happened, as far as I could see and hear.

Sekani's Recollections

I described the summer encounter to another section of the diversity class the following fall as follows: "When I gave the presentation, I was honest about my politics. I assumed the students would take what they needed and leave the rest. The whole issue of how to teach Black children and what the district and the department don't teach you got completely dismissed. What got many students' attention was me as a Black woman and the anger I obviously felt and my clear 'reverse racism.' It didn't take me long to realize that race was the number one issue on these students' minds. It was ridiculous how a total stranger could walk into a room and in two hours get two people crying. In two hours I was able to do what I sometimes saw Black kids do to their white teachers in a day.

A few months after the Boot Camp presentation I wrote the following account of what happened that day.

My reaction is much different now than it was immediately following the presentation, given that quite a few events have transpired since then. These included watching as less than quality teachers blew out of their jobs and moved to other schools, still teaching, just as badly, I'm sure, but able to find work because the district is desperate.

So I have to go back and try to remember.

I have to notice my lack of memory of these people and examine why they don't burn into my mind. White people become less notable to me in time. Their patterns of behavior become so repetitive that they fade, as people, into the background, and all I can recall about them is their fear, anger, or deceit. Not very flattering, is it? I suspect, although I don't feel it, that my inability to see white people as individuals is, in a sense, a form of denial.

I find myself wondering, "What does it feel like from the other side, to be a bigot, to be a racist? Do you feel angry? Frightened? Empowered? Does it feel good to discuss white supremacy and color-blindness? Bad? Or is there no feeling connected to these issues at all?"

I remember first and foremost the angry white man. I would walk right past him now if I saw him, although I suspect he would walk right up to me and know my name. I never confess this to white people because they would be unduly hurt. My inability to remember has more to do with my defense mechanism than with who they really are.

I view and measure white people by the degree of danger they pose to me and those I choose to protect. The couple of white friends I know and love are not white to me. They are Jewish or Black. That is, they can think from a Black point of view.

During the role play I remember being startled by the Chinese man. I was sure he would have trouble acting like a Level 4 child. Instead I released a Nicholas Cage. Live and learn.

None of the issues that came up were a surprise. Jim's feelings of being set up. The white woman who cried. The expression of "Why don't you feel our (white people's) pain?" The expression of the "Don't be so mean to us and to the kids" philosophy of teaching. The illusion that good intentions will somehow protect their own psyches. The blatant falsehood that children inflict less pain than adults when they call you on your shit. No surprises. Not even a good rebuttal to my remarks.

This was not because they weren't bright. It was because there had been no vehicle in their lives for discussions like this to take place. They need a Black person to confront them with these issues and to illustrate what will happen if they go into teaching with their philosophy and what can happen when someone Black confronts their philosophy head-on. I hope at least some of them took my viewpoint seriously and will use it as a jumping-off point to develop a more realistic and effective teaching strategy of their own.

I believe that as an African American I was far better equipped to go through the encounter than whites because, since I must live within a culture different from my own, my reality is questioned daily. I have, therefore, developed a semipermeable mentality that allows for my reality to be challenged without my losing sight of who I am. The white voice lives in my own psyche, constantly arguing and debating all that I see, hear, think, and feel. So by the time a real white voice speaks out, I have already processed it with a response. This is an advantage in the face of rational and legitimate debate. So none of the students' challenges, when they came, were new. I had heard all these arguments before, both from calmer and far more irate sources. But the vast majority of the students in the class that day had not.

4 Ann: Picking Up the Pieces
Processing Is Everything

Students' Journal Entries

Kathy *White, female sociology major from a high-status university*: "I am a third generation San Franciscan, so I am pretty far removed from my European heritage. . . . I never thought of myself as anything but 'American' " (*journal entry, first day of class*).

Needless to say, I was pretty upset and angry after today's class. I loved *The Color of Fear*. I learned so much from it, particularly from Victor. He eloquently expressed his anger *and* he was the only person who mentioned women in the film.

In contrast, I am upset and enraged by the message I heard from today's guest speaker. (I do not know how to spell her name.) After seeing *The Color of Fear*, which was a tremendously emotional experience for me, I was open to discuss issues of racial inequality in society, particularly in the classroom. I feel privileged to be taking this course with such a diverse, intelligent, articulate group of people. I am feeling connected to my classmates, and I believe that we have built a community based on our shared and differing experiences in these areas and that we are respectful of what we can learn from each other and open to civil discussions of differing opinions. I found S. (this is the best way I can think of to represent her without knowing how to spell her name) to be hostile, condemning and close minded. I was interested in learning about her experiences in life, especially as a teacher. I was also intrigued by the exercise she had prepared.

I don't know if she was aware that some of us were teaching already but I found her attitude extremely condescending. I am aware that she visited our class to share her experiences but I felt she completely dismissed any of our experiences, particularly Jim's. I am enjoying learning from a professor who practices what she "teaches" (not preaches). I appreciate that you tell us how much you are learning from us. You validate our experiences and foster an environment that allows us to create a true community of learners.

If S. had this class last semester I am guessing that she has not been teaching much longer than some of us. I felt she was extremely insulting to Jim. I understand the point she was trying to make about the chaotic nature of many classrooms. . . . I believe it was unprofessional of S. to [make] the sweeping generalization that white middle-class women do not know what they are in for, can't handle it, and have not experienced violence in their communities. How dare she? She claims she can not be racist because she does not hold a position of power in society. When she entered our classroom, by taking on the role of "teacher," she *was* in a position of power and she used that power to judge people and make disparaging comments on the basis of the color of their skin. Hmmm. Sounds like RACISM to me.

I got upset and I was overcome by tears of rage when she said that white people do not experience violence. I would love to share my white experience of growing up with an alcoholic father with her. . . . I do not believe that she is qualified to comment on this subject for, if she had experienced violence, alcoholism and drug addiction she might be aware that these diseases know no boundaries of race or social class.

This is a particularly painful issue for me right now because I have spent most of my life shutting off my feelings as a mechanism for coping with pain. For me to feel that degree of pain, rage, fear and frustration represents major progress for me. Today I felt that my experience, my suffering, was being minimized.

Jennifer *White, female.*
Whew!!! What a class!!! It was one of the most valuable I have ever had. Sacony (sp.?) deserves a lot of praise for her willingness to be so up front about her "agenda" as a teacher and her classroom practices. I think the exercise she developed was a huge success at beginning and inviting an open discussion on an endless number of very important issues (as we all witnessed!!!).

The experience is probably the closest I have ever come to feeling like I know what I look like or could look like through the "lenses" of an African American woman. This information is *so* valuable to me. I am a white middle class woman. How many people who share this part of my identity can say that they have had the opportunity to see themselves from the point of view of an African American woman? Very few, I'm sure. We can see videos and read books or make wild guesses—but this experience was much more real. Sacony told me how her lenses were made, and then allowed me to peek through them—for a second—at myself. She did not have to share this—it was her *personal* life. I respect her for her honesty—for *not* sparing my feelings—for *not* giving me a watered down version of her "truth."

During the INTENSE discussion after our role playing game with Sacony I looked over at you [at Ann, the teacher] and noticed the role that you were taking. Basically you became an observer—watching critical thinking, communication, discoveries and learning happen. This is the sign of a "successful lesson." We were so absorbed (at least I was) in our activity and discussion that I completely forgot about your role as a "guide" in our classroom.

I remember looking at the faces of other students in our class and noticing them glancing over at you, wondering if you might stop the discussion, add to it, redirect it, or intervene in some way. I wondered this myself, and I am glad that you decided to let the conversation (the learning) continue. As future (or present) teachers, the last thing we need is to be sheltered from the conflicts that may arise between teachers because of their different agendas and cultural "lenses." Thanks for providing a safe space for these kinds of conversations to take place, and for letting them take their course— regardless of how unsettling it may be for some. As teachers we cannot expect to be settled. . . . I'm sure you must feel that this class (our interaction with Sacony) was a great success as well.

Jennifer's third journal entry, late June: "After doing the White Privilege exercise I realized I spend time talking to and working with people who are very much like myself; white people. . . . How could I live so much of my life this way? . . . I remember when I was about ten my father thought that my sister and I were being unappreciative of all the 'things' he gave us—so he drove us through a ghetto in Cleveland, telling us to roll up our windows and lock our door and be glad we didn't have to live there. All the people I saw were African American. So I was scared into being proud of my whiteness as if my life would stink if I weren't."[1]

Jim *White, male.*

WOW!!! Today's class was very interesting and *worthwhile*. When thinking what took place I continuously come back to the concept of individual difference. I appreciated the point that the exercise was trying to establish. I believe it was an attempt to open our eyes to *all* of the complex issues that children bring with them to school. However, I don't agree with several of the methods that were used in conveying the message. In reality, it's hard to put into words exactly what I do feel in regard to the exercise and the mannerisms of the woman facilitator [Sekani]. I should begin by saying that I don't feel she is sensitive to the feelings of everyone, which is something that I think any teacher, even at the college level, needs to be. It seems to me that she was telling us "the way it is" from a very one sided point of view. Even though she may have genuine experience from her upbringing, from her ethnicity, and from the inner city school she works at, it doesn't mean everything she feels is going to apply to all of us in quite "her" way.

Right now (as I write) the feelings I have make it hard to convey the thoughts that are running through my head. . . . I imagine the emotions that I'm having are probably very similar to the emotions that many people of color have in regard to the way they have been treated in the past and present.

I look forward to hearing the class discussion that will certainly follow today's class. Hopefully *everyone's* personal concerns will be *recognized* and *respected.*

Jim's journal entry the first day of class: "In all honesty, . . . while growing up I was socialized to be very racist and almost hateful towards people who were not the same as my family. . . . Together my early experiences instilled many almost irreversible feelings and concepts regarding . . . anybody different from myself. I say this because these feelings from my youth can rise up at times (which I'm not proud of). . . . I almost feel as if I was raised without much culture. . . . My problem is that I don't really know where I come from. My family moved from Iowa to California and my parents worked for everything they had. . . . When

I return to 'Dear Old Simi Valley' I often feel relieved to have escaped a place where the culture consists of shopping centers and fast food restaurants."

Martha *White, female.*
I don't think many of us walked out of class today without feeling emotionally charged. I would first like to say I found our guest speaker to be extremely interesting and informative. At the same time I felt she definitely had some strong feelings about Whites. [Ann, responding to this journal entry, circles "strong" and writes, "negative?"] Right from the start she expressed that she was doing us a great favor by giving us inside information that is not taught here at SFSU regarding the way it really is in the inner city classroom in The District. While I do believe she does indeed have great ideas . . . I found that many of her remarks put me on the defensive. As I listened to her story of her second grade experience with the blond white girl I realized that her anger and hostility, although justified, go way back. . . . I feel she was almost saying at times that because you can not possibly relate to these children's lives you've got no business in the classroom. I do not wish to make judgments, but rather I feel that my feelings are extremely important ones to get out if I am to become a teacher and work in a field that our speaker herself described as a place where Whites are sometimes a minority. I found myself asking the questions, Will Black students listen to me? . . . Can I give them anything?

I feel our very articulate African American woman speaker wanted us to ask these very questions of ourselves, now, before we enter a classroom wearing rose colored glasses. . . .

I realized that when our speaker mentioned her politics and the word "militarism" that this term has very different meanings and evokes different feelings with different ethnicities in our class. I also find the term to be negative, and a word that emphasizes the need to fight and remain as separate and hostile groups, one seen as victims and the other as oppressors. I feel this attitude may only increase racial hostility and keep us separate. . . . I understand (I think) that our speaker means to imply the need to strive for justice and stand up for oneself. . . . I just hope all teachers, of all colors, teach in addition to self pride and respect, a sense of openness and lack of judgment towards all people. [There is no further mention of Sekani in Martha's journal.]

Julia *A teacher in New York City for twelve years:* "During the 'Power Shuffle' when the professor called out biracial I didn't go forward, because my initial thought was, 'I'm pure Filipino.' But upon deeper introspection I got to think about how my grandfather was partly Spanish, my other grandfather was partly Chinese" (*journal entry, first day of class*).

To be honest, at first I was taking in Ms. Sauconoy's (I don't know if I spelled her name right) introduction just like that of any other guest speaker. I don't know whether Prof. Berlak had any intention of pairing the film [*The Color of Fear*] and the speaker activities in one day. But as the experience began to unfurl, I felt some strange feelings as if the film was suddenly juxtaposing and coming to life in our classroom. I can't claim to have been neutrally affected by the whole proceedings. And although I was sitting there quietly taking it all in, a whole range of emotions came and went inside me. Watching the movie evoked sympathetic emotions. Some of my classmates were teary eyed and were sobbing. But when the movie came to life in the person of Saucony, who articulately recounted her own experience, and in the life of LaTipha— so well acted out by Nora [in the role play]—I felt that the emotions took on a more intense color. Its different when you see people on screen, outside of yourself, debating with one another. . . . It becomes personal when it stares you right in the face and, in a sense makes you accountable for what may seem to be the breakdown of a class, in particular, and of a future society, in general.

There were times when I felt that Saucony had too big a chip on her shoulder when she came into the class "setting it (the teacher in the role play) up to fail." But I could understand her experience and I knew that she has had some very real lessons from which we could all learn. I felt bad for Jim and in a way for the other girl who spoke up about feeling personally offended. Although it was a class activity . . . it cannot but get personal because, as Saucony said herself, we bring into our teaching all of our history and all of what we learned and all of what we hope life will be.

I admire all that she had to go through and cannot begin to think of how my life would have been had I been in her shoes. I can also see Jim's point as he tried to argue with her . . . I guess, as Saucony taught us, best and sincere intentions are not enough to make one last a month, much less a year, in terribly difficult and frustrating situations.

I guess the activity succeeded in deepening my awareness that this issue of racism is not out there in the streets, or out there in the schools, but in here—in every person's heart. Its easy to deal with it in readings and lectures and even to some extent, in relating past experiences, but when it . . . faces our very being—how we see ourselves as persons committed to making this world a better place—it takes on a more frightening dimension.

Daren *White, male; African American studies major.*
I hope you're not too tired of hearing about the topic by the time you get to my entry but—whew—Tuesday's class. The dynamic especially between Jim and the speaker (I don't remember her name) was an interesting one but I also wished it hadn't gone on quite so long. I'm sure it will be the topic of much discussion in class tomorrow.

What I would like to say to Jim (though I'm not sure that it would be helpful to him or anyone else) is that he seemed to have it in his mind that he was going to succeed even though the speaker told him that he was being "set up to fail." James seemed to think that based on his years of teaching experience and his self confidence that he would be able to "win." I don't think that he realized that the role playing activity was designed to be a springboard for discussion and not a test of the "teacher's" management skills. The other dynamic that I believe was in effect (but that I will absolutely not bring up in class) is that James was not prepared to accept that sort of critique from an African American woman, especially one as strong and militant as today's speaker. (I wish I could remember her name.)

Denise *White, female:* "My (social) class allowed me to see I had every opportunity available to me. . . . 'Couldn't AFFORD?'—in my entire life I never heard those words" (*journal entry, first day of class*).

I don't know if you noticed but I left class early—not because I had some-where else to be. I simply chose to leave. I felt the content was turning a corner I did not want to be part of. I was afraid you would think I was abandoning the discussion which would be the same as turning my back on "refocusing my lenses." I felt the information became personal, not educational.

What a strange day for our class. I felt the warmth of our community was stormed by the militia.

I was writing my notes on *The Color of Fear* when Sekani walked in. . . . I remembered we were going to have a speaker. That must be her, I thought . . . I felt a sense of anticipation. . . . Her intro to her presentation was intriguing. However, I distinctly remember her saying that her goal of teaching was to create militant African Americans. Militant. That word did not sit well with me. I struggled with the question of whether it didn't sit well with the white me or me. At this moment I know my instincts are right—my perception of her use of the word militant was adversarial. . . .

When she was explaining her experience in the school where she was teaching she spouted off an extremely chaotic school situation. . . . But that was okay. I was hearing and adjusting my lenses as I heard her experience. But it hurt when she callously put down our readings from class. I felt this was an insult to you, her former teacher. I am getting a lot out of what I am reading. . . . Her mention of the white females in her life—the little girl with the swinging hair and the teachers she deals with in her work place—were all negative. That was her experience. Her comments didn't hit me the way they did some women in the class. But towards the end of the session she got louder and angrier. I felt she started to lash out.

Jim took his role in the role play way too seriously. It became a debate between him and Sekani. . . . His ego was shut down and he was trying to build it back up. . . . At first I thought he was going overboard, but when I heard his passionate reasoning I understood why he wanted to be heard.

He wants to give back to the kids and schools of today. Why should his ideals be challenged by a stranger? . . . The fact is she is not an expert.

As Sekani was talking before the exercise we exchanged a lot of eye contact. I was nodding in agreement with her monologue. Now I wonder why she was looking at me. Was she seeing a middle class white woman who was going to get her ass kicked in The District's schools? . . . I think so. I feel she was laughing to herself, saying, these girls don't have a clue.

When the hostility rose sharply I had had enough. I wanted to listen, to hear her experience since I have not had that exposure. Lois echoed the same feelings. But the discussion became invasive and violent. . . . Militant.

As a guest in the classroom I feel the end result was a disservice. How are teachers supposed to work together with this teacher's attitude? She needs to check her "chip on the shoulder" at the door. As your guest her opinions are validated. . . . That alarms me. . . . I wondered why you didn't intervene.

Lois *White, female:* "When we moved to Southern California, I was 8. I grew up in an extremely homogeneous area. I know there were not many Jews and always felt a little different because I was the only one of a handful of kids that missed school on the Jewish holiday" *(journal entry, first day of class).*

[When Sekani told the blond-haired girl story,] I sensed some resentment towards cute blond-haired girls that she may have felt or still feel, but that is her right. . . . It doesn't offend me though I am blond. In fact I would rather have children develop pride, strength, maybe even [become] a bit militant, than to internalize racism . . . I want to be prepared to handle these classrooms, to try and relate to these kids so I can teach them. Please let me know if she gives lectures or trainings and where I can learn more.

Isaiah *The only African American student in the class:* "I can't stand the idea of racism and I can turn into that angry 'negro' boy who will lash out. My mother (A SINGLE BLACK WOMAN) raised three children. . . . She often told myself and my siblings, 'You were born BLACK. You're going to die BLACK! So you better get an education and fight for what ever you believe in' " *(journal entry, first day of class).*

Damn. "The Color of Fear," realism, fear, anger. What to do? Can I do this job? Where can I buy that tape [of the film]? Men of all colors need to view that movie. Victor is real. His insights are unmatched.

Sekani touched a nerve in our classmates. Here's my view. Some of our classmates, Professor Berlak, need to take a look in the mirror. They didn't like what Sekani said because it [the statements] attacked what they are in school for—TEACHING. Now, are Sekani's facts about white middle class women teaching children of color true? Do those types of teachers have a difficult time teaching children of color because that type of teacher can not relate to the child? Sometimes YES and sometimes NO! It really depends on how they and the child were raised and what cultural facts they both were taught. But Sekani gave our classmates some knowledge, she gave them some insights, she gave them more in two hours than they will get from any course or class at this university. She stated her AGENDA and Jim and others attacked that agenda and forgot about the issue of teaching children of color. Our classmates should be grateful, not ANGRY. . . . Sekani was great for our class. She opened or made people take their lenses off and LOOK! LOOK AT YOURSELF! LOOK AT YOUR STUDENTS! LOOK!

Carol *White, female.*

I found Sekani's role playing activity the most relevant thing that I have had to participate in while in the credential program. I was with Lois when she stood up and said that she wanted to hear what this woman's ideas were for how to deal with this classroom. . . . I appreciate that the people who were frustrated with Sekani's statements felt they weren't being seen as individuals, like Kathy being upset saying, "You don't know me." But you know what, those students aren't going to know her either and they are going to behave and treat her how they behave any time any white middle class woman subs in their classroom.

It was good advice she had and I feel many members of class were so worked up about their own issues they weren't hearing her. I found Jim's reaction to her statement before the role play began very male (yes, I said that) because when she stated that he was being set up to fail he asked her if he could try to affect the outcome. He couldn't fail and learn from his failure even though it was a safe place to fail. I had an interesting comment from my husband today when he so unsuspectingly asked, "How was class today, honey." When I told him our speaker referred to her agenda in the classroom as teaching [children to become] Black militant men and women he said, "Powerful semantics." . . . She's a strong woman

Ann: Picking Up the Pieces

and I would recommend you utilizing her for your future classes if she's up for it.

Margie *White, female.*
All things considered I think it was a good thing to have the guest speaker join us in class today. The heated debate that happened towards the end of the class would most definitely have happened somewhere and at some point in time and I'm sort of glad it happened in class. . . . I can only speak for myself and what I was feeling. I did feel intimidated, daunted and scared. Maybe that's what she wanted us to feel. She did imply and perhaps state outright that a white teacher would have a particularly difficult time in such a situation. I think that may have put some people on the defensive.

Sally *White, female.*
One part of her politics that caught my attention was when she explained that her goal as a teacher was to bring up "militant" girls and boys. Initially, I was not totally clear on what that meant. Off the top of my head I assimilated it with words like military and war.

Tim *Chinese immigrant, male*: "I was brought up and raised in Hong Kong, a British colony with English occupied most administrative positions. . . . I remember, when I was young, whenever we passed an Indian watchman in front of a bank my mother would say if you don't work hard in school and find a good job you would probably end up like this "dirty" "stinky" "worthless" watchman. Up to now I still got this uneasy feeling when I come across an Indian American" (*journal entry, first day of class*).

Thanks to Ms. Sigouney lesson all teachers realized to a certain extent the reality in the real inner city. . . . What you learn may not work. . . . In heated argument (Ms. Sigouney, a clear minded, logical and experienced orator is gaining a lot of ground in the argument), it also made another female white student cry in tears.

Whether Ms. Sigouney did it on purpose or not is not the crucial point. The reality is the "white" felt unfairly "picked on" and categorized for not being able to do the job. They probably felt more hurt since the comment came from a Black female teacher who they might unconsciously consider to be not that intelligent, or to be highly discriminative against whites.

I think the lesson was great for it has combined the video (*The Color of Fear*) and real life drama. It proves and confirms that the emotion and pain experienced by individuals of minority group in racist society are concrete and real. At this moment you can also see it on the face of our white folk who felt they are on the receiving end of it. The emotion and pain from the minorities and Blacks on video is one more time vividly experienced by the white folk in our actual classroom. . . .

It is never the intention to do this to our white folk. But if you design a course to fight [for] social justice it is inevitable [this] would be the scenario. . . . I don't know if the white folk have got the message or not since they are busily defending their position. . . . If all of us listen hard enough, we would know that we have to prepare ourselves well by developing sensitivity towards Blacks and minority kids in the inner city. After all, this is the main thing this course is supposed to teach. . . . There are a lot of insights for our white teachers in our room. She [Sekani] knows the white culture and she has gone through all the experience of all the kids in her classroom. You can't argue her ability and eligibility. She is an asset and blessing for the Black because Black teachers are so much under-represented in the schools.

Ann: Processing the Encounter in Class the Next Day

The evening of Sekani's visit I think primarily about what I will do in class the next day. As the journal entries I will receive the next day indicate, I am not the only one thinking about what comes next. When class begins the following morning I have decided to ask everyone to write answers to eight questions I dictate. After the students have written their answers to each question, I go around the circle, asking at least four students to read their answers to the question aloud. No one is to speak to what she hears her classmates say: "No cross talk." Everyone has "the right to pass." I ask:

1. What do you think Sekani wanted to teach us?
2. What do you think she meant when she said she wanted her students to become militant?
3. What do you think she wanted us to know about white teachers working with Black children?

4. How do you *feel* about the presentation?
5. How did you *feel* about Sekani's story of the blond girl?
6. How do you think Sekani *feels* about white people?
7. Should I invite Sekani back, and if so should I ask her to change her presentation in any particular way?
8. Where do you disagree with Sekani?

The number of responses I solicited to be spoken aloud after each question was, as I see it now, based upon my only dimly understood intention to make sure that the students and I could get a feeling for the range and variations in thoughts and feelings about Sekani's presentation that existed in the class. When I later look at the students' written answers to my questions I see no evidence that any perspective even one student had written had been left unspoken.

I recall that, after four or five students had read their responses to a question, I expressed my own thoughts about it. At the end of the processing session I also said something about how we all, myself included, need to reflect upon how we respond to anger, and to hearing it expressed in classrooms, particularly when it is directed at those who are members of privileged groups by members of groups that are less so. According to what I can reconstruct from my "lesson plan," we then moved on to another topic: a discussion of language oppression and the implications for us as present and future teachers.

In response to the question about what Sekani wanted us to know about white teachers working with Black children, eleven say she wants them to know that white teachers will have difficulty relating to Black children because of *cultural differences*. (They do not mention racism.) Daren wrote: "White teachers may be unprepared for working with African American students because of their *different* backgrounds and cultures.") Six others mention that Sekani wants white teachers to recognize the various effects of racism on their students that may be manifest in children's lack of trust of and perhaps even hatred for white teachers. Included in this group are Kathy, Sally, and Julia. Sally wrote: "Black children may view white teachers almost as the enemy; they will not respect you unless you earn it."

In response to the question about how they felt about the visit, six students, including Margie, used words such as "intimidated" or "tense." Margie added that less than twenty-four hours later she sees

Sekani's visit as having been a rare opportunity to see through Sekani's lenses. Julia, though she had felt defensive, said she later felt "forgiving." Others wrote that they had felt stimulated and grateful. Isaiah, emphasizing his response with capital letters, wrote: "I FELT HELLYA (GOOD) BECAUSE I KNOW WHAT'S NEXT. What comes after the course work here in college, when they start to teach."

Responses to the question about the Blond Haired Girl Story surprised me most: A number of students indicated they did not think the story had anything to do with racism. Julia, Margie, Christina (a Latina), Debbie (a Chinese American), and Jen (a Japanese American woman) expressed these doubts. Julia: "I don't think this had anything to do with racism. It would not have made any difference if the little girl who did that or the teacher was Black, white, or brown." Carol expressed a very different understanding: "I felt sympathy . . . this stood out to her [Sekani] as an event that taught her about society, values and how the racist system failed her."

By the time students wrote their responses to the question of whether Sekani should be invited back and, if so, how she should change her presentation, they had already listened to a sample of their classmates' views. Only Denise wrote that she believed Sekani should not be asked back. Martha, Margie, Daren, Christina, Debbie, and Jen thought she should be invited again but next time should put aside her personal and political agendas. The others (including Isaiah, Carol, Jennifer, Lois, and Sally) thought nothing should be changed.

Reverberations: Students' Journal Responses to the Processing Session

Jennifer People who have been ignored, abused, devalued, harassed and stripped of their identity will naturally become angry. When this abuse comes from and permeates all the systems and structures in your society, it becomes very, VERY difficult to find a way to direct your anger. Even if you *do* find a way to express your anger . . . it is very likely that this expression will get you into "even more trouble" with the dominant culture. Many people in powerless "target" groups are taught to bite their tongues, sit down, keep smiling, be "nice," regardless of the rage that is building up inside them. Victor *(Color of Fear),* Sekani and the children are pissed off—and rightfully so!!! I think it is very important to think about what it means to be angry. We touched on it a bit in class—but it needs to be taken further. . . . You know the phrase "If you can't say anything nice, don't say anything at all"? How oppressive!!! Anger is an emotion which is just as valid as any other. . . .

Some people in our class felt attacked and uncomfortable when Sekani expressed her anger in front of them. . . . I suppose she pushed some of us out of our comfort zones—the safety and security that comes along with privilege. It reminds me of one of our first readings—"Beloved Community" [by bell hooks] which tells us that "White people who commit themselves to living in anti-racist ways need to make sacrifices, to COURAGEOUSLY ENDURE THE UNCOMFORTABLE, to challenge and change."

Sekani's anger (and Victor's) is challenging—it is difficult to accept and absorb. I guess we have to ask ourselves if we are willing to stomach it—are we willing to do the work that is required to live a truly anti-racist life? We have seen that it will not be easy.

Jim   Today's class [the debriefing session] helped me internalize the messages that were hard for me to grasp yesterday. While the role play exercise was in progress, and while I was listening to Sekani it was very hard to look beyond the feelings I was having. I have to admit that I was angered and defensive towards her methods of presentation. Therefore, having an evening and a class discussion definitely helped me look at and comprehend the underlying and important messages.

The major message that I was awakened to was Sekani's attempt to teach people the reality of behavior in inner city schools. While the exercise was in progress I was much more aware of how *I* was feeling and not really in tune with the feelings and needs of the other students. After giving everything a chance to digest it was much easier to see the benefits on a holistic level instead of a personal and defensive level.

Final journal entry: The last comment I want to make is that I feel I'm really starting to "GET IT." The comment in the class the other day about how others perceive you really hit home. . . . What I'm starting to realize is that no matter what I feel, others have feelings and images that are just as real, and also based on years of experience.

Daren *Final journal entry*: It was not until I began writing [the journal] that I realized that Jim and Sekani's different races and genders were probably a big part of why he became so defensive.

Kathy I felt much better after today's class. I enjoyed the debriefing exercise. I had such a violent reaction on Tuesday night that I was unable to focus on any positive aspect of Sekani's presentation. After I had the experience of hearing other people's perspectives I realized that I had learned and gained more than I thought. I think it was good for me to hear her anger and to examine the deep feelings it brought up for me. I do admire her strength, her conviction, her honesty and her ability to express her anger. I think politics definitely influences pedagogy, whether we acknowledge it or not, and I appreciate her willingness to openly identify her biases.

I still feel that interpersonal relationships need to begin with a basic sense of respect. I guess Sekani's point was not to establish quality relationships with us but to share her classroom experience. I am still upset with some of her attitudes but at least now I can identify some value in the experience.

Denise I wasn't sure how the class was going to launch into Tuesday's experience. I thought the way you approached tackling our feelings was a successful method. My heart rate increased as the questions progressed.

It wasn't until we were talking that it dawned on me that my reaction to Sekani was so complex. In addition to the "reasons why" I wrote in my journal I also know now that I tune out when I am in the presence of loud anger. I am not very adept at dealing with confrontation . . . I now see that Sekani's aural/verbal expression/anger/aggressiveness . . . are all expressions of "being" that I may encounter as a teacher and as a person at some point.

At the first break Margie commented that I expressed her feelings and probably a lot of others in the class who were not speaking up. We talked about how we probably would not be teaching in the district. Sekani confirmed that we would almost "avoid" a situation like that. . . . I know there are multi cultural schools out there that are not infested with the negativity that Sekani depicts.

Ellen said something that has stuck in my head . . . that she has done a lot of work on herself to get beyond certain things and that Sekani's anger didn't affect her. . . . The fact that I didn't get beyond Sekani's anger—I don't think that means I need to work on myself. I am not sure what it means other than that she is the way she is. I am the way I am. My lenses are changing, yes. I will have to learn how to respond to someone like Sekani and not let her words cause me to breakdown (at least in front of her).

Lois I agreed with Daren's point that her (Sekani's) personal politics were fine to introduce but she should not have let the class focus on them. That is sort of what I meant when I said that the blond-haired girl story might alienate people and she should anticipate that and avoid it if her goal was to get through the "lesson." Even though Leslie experienced self-doubt (and so did I a little) this experience made me feel even more determined.

Isaiah Professor Berlak, I really feel some of our classmates were intimidated by Sista Sekani. . . . I'm really glad you did the [debriefing] exercise so the many emotions of our classmates could be heard. . . . I know you would like me to speak more when we have open discussions, but I don't believe our classmates can even hear ME. . . . I feel totally shut out sometimes in our class and that may be ME "trippin." Sometimes I have a hard time articulating my message, even though I have a college degree, even though I have worked in a classroom for six years in the district, even though I have worked in a community program, even though I have written grants and received many awards, even though I know I belong HERE! This is how I FEEL right now. ANGRY. Thanks Professor Berlak. I needed to know how people really see me. . . . This class has been an awakening for me . . . I hope it awakes my fellow classmates. But my lenses have been opened as well.

The following paragraph was part of Isaiah's rewrite of the conclusion to a paper on what to teach Sam, a Black child he had interviewed. He submitted it the last day of class and wrote across the top in giant letters, "NOW I GET IT":

Finally, my goal for Sam is to be a "soldier," NOT a ghetto soldier but a soldier. My soldier will learn tactics of survival, fight the injustices of people who are racist . . . know who your enemy is and confront your enemy, know who your allies are and talk to them always. Sekani was honest about her agenda. So I guess my agenda is to teach a little soldier who will be smart, real tough, (physically and mentally) and educated.

Margie I'm going to write a bit more about Sekani's visit . . . I have to admit I'm still processing it. I know it will take some time. I feel a bit better today after listening to others in the class talk about their impressions. In particular I related to one woman's statement that she felt discouraged and upset when she left class yesterday. That's the way I felt. I went home thinking maybe I'm not the right person to teach in a classroom like Sekani's. And maybe I'm not. I think that's okay to admit. . . . How would I deal with the anger I most likely would be confronted with? I don't know.

Final journal entry: I'm still thinking of Sekani's visit. Of course I am. I feel like my insides have been ripped out and have been replaced, and I think it will take some time to heal! So far, this has been my range of emotions: Intimidation, fear, defensive attitude, hopelessness, realization, guilt, confusion, hope, understanding, admiration, respect. And I would say that's just the tip of the iceberg.

Sally In reflecting on today's class I have to say that I appreciated that Berlak (you, Dr. Berlak) took the time out of our busy class "discussion schedule" to give us her opinion. I think many teachers go through an entire semester of lessons and lectures and discussions without opening up to their students about their viewpoints . . . I feel that when Dr. Berlak gave her opinions [on Sekani's intentions and on her feelings about white people] that she was contributing a lot to her students. I feel we as students highly respect many college professors. When one talks, I listen.

Tim *Final journal entry*: In my opinion one great achievement in this course is that all of us are getting emotionally involved. Teachers nowadays may have paid too much attention to the cognitive development of our children at the sacrifice of . . . genuine love and passion for people different from ours.

I felt, experienced and learned most during my personal "encounters," quoting Dr. Berlak's words, with people of different ethnicities, in watching the film "Color of Fear" and in subsequent "encounter" with Sekani.

Wong Wan Shan *Male, emigrated from Hong Kong.* The journal response Wong Wan Shan wrote the evening of Sekani's visit had not mentioned Sekani directly at all.

As our classmates continued to react to yesterday's situation when we have a visitor to share with us her very genuine experience . . . there is one single but very important thing that might have been overlooked. The point to make here is that as a teacher we must never at any one time while inside a classroom be carried away by our emotions. Teachers are like postmen, they are all supposed to deliver. . . . If teachers are to fulfill this holy job of theirs . . . while a teacher is teaching he/she then should be the one in control, not only controlling the class situation, but also controlling himself/herself by not losing control of one's emotion. But yesterday for that short period of time the guest speaker and some of us let our own emotions take over. That is bad. While it is understandable that at that particular moment in time all anger and frustration and long-suppressed emotion have fused together and finally exploded, yet one has to remain under control, letting not our emotions to take over. We are all eye witnesses to the result—the original good intention of the guest speaker got totally washed down. . . . The very valid lesson I learned once again is: no matter how good your teaching materials are, if your message failed to get through it's wasted.

Final journal entry: A week ago Dr. Berlak asked for my agreement to read out in class my autobiographical writing on social class. . . . If this had happened six years ago I would have politely turned Dr. Berlak down, saying this is a rather personal matter. . . . But now I have been in America long enough to allow change to occur without myself even noticing it. I am not a shy person, but definitely not as outgoing as the Americans. There is this distinctive difference between the Chinese and American culture. Later when my piece was being read out, I blushed. I blushed because I have such mixed emotions. Time has overpowered me. I still remember when I left Hong Kong and while I was on board the plane, I kept asking myself, "How much are you going to change?"

The film *The Color of Fear,* the book *School Girls,* the articles, the words from my peer Isaiah and our guest visitor all pointed to one fact—racism existed in the past and it is still very much alive despite disbelief by so many. I sensed the pain caused to us last week after we did the role play in a classroom situation. The tension grew, the anger exploded, the self-image challenged, the fear and distance created, and yet the feelings so true. It was through pain that we learn more about pain [caused by racism] and that we learn to avoid causing it. Through argument we see truth and through struggle we see hope. It may take human beings another hundred years or more to eradicate racism if we don't educate our young. Only true respect for another race will get us out of trouble—a lesson now deeper and internalized in me. . . . I rarely look at ethnicity and culture like the way I do now than before I studied the issue. I took it very superficially and have never ventured far enough to get to its core.

Final project on African American culture, July 15: My first impression I had about Black people is: they are dark-skinned, have big eyes, thick lips, strong built and have curly hair. When I was about nine I went to see the Harlem Basketball team from USA in Hong Kong. These guys' skills really amazed me. However, when I asked my relatives about who these people are, they told me that Black people were mostly illiterate, lazy. So growing up, negative images of African Americans continue to build up. In American movies, Black people had always been portrayed as lazy, dishonest, hateful, poorly educated. They are the bad guys. . . . Therefore, in the sixties when I saw the movie, *To Kill a Mockingbird*, in which Gregory Peck played the part of a white lawyer defending a Black man who was accused of raping a white woman, I thought, why should the white man defend the Black man? The distorted image continued to grow as I grew up. In the foreign news pages we often read news about Black people being convicted of all major crimes . . . and they always took part in riots. Those news came from the American news agency, the Associated Press. . . . So powerful was that silent message that I too was tattooed. . . . Since the issue of racism had no bearing in my life in those days, so I never attempt finding any information about it.

Glimpse of the Tip of an Iceberg: When I first came to this country the distorted image of the Black people continued to stay in my mind. Then one day I saw a documentary film about the assassination of Dr. Martin Luther King. This aroused my curiosity about racism. Few months later came the Rodney King case, followed by the L.A. riots . . . I began to realize racism is of major concern in this country.

Close Encounter of the First Kind: A year ago I became a teacher working in the District. The day was September 16. I have just finished my preliminary interview by the head of the District, and was told to see the principal of a nearby elementary school right away because they needed a bilingual teacher there. In the cab, I was still enjoying the sweet success of being recommended for the job. But that moment was short lived when I walked into the school office. I was met by a Black lady and sitting next to her is another Black lady talking on the phone. But that's not it, I saw five Black children sitting in another room waiting. Then came the biggest surprise of all—the principal's door opened and out came the Principal, a Black lady in a Black dress (my Principal loves to wear Black.) My throat got stuck. The first encounter was brief, but the effect everlasting. I had met eight African Americans at one time!!! The dose was too heavy for me. When I finally emerged out of the principal's room, I asked myself an honest question, "Do I want to teach here?" But I accepted the job, a job that helped me to change my view towards a race I barely knew.

Part 3

What's Going On Here?

Analysis

5 Ann:
What Makes You Think She's Not an Expert?

We must keep the perspective that people are experts on their own lives.
—Lisa Delpit

My students and I had been discussing racism, class injustice, and sexism together for nearly thirty hours in the two weeks before Sekani's visit. About ten hours of that time had been devoted to learning about racism. I had begun the segment of the course that focused on racism by asking the students to write their racial autobiographies. Like many other teachers of such classes, I asked them to do so because I hoped that excavating and reflecting upon the experiences that had shaped the ways they made sense of "race" and racial differences would promote awareness that their images, views, and beliefs are not reflections of reality but have been learned and are therefore subject to change.[1]

I had encouraged the students to consider how both the media and schooling from elementary school through college—what the teachers and textbooks said and did not say, the prescribed curriculum, the tests that were used to assess what students had learned—affected the way they saw and thought about race and racism. We had discussed how all of us, white and of color, have been and continue to be exposed to a multiplicity of racist images and misinformation from all the social institutions of the society, including the health care system, the legal system, and churches and synagogues; we had noticed how the vast silences about racial injustice often speak louder than words.

I had shown videos naming and documenting instances of racism, both individual and institutional, including a video clip narrated by Diane Sawyer that shows, through the use of hidden cameras, the different ways a Black and a white man are treated by the police, salespeople, and potential employers and landlords. Some members of the class had related instances of racism they had observed or experienced firsthand.

We had talked about a variety of consequences of institutional racism,[2] including the disproportionate number of African Americans and Latinos who are incarcerated and receive the death penalty, and the miniscule number of African Americans and other students of color in our class and in the elementary education program at our university.[3]

I had shown a video portraying two young Black men, one light-skinned, the other dark, whose friendship was affected by the messages the two of them, like the rest of us, received about the negative valuation of darker skin. We had labeled one effect of these messages on people of color—the internalization and acceptance of racist messages—"internalized racism."[4] The students had read firsthand accounts documenting the ways racism has been experienced by people of color, and the ways racist conditioning has often been resisted by both people of color and white people.

I had asked the students to engage in a "White Privilege" exercise: First, they circled those items on a list of "privileges" they believed they could exercise if they chose to do so. The "privileges" include such items as never being asked to speak for all the members of one's race, and being able to use checks, credit cards, or cash and to count on one's skin color not to work against the appearance of financial reliability. Because white women often use the occasion as an opportunity to think about *gendered* privilege, I had emphasized that for this exercise everyone is to answer on the basis of race, not gender. After the students circled those privileges they thought they could exercise and tallied up their scores, I had asked the highest scorers (those who circled 35–46) to stand along one wall, the moderate scorers to stand opposite them, and those remaining to stand along a third. We then observed the results: With one exception, we had recreated a visual representation of the category system known in the English language as "race." We then processed the activity by discussing what each felt about and learned from the exercise, and possible reasons why the one white person who claimed to have only a moderate number of "privileges" might have "gotten lost."[5]

And, in the moments preceding Sekani's visit, we had seen the video *The Color of Fear*. If it hadn't been for my having invited Sekani to make a presentation, after having processed our responses to the video, we would have turned our attention to the next topic on the syllabus, language oppression.

We're Not Speaking the Same Language

> A multiplicity of languages make up the apparent unity of a "national language." Bakhtin's word for these various languages is heteroglossia. Heteroglossia alludes to the variety of actually spoken languages of social groups and classes, professional groups and generations and the different languages speakers adopt for different occasions even within these broader distinctions. Every word spoken in any of these languages is charged with multifarious and conflicting meanings. No word can be spoken without an evaluative accent, without an attitude adopted towards that of which it speaks.[6]

On the day of Sekani's visit we were, of course, speaking English— English learned in New York in the Seventies, Hong Kong in the Fifties, Iowa, the Philippines, and California (Simi Valley, Hunters' Point, Palo Alto), in Black, mixed, Latino/a, Chinese, and white neighborhoods. On the evening of the encounter the students wrote their reflections on the visit in English. They spoke or wrote the words "civil," "quality relationships," "chip on her shoulder," "redneck," "lash out," "unprofessional," "one-sided," and "militant." Since we were all English speakers, we took it for granted that we knew what one another meant.

Let us consider this supposed mutual understanding by looking at the fortune of the word "militant." In her introduction Sekani told us her agenda was to teach Black boys and girls to become militant. At the time I did not give this a second thought. After all, we had already discussed James Baldwin's proposal to teach every Black child that "those streets, those dangers, those agonies by which [he is] surrounded . . . are the result of a criminal conspiracy to destroy him and that he must never make his peace with it."[7] I had been left with the impression that most if not all the students supported Baldwin's agenda. (The same Denise who would on the evening of the encounter describe Sekani's views as invasive and violent had written in her journal less than two weeks earlier: "Unfortunately, Baldwin's message is still as urgent in today's world. . . . It stirs me, a white female teacher, to be more of an advocate to all children.")

Until I began to ponder our class's encounter with Sekani, I did not see her use of the term "militant" as pivotal. I had not considered that the word was seething with multifarious, highly charged, and conflicting meanings. I was not tuned in to the fact that it, like all words, had different meanings when spoken and heard in the context of each of the many different languages that on that day in our classroom huddled together under the canopy of what we call the English language.

I find Bakhtin's term "heteroglossia" useful for thinking about the different meanings we take from a word such as "militant." "Heteroglossia" refers to the babel of languages, perspectives, or worldviews that are spoken by people of different generations who learned to speak what we commonly think of as a single language in different geographical locations and different social classes and different religious and political milieus. The term provides a context for understanding that every word in any utterance or dialogue inevitably has multiple, often contradictory, meanings depending upon the language in which it is heard and spoken.

Critical Multiculturalism

The encounter had occurred after a series of activities, including videos, class discussions, readings and exercises, that had been designed to encourage students to think in the languages, perspectives, or traditions that have been given a variety of labels including "antiracist" and "critical multicultural."[8] That is, I had been trying to teach students to use a framework in which systematic group differences in institutional power are central.

The language of critical multiculturalism is structured to convey that the entire social order is shaped by institutions that tend to preserve and reproduce prevailing racial, gender, and class inequities. From this perspective social rules and institutional practices are set up so members of more powerful groups have inordinate influence over schools, as well as other political and social institutions, including the media. And, whether wittingly or not, they use their power to preserve and enhance their privileged positions.

Central to critical multiculturalism is naming and actively challenging racism and other forms of injustice, not simply recognizing and celebrating differences and reducing prejudice. Because this perspective is built upon the assumption that being nonracist or nonsexist is insufficient to dismantle systematic institutionalized injustice, "social activist" and "antiracist" are key terms of critical multiculturalism.

For those who think in the language of critical multiculturalism, the central issue when evaluating institutional patterns and individual actions is their consequences. If, for example, Black or brown or immigrant children are disproportionately suspended or Black or brown men are disproportionately incarcerated, the schools and courts and their agents (teachers, principals, police, judges) are responsible for perpetuating white supremacy, whether or not they intend to or are even aware that they are doing so.

Before the session ended on the day of the encounter, I had asked the students what they thought Sekani meant by "militant." I then told them I placed Sekani and her use of the word "militant" in the tradition of James Baldwin. I was trying to influence the students to accent militancy, not as random and senseless violence, but as action intended to bring about institutional change in order to increase the degree of justice in an unjust world. I was using my authority as teacher to encourage the students to hear Sekani's use of the word "militant" in the language of critical multiculturalism.

The students had seen the film *The Color of Fear* in the hour and a half preceding Sekani's visit. At one point in that film a white man claims, "The field is wide open and each man (no matter what his race) can stand on his own ground." Victor, an African American, responds with fury:

> No. Each man does not stand on his own ground. Some men stand on other men. Light skin men and men from Europe stand on the heads of men and women and children of color. (And of course also on the heads of white women.)
>
> Damn near all of the ground on this planet has been taken from almost all of the people of color on this planet. Australia was a Black continent. Africa was a Black continent. North America was a red continent. South America was a red continent. You're not standing on your own ground. You're standing on red ground. And that's what it means to be white. To be standing on someone else's ground and then mystifying the whole process so it seems you're not doing it.

Had I known that there were students like Denise who had been able to hear Victor's as well as Baldwin's anger, but not any of Sekani's, in my effort to encourage the students to use a critical multicultural language for making sense of Sekani's use of the word "militant," I would have enlisted, in addition to Baldwin's, Victor's support as well.

Liberal or Mainstream Multiculturalism

As I read the journal entries written on the night of the encounter I realized that most of the students had not used the critical multicultural categories I had offered them to interpret what Sekani meant by "militant," in spite of the fact that I had urged them to do so. What I hadn't understood was that—although after more than twenty hours of classroom conversation, films, and exercises, many students had become facile in the language of critical multiculturalism—liberal multiculturalism continued to be the primary language through which Margie, Sally, Denise, Kathy, Martha, Jim, and others made sense of their social worlds.

Central to the language of liberal or mainstream multiculturalism is the belief that people are, with a few exceptions, rewarded on the basis of their merit. Those who see and speak about the world in terms of liberal multiculturalism do not have the language or lenses for perceiving the institutional and systematic racism that belie claims of meritocracy and equal opportunity both in and outside the classroom.

The language of liberal multiculturalism supports white privilege by rendering institutional racism invisible. It does so by marginalizing systematic and institutionalized differences in power that are related to race, as well as to class, culture, language, and gender. Those for whom liberal multiculturalism is the primary language therefore take for granted that if individuals are taught to give up their individual prejudices and treat everyone the same, we will all "get along," and any remaining limits to equal opportunity will simply disappear.

Because most of the students, initially at least, used the language of liberal multiculturalism to interpret what Sekani was saying, they could not entertain the possibility that she did in fact experience racism every day and that racism was operating in her interactions with the little blond girl and their teacher, and with Ms. Crutch.

They could not, therefore, see any alternative to interpreting her militancy as irrational violence initiated by her and other angry Black people who were, as Denise put it, "infested with negativity." It's not surprising then that Margie, Martha, and Sally associated Sekani's use of "miltant" with militarism, fighting, and "remaining separate and hostile."

Unquestionably, the language of liberal multiculturalism was the language most available to most of the students for interpreting Sekani's use of "militant." However, Sekani, I think, both wittingly and not, mobilized that language as *The Color of Fear*, to my surprise, had not. She did this by her living presence, her African style dress, her confident-appearing, assertive manner, her imposing demeanor (though she was nervous, she did not appear to be so), by the very title of her talk, "Boot Camp for Teachers," and by her stories of the blond girl with the swooshing hair and the white teachers at the school where she was teaching. In retrospect, I think it would have been remarkable if more than a few of us had heard Sekani's use of the word "militant" in the language she was speaking. There were, of course, some—Carol, Daren, Jennifer—who comprehended "militant" primarily in terms of an antiracist/social justice/critical multicultural language.

"I Really Don't Know What I Think": Languages in Conflict

Every student in the class had been exposed to and was familiar with a number of the languages that make up the apparent unity of the national language. The journals provide evidence of the struggles among these languages within the students as they grappled with how to make sense of what was happening.

Jim, who felt that "the woman facilitator [Sekani] . . . is not very sensitive to the feelings of everyone" and has "a very one-sided point of view," wrote that he had many thoughts running around in his head. For a moment, at least, he thought in the antiracist language that was less familiar to him: "The emotions I'm feeling are probably very similar to the emotions that many people of color have in regard to the way they have been treated in the past and present."

Julia, herself a woman of color, at first accented Sekani's militancy as justified anger and described her sympathy, after seeing *The Color of Fear*, for the men of color. However, after having "the film come to life" in the person of Sekani, she wrote that the person speaking out for militancy "has too big a chip on her shoulder," and that she feels sorry for Jim. Like many people of color often do, Julia, at least in that moment, identified with the dominant race, though ambivalently.[9]

Kathy, the white sociology major, well schooled in antiracist languages before entering the class, also experienced an internal battle between contending ways to accent militancy. She initially responded to *The Color of Fear* in terms of an antiracist framework (perhaps in part because Victor briefly acknowledged awareness of the difficulties facing white women). She wrote, "I learned a lot from Victor." However, the evening of the encounter with Sekani, Kathy resolved the battle between contending ways to interpret militancy that was raging inside her by hearing and portraying Sekani as hostile, condemning, and condescending. She interpreted Sekani in the terms of the dominant language of the white privileged.

Denise, who is also white, recounted *her* internal battle: at first, anticipation, then doubt: "Militant. That word did not set well with me." Then her struggle to see through Sekani's eyes: "Her mention of the white women in her life . . . were all negative. That was her experience. Her comments didn't hit me the way they did some women in the class. But towards the end of the session she got louder and angrier. I felt she started to lash out."

Though Denise wrote that initially she felt Jim was defensive, a few seconds later she came to see Sekani through Jim's white male eyes: "I understand why he wanted to be heard . . . his ideals should not be challenged by a stranger . . . she is not an expert." Sekani becomes "the militia" storming "our warm community," a woman who wants to humiliate Denise and other white women aspiring to be teachers. Like Julia, she reads Sekani's anger as "a chip on her shoulder."

Lois, within whom liberal and critical multicultural languages were also contending, expressed her ambivalence about teaching children to become militant: "I would rather have children . . . . maybe become *a bit* militant."

We each have multiple selves, each speaking a different language. Many factors influence which self in any given moment will speak or listen.

Why Aren't You Listening?

> Any utterance takes place between language users who are socially
> marked in the very languages they use.[10]

Twenty-eight of us, twenty-five of whom are women, engage on this day in a two-and-a-half-hour conversation. But we are not simply teacher, students, and guest lecturer. We each bear marks of historical forces of oppression and privilege, and these affect how we hear one another, and the languages we speak and understand.

The two white men enter the class bearing the privileges and prestige that sexism and racism confer upon them. Their statuses predispose us to see what is happening through their eyes. Had they wanted to, they could not have completely divested themselves of the power accorded to their white male views and voices. Some of the women struggled against it on the evening when they wrote their initial responses to the verbal exchanges between Jim and Sekani. After the dust had settled, many had come to see the events as Jim had seen them. Had the other white male student, Daren, for whom critical multiculturalism had become a primary language, expressed his views publicly, things would surely have gone differently.

White and middle class, I carry the power invested in me by the state to award the grades and credit that permit students to teach in public schools. My authority is enhanced because the course is state mandated, a fact I had not failed to emphasize the first day of class. I garner additional power by virtue of the prestigious academic languages my students sometimes hear me speak. All this accords me respect, so when I speak, as Sally wrote in her journal, students listen. (Few students recognize that as a lecturer, particularly in a department of elementary education, my voice actually carries little prestige in the academic hierarchy.) My race and native social class have facilitated my "earning" their presumption of my expertise.

My gender and perhaps my Jewishness dilute some of my authority. Had I been Christian and male, it is likely that at least Jim's reading of the classroom conversation would have been different.

Though I enhanced Sekani's credibility and legitimated her perspective by "handing" her the class (Denise: "As a guest her opinions are validated . . . that alarms me . . . I wondered why you didn't intervene."), her words were still heard by many as less legitimate because she was Black and female. Tim and Daren knew this. Tim: "The 'white' probably felt more hurt since the comment came from a Black female teacher who might unconsciously be considered to be not that intelligent." Daren: "A dynamic (that I absolutely will not bring up in class) is that Jim was not prepared to accept... critique from an African American woman, especially one as strong and militant as today's speaker."

It was given to me, privileged by race, class, and schooling, to legitimate Sekani's right to teach children in public school classrooms to be militant, and to put her into a position to raise the issue of militancy so powerfully in "my" class. I used the prestige of my position to attempt to encourage students to re-accent civility and militancy, to take particular meanings from Sekani's words, to read Sekani's views in an uncommon way.

There's a First Time for Everything

> Verbal communication can never be understood and explained outside of its connection with a concrete situation.[11]

> There are at any given time, in any given place, a set of powerful but highly unstable conditions at work that will give a word uttered then and there a meaning that is different from what it would be at other times and in other places.[12]

How to understand the absolute uniqueness of the concrete situation—this particular two-and-a-half-hour conversation set within a more extended conversation of forty-five hours? One factor of great significance, the one over which I have the least control, is who is present: the racial, ethnic, cultural, class, and gender mix;[13] and the presence or absence of students who are willing to express their thoughts and feelings openly, and who have witnessed and are willing to bear witness to various forms of racism.[14] All this is beyond my control, with one exception: I can invite a guest speaker. An invitation to a militant (or mainstream) Latina, or Chinese or Filipino American, would have changed what happened significantly.

The overwhelming whiteness of the class shaped and gave all words spoken particular accents. There was only one African American student. Had there been even a few more, perhaps Kathy, Denise, and Jim would have been less willing to express their feelings about

Sekani and Isaiah would likely have felt less shut out, less invisible, more comfortable exploring to what extent his feelings of invisibility were the result of his "trippin'." Had I not invited Sekani, I am certain Isaiah would have engaged in our classroom conversations even less than he did.

The context of Sekani's visit also included the in some ways random accident of scheduling that juxtaposed viewing *The Color of Fear* with a live encounter. Knowing the students had just seen the film, Sekani entered "feeling she was (perceived as) Victor." Julia wrote, "I had some strange feelings as if the film were suddenly coming to life in our classroom."

Significant as well is that this was a summer class, telescoped into three weeks; we could not go home after class and put thoughts about the course aside until the following week. Distractions of work and family that might divert our eyes from the issues we were engaging were limited.

Silences Can Speak as Loudly as Words

> Utterances . . . depend upon the historical forces at work when they are produced and when they are consumed.[15]

On the day of Sekani's visit I step back and watch what I now see as, in part, a struggle over the meaning of "militancy," a conversation that has been carried on across decades, in many venues, and in a great variety of social/historical languages in which various meanings of "militancy" (or some synonym for it) are embedded.

The meanings of "militancy" each of us brought into the classroom on that day and the languages in which they were embedded were the effects of our social as well as personal histories. Sekani, whose mother had been a Black Panther, and I had both learned to accent militancy as an active challenge to injustice in the late Sixties and the Seventies, though I was in my thirties and Sekani in her teens. I had come to identify militancy with racial consciousness, Black Power, and social justice by listening to and reading the marginal languages of protest spoken by people like Sekani's mother, languages that often inspired fear in—and were often ignored, stigmatized, and discredited by—the dominant culture.[16]

In an earlier moment the Allied victory of World War Two had ushered in the U.S. domination of the globe and with it the spread of

U.S. culture, which brought to Hong Kong the Harlem Globetrotters, *To Kill a Mockingbird,* and the Associated Press newscasts that had "tattooed" Wong Wan Shan and his elders with racist images of African Americans when he was a child.

As a result of a treaty requiring the return of Hong Kong to China at the end of the century, Wong Wan Shan and Tim arrived on the scene from Hong Kong, bringing with them a colonial legacy of a British education and the residue of conversations about race that had begun long before they had ever met an African American.

All this had come into internal dialogue with Wong Wan Shan's more recently implanted images of "riots" and civil rights marches, and his "close encounters" with African Americans. The close encounters resulted from a court decision that, almost two decades earlier, required the district's schools to desegregate. This Chinese immigrant who had become certified to teach in a Cantonese bilingual classroom was, to his utter surprise, being assigned to a school that had a large proportion of Black children, teachers, and administrators because the Court had ruled that, in each and every school, there could be no more than 45 percent of any given racial/ethnic group, and at least four racial/ethnic groups had to be represented.

These are just a few of the historical forces that were present as the students encountered Sekani, who arrived in class that day in July bearing the imprint of the Civil Rights and Black Power movements.

Most of the U.S.-born students in the diversity class, still less than thirty years old, had come of age in an era when job and housing discrimination had long been illegal. The public world that shaped their understanding was one in which "We shall overcome" was thought of in the past tense, "We have overcome."[17] It was an era of backlash to the Civil Rights and Black Power movements.[18] The common wisdom of most white people and a few people of color as well was that the only racist policy that remained in a now colorblind equal-opportunity society was affirmative action.[19]

Various forms of media, each in their own way, conveyed the demise of racism. News media did so by showcasing people of color who "made it," such as Oprah and Colin Powell, and portraying Asians as a successful racial/ethnic group (though 50 percent of Asians continue to live below the poverty line).[20] On TV, "celebrations of difference," such as Black History Month programming, paid far more attention to past institutional inequities than presently existing ones. The perspectives of the viewing audience, including most of the students in the class and their families and peers, bore the imprint of high school American history texts that with rare exceptions had made both racism and antiracism in U.S. history invisible.[21]

The students in the class were coming of age in a period of modern racism, at a time when overt claims about the biological superiority of white people and the superiority of Anglo-European culture were considered unacceptable in polite company. However, the long history of media portrayals of African Americans as violent continued unabated. Newspapers, magazines, TV, and Hollywood films focused viewers' and readers' anxieties on those of darker skin by featuring not the daily lives of the vast majority of law-abiding and self-supporting members of disempowered groups but their degeneracy, moral decrepitude, and welfare dependency.[22]

The ubiquitous portrayals of gun violence in inner cities perpetrated by tough Black as well as brown and Asian urban hoodlums whose parents are to blame for failing to instill values in their children contrasted sharply with the media spin that accounted for the white teen killers at Littleton in terms of a culture of alienation.[23] The videotaped play and replay of the beating of Rodney King had created an image of King, not the white police, as the object of fear.[24] It is likely that media-implanted images of African Americans setting fires in Los Angeles after the acquittal of the policemen who beat Rodney King were attached in some students' minds to the word "militant," even though Asians and Latinos were the major groups involved.

The social/economic climate in which the classroom encounter occurred was one of considerable economic insecurity. Factories were downsizing, and relatively well-paid factory jobs were continuing to move out of the country. Many middle-class people felt a sense of desperation as they realized they could not count on the quality of life their parents had enjoyed. While the incomes of the few soared along with profits, people earning minimum wage lived below the poverty line, and decent-paying jobs with benefits were scarce.[25] Teachers were often justifiably afraid they would be unable to afford to live in the communities in which they taught and often despaired of being able to buy homes.[26] It was in this climate that Denise, who "had never heard the words 'Can't afford,' " was fearful that because of the need for teachers of color, she wouldn't get a job. She saw the threat to her economic well-being as coming from people of color, rather than state and national governments that refused to provide funding to educate and hire teachers in sufficient numbers and pay them well.

It was in this milieu, replete with messages that racism in the United States is dead or dying, that David Shipler conducted a study of white middle-class American views about race. Wherever he looked, in schools and college dormitories, factories and churches, police stations and corporate boardrooms, he found the notion that Blacks are not as smart, not as competent, not as energetic as whites. He found these views woven so tightly into American culture that they could not be untangled from everyday thought, even as they were largely repressed in polite company. Shipler concluded that color is the first contact between Blacks and whites. It comes as the initial introduction, "before a handshake or a word, before a name, an accent, an idea. It is the announcement, the label, the badge, the indelible symbol that triggers white assumptions about a Black individual's intelligence, morality, reliability and skills."[27]

In this world Susan Smith, a white South Carolina woman with a sure grasp of American racial beliefs, set off a nationwide manhunt by inventing a fictitious Black kidnapper of the children she herself had just drowned. She knew that white people would be only too ready to believe a Black person did it.[28] Perhaps the world the students in the class lived in was not really one world but two: In the Black one, 85 percent agreed with the jury that acquitted O. J. Simpson, and in the white one, 34 percent agreed.[29]

Most of the U.S.-schooled students in our class had attended elementary and secondary schools that were overwhelming racially segregated.[30] The majority who had not had experienced segregation within schools because of tracking or curriculum segregation.[31] Therefore, few of the students of any race had had close cross-racial friendships, even during college. This insured a great experiential gulf between most of the white students and the mostly poor Black, brown, and Asian immigrant inner-city residents most of them would be teaching.

The historical context in which they had grown up had provided hardly any multicultural and essentially no antiracist education in elementary or high school, and only a few felt they had had their Eurocentric perspectives challenged in college.[32]Given the dearth of firsthand experience—and with few exceptions, no education, formal or informal, to the contrary—most of the students had come to take for granted the prevailing explanations for racially differentiated school success: Class and race differences in achievement were the result of parents' limitations—their irresponsibility, their low levels of education, their apathy toward their children's schooling—a perspective social theorists label "cultural deficit" or "cultural deprivation" theory.[33]

The students in my class, like others in the society, had not been exposed to and therefore did not bring with them into our classroom alternative explanations for race and class differences in school success. For the most part, they were aware neither that a disproportionate number of Black, brown, and immigrant children went to schools that were savagely unequal in per-pupil expenditures, in facilities, and in the preparation of their teachers, nor of the effects of this on school success.[34] They had not thought about whether schools for poor children should receive not only equal but greater expenditures to help compensate for the educational liabilities that poverty incurs, for example, frequent moving from school to school and inadequate nutrition and health care.

They did not know that one effect of official school desegregation was that, though they most often continued to attend segregated schools, students of color were being taught by an increasingly white teaching force.[35] Nor had they had the occasion to consider that as a result, students of color were being taught a curriculum that was ever more closely scrutinized and controlled by white administrators or administrators of color who had most frequently been educated in white-dominated institutions, and they had not thought about how this might affect the school success of Black and brown and other poor children.[36] They had not, for example, entertained the possibility that the academic difficulties of many Black and brown students might result in part from the beliefs of teachers and administrators, primarily but not only the white ones, that these children couldn't learn as well as whites.[37]

Nor had they considered that the competitive logic of school success and the Eurocentric and implicitly if not explicitly racist curriculum of these post-desegregation- era schools required academic and social behaviors that were not merely different from but at odds with the ethnic/cultural heritage of many African Americans.[38] They therefore could not consider the possibility that conforming to school norms might result in alienation from the communities from which many Black students derived their sense of belonging, a consequence so hurtful it has been labeled "social death."[39]

Nor had they been exposed to the view that some Black students' low academic performance might therefore reflect not an inability but a refusal to adopt the Anglocentric perspectives required to succeed in school.[40] They had no idea that it was possible to teach a culturally relevant curriculum that would not force students to choose between achieving academic excellence and identifying with African American culture.[41]

Since neither the media nor any of their prior teachers had reported it, the students in my class did not know that there is evidence that children and youth of color who are able to identify racism and are prepared and committed to resist it—those who are "militant," as Sekani and I use the term—are more likely to succeed in school than students whose teachers promote assimilation into existing power relations.[42]

Nor had my students entertained the notion that antipathy to school might often be both stimulated and reinforced by the growing sense of hopelessness of many Black and brown children and youth and their parents. Given that most of them were unaware that the school success of poor Black and brown children and youth is unlikely to be rewarded with employment opportunities equal to those of whites—that the promise of equal opportunity that accompanied the end of official segregation was, with some very visible and highly publicized exceptions, illusory—they came into our classroom on the first day of class assuming they would find Black antipathy to school that had its roots in children's home ethnic culture.[43]

Though well-regarded by many in the scholarly education community, the view that good teaching practices for middle-class white children might not be identical with those for children who arrive at school without knowledge of the culture of power had received a very limited public hearing.[44] The students were therefore unaware of this explanation for racially differentiated school success, as well.

In light of their failure to be exposed to any of these explanations, it is easy to understand why the students brought with them the "common-wisdom" view that the reason for differences in achievement resided in the children and their parents, not in the society and its major socializing institution, schools. It is therefore not surprising that most of the students brought with them into our class the view that what is required to be a good teacher to children of color is simply to care about them. This meant caring about children as individuals; it did not mean promoting the welfare of the communities the children came from by addressing the unjust social arrangements of the broader society that powerfully influenced the children's lives.[45] Their notion of caring was a far cry from the kinship, connectedness, and solidarity that Foster deems essential for effective teachers of African American children.[46]

How could our students arrive on the first day of class with an understanding of the limitations of mainstream explanations of Black students' failure to thrive in schools, when critiques of the dominant perspectives had been so publicly and academically silenced?

* * *

Thus, the schools and the media, by what they said and what they failed to say, provided the context that shaped the thought and language that students, both white and of color, brought with them to class, and informed their attempts to account for the overwhelming realities they were aware of: disproportionate amounts of Black and Latino poverty and unemployment, high drop-out and expulsion rates, racially differentiated school success, and high incarceration rates of Black and brown people. It was in this political, cultural, historical, and economic context that Denise, Jim, and others encountered Sekani's views and struggled to come to terms with her claims to expertise.

6 Ann:
Fantasy and Feeling in the Classroom

Conversations Across Time and Space

> Every utterance must be seen as a response, and every utterance
> expects a response. An utterance is shot through with anticipations of,
> and responses to, the words of an other.[1]

Multiple conversations converged in the moments we are telling
of, each composed of innumerable responses to and anticipations
of the responses of others. These conversations reverberate across
time and space. At the moment of the encounter between Sekani
and the class, I was aware that my invitation was a response to my
conversation with her about the relevance of the diversity course and
of the teacher education program more generally. Though I was only
vaguely conscious of it at the time, I now see that I also invited
her because I wanted the students to engage with her militancy.
What I wanted, among other things, was for the students to join
a conversation I had first participated in with Inuka Mwanguzi, who
had been my student more than three decades before. I remember
watching Inuka interrupt her own graduation ceremony to insist
that the president of the university, who was awarding the diplomas,
pronounce correctly her chosen African name.

On the day following the encounter I initiated a discussion of
Sekani's visit so the students could hear their classmates' responses
to what she had said. My intention, again only partly conscious, was
to spur ongoing conversations within themselves, with one another,
with friends and family, and with me through the journals. (Because
of time constraints, this was the last time we would talk about the
encounter in class.)

I took sides in these complex negotiations in the politics of language cautiously: I chose my battles. I did not intervene during

Sekani's presentation, though I closed the class on the day of the encounter by telling the students I thought Sekani, like James Baldwin, accented militancy as action for social justice. I expressed this view again in the processing session the day after the encounter and in some of my written responses to the students' journals. My comments were both anticipations of the students' views and rejoinders to the views they and former students had already expressed.

In response to Sekani's presentation, Wong Wan Shan had written: "Some of us let our emotions take over. That is bad. . . . The original good intentions of the guest speaker got totally washed down." I responded in his journal: "One lesson I take from what you say here is that there are significant differences between you and Sekani in cultural style."

My words were intended to encourage Wong Wan Shan to listen to Sekani's anger and, more generally, not to discount what people say just because their voices are filled with passion. My intentions had been shaped in part by a paper about Chinese immigrants Sekani had written while she was a student in my class. In that paper she had told of two Chinese immigrant women who had become her aunts through marriage to her uncle and the difficulties these women faced dealing with the complexities of an African American culture for which they had no frame of reference.

Sekani's written reflections on her aunts were in response to an assignment I had given her in the diversity class in which she was, officially, my student. That paper had shaped my grasp of the difficulties and importance of understanding between Chinese immigrants and African Americans. What I learned from it was alive in my response to Wong Wan Shan.

Is This the Way You're Supposed to Behave in a Classroom?

Some versions of a language enjoy prestige and others do not. The history of any national language can be written as an account of a tension filled heteroglossia that is pulled towards uniformity by the normative language created by education and the national media and towards variety by the centrifugal pulls of social, geographical, ethnic and generational differences. One component of each of the languages of the heteroglossia is its genre. Genre determines the ways people speak in different circumstances. Genres are the drive belts from the history of society to the history of language.[2]

In our class I had spoken and wanted the students to learn to think and speak in an antiracist or critical multicultural "language." Most of the students, like me, had been schooled in—and took for granted that we would be speaking in—one of the liberal or mainstream "languages" that are more commonly used in classrooms at all levels of instruction. Though the languages the students were most familiar with and the critical antiracist talk I was introducing and expecting students to become conversant in differed in important ways, they had in common that they took for granted that classroom talk should be "civil," "polite," and "respectful." And what this meant in practice was that we should speak to one another without expressing feelings, particularly feelings of anger.

The critical multicultural and mainstream languages both rested on the assumption that classroom talk should be rational and dispassionate,[3] and that the rule to exclude feeling applied to everyone equally: to those who experience injustice and those who may have benefited from it. For example, the person who is the target of a racial slur and the one who speaks it are both subject to the same prohibition against expressing anger.

Defining politeness in terms of masking anger is of course neither inevitable nor universal. We *learn* when it is appropriate to feel and express anger; we *learn* to consider bombing civilian populations or imprisoning increasingly large numbers of African American males worthy or unworthy of anger. In Audre Lorde's view, for example, it is often inappropriate to *mask* one's anger. She writes: "I cannot hide my anger to spare you guilt . . . for to do so insults and trivializes all our efforts."[4] Wong Wan Shan's, Denise's, Jim's, Isaiah's, Sekani's, and my feelings about expressing anger are products of our social, historical, and cultural experience.

Denigration of the passionate expression of anger by those who set and reinforce social norms weakens dissent and drains the energy from challenges to the status quo. But because they are so ubiquitous in our society, prohibitions against expressing anger eventually come to seem normal, and the ways in which they are embedded in power relations and are shaped by and serve the racial, ethnic, gender, class, and academic hierarchies become invisible.

As I revisited the encounter and its aftermath, I saw anew how deftly the powerful national and academic languages of genteel po-

liteness most of us learn to speak reinforce and perpetuate orientations to expressing anger that are endemic to particular ethnic cultures. Denise's feelings about Sekani's expressing anger likely reflect
an Anglo-European tendency that is closer to Wong Wan Shan's home
culture, and to the dominant cultural definition of politeness, than it
is to Sekani's.[5]

Though Wong Wan Shan had written: "Some of us let our emotions take over. That is bad," Tim (also a Chinese immigrant) had
written immediately after the encounter: "In my opinion one great
achievement in this course is that all of us are getting emotionally
involved. Teachers nowadays may have paid too much attention to
the cognitive development of our children at the sacrifice of genuine
love and passion for people different from ourselves." This initial
difference between Tim's and Wong Wan Shan's orientations toward
expressing feelings is a reminder that there is no simple correspon-
dence between ethnicity and the speech genres deemed appropriate
in classrooms.

If the encounter had occurred in the Sixties or early Seventies,
when the standard of dispassionate speech was frequently challenged
in, as well as outside, many university classrooms, perhaps the norms
for expressing anger would have been different in our class. What
forms of speech are deemed acceptable in what venues is subject to
historical change.

Anger (Moral and Defensive)

Until Sekani's visit, the students had discussed racism in tones that
might as easily have been used to talk about the weather. However,
on the day of the encounter, Sekani broke the rules of "polite"
conversation by telling stories of racism she had experienced and
expressing the anger she felt about those experiences. (This was
something she had never done when she had been a student in
my class.) She expressed her anger in a relatively intimate setting
while looking directly into students' eyes. (Denise: "As Sekani was
talking . . . we exchanged a lot of eye contact. . . . Now I wonder
why she was looking at me.")

On that day, for the first time, a number of the students also
expressed anger, either in their journals or in the open forum of
the class. It seemed to me that Sekani's breaking of the cultural

and classroom norms against expressing feeling gave permission to some of the students to break the norm as well. However, with only two exceptions, the anger the students expressed was of a distinctly different sort than Sekani's.

During the encounter I wasn't thinking about the distinction between moral and defensive anger. What I call "moral anger" is anger at socially induced suffering. "Defensive anger" is a response to being held (or feeling one is being held) accountable for the injustice that provoked the moral anger in the first place.[6]

Only Sekani expressed moral anger aloud, though Jennifer and Isaiah wrote about it in their journals.

Jennifer (the white student whose father had given her a lesson in race relations by driving her through a "ghetto" in Cleveland) wrote:

> People who have been ignored, abused, devalued, harassed and stripped of their identity will naturally become angry. When this abuse comes from and permeates all the systems and structures in your society, it becomes very, VERY difficult to find a way to direct your anger. Even if you *do* find a way to express your anger . . . it is very likely that this expression will get you into "even more trouble" with the dominant culture. Many people in powerless "target" groups are taught to bite their tongues, sit down, keep smiling, be "nice," regardless of the rage that is building up inside them. Victor [in the film *The Color of Fear*], Sekani and the children are pissed off—and rightfully so!!! I think it is very important to think about what it means to be angry. We touched on it a bit in class—but it needs to be taken further. . . . You know the phrase "If you can't say anything nice, don't say anything at all"? How oppressive!!! Anger is an emotion which is just as valid as any other. . . .
>
> Some people in our class felt attacked and uncomfortable when Sekani expressed her anger in front of them. . . . I suppose she pushed some of us out of our comfort zones—the safety and security that comes along with privilege. It reminds me of one of our first readings—"Beloved Community" [by bell hooks] which tells us that "White people who commit themselves to living in anti-racist ways need to make sacrifices, to COURAGEOUSLY ENDURE THE UNCOMFORTABLE, to challenge and change."
>
> Sekani's anger (and Victor's) is challenging—it is difficult to accept and absorb. I guess we have to ask ourselves if we are willing to stomach it—are we willing to do the work that is required to live a truly anti-racist life?

The evening of the encounter, Isaiah, the only African American in the class, wrote in his journal: "I don't believe our classmates can even hear ME. . . . This is how I FEEL right now. ANGRY." It is not surprising that Isaiah failed to express moral anger in the classroom and only began to write about it in his journal after Sekani's visit. He had been well socialized to "proper" Black—particularly Black male—student behavior in white-dominated classrooms such as ours. But why was it that none of the other students expressed moral anger in the open forum of the classroom?

There are at least two possible reasons. One is that they felt constrained by the dominant social norm regarding expression of emotion in classrooms. Jennifer, though she condemned the norm against expressing anger (" 'If you can't say something nice. . . .' How oppressive"), was likely still restrained by it. But the second possibility is that most of the students didn't express moral anger because they didn't feel any. Why not? Perhaps because moral anger requires empathy, and empathy can so easily go awry.

Several of the responses written by Kathy, Jim, and Denise ex-emplify one way empathy can go wrong. After seeing the video documenting surveillance by store detectives who target African Americans, Kathy volunteered: "I know how that feels. I get fol-lowed around a store if I don't dress up when I go shopping." Jim told us he had experienced harassment "like the (Black) man in the video." He too, he told us, was often stopped by the police, because he drives an expensive car. Denise assumed that the differ-ence between her experience growing up with an alcoholic father and what the experience would have been if she were Black was inconsequential.

These white students were denying the differences between the suffering of African Americans and their own, thus in effect discount-ing or minimizing the role racism plays in this society. They were, in essence, thinking, "Their pain is just like mine," not "My pain is like theirs in this one way." These students' claims that they know how those others feel are expressions of a distorted form of empathy that does not acknowledge the limits to their abilities to understand the experience of people who live in a different relationship than they do to the structures of power. This blindness to the difference race makes is, of course, one of the effects of social institutions (the media, schooling) rendering white privilege and institutional racism invisible.

Denying shared suffering is, like claiming it, another way that empathy can go wrong. For example, women of dominant races and social classes can, through experiences of their gender, understand *something* of the suffering of poor women of color because these women share the common experience of sexism, in spite of the fact that their experiences differ profoundly as a result of their race and/or class.[7] For these racially and class-privileged women to fail to see what they have in common with women of color is as dehumanizing to these women as is a claim that their suffering is identical.

Jennifer recognized that she shared with Sekani the experience of exclusion by "popular" blond girls, but she also acknowledged that her ability to know what Sekani felt was limited. Implicit in Tim's statement, "It is never our intention to do this to our white folk," is an acknowledgment that he shared something of the suffering African Americans experience as a consequence of racism, though he seems to recognize that racism directed toward Chinese Americans is also different in kind: "If all of us listen hard enough, we would know that we have to prepare ourselves well by developing sensitivity towards Blacks and [other] minority kids."

Wanting to "help the unfortunate" (by, for example, offering them "charity") usually indicates pity, another form of empathy distorted by denial of shared humanity. Those who pity others demean them by seeing and treating them as less—less motivated, less capable, less intelligent. They take for granted their right to define and evaluate whether or not the sufferer deserves to be treated with kindness and generosity. Pity is an emotion once not uncommonly exhibited by slave owners for their chattel. It directs attention to the objects of pity and away from those who may be causing the suffering.[8]

Jim wants to "help" children who are more unfortunate than he is, and Denise supports his desire: "He [Jim] wants to give back to kids and the schools of today. Why should his ideals be challenged by a stranger?" Though he claims he wants to "give back" to poor African Americans by teaching them, Jim's disrespect for Sekani's knowledge suggests he had no idea what he had received from African Americans (or what he could get from them in the future). It is therefore unclear what he wants to offer restitution for by "giving back." When Sekani tells Jim, "No one should try to heal his conscience by saving poor Black kids," she challenges and rejects Jim's pity.

The reflections students wrote the night of the encounter indicate that on that evening some of them were angry. With the exception of Jennifer and Isaiah, however, the anger they felt was not moral anger directed at the injustices Sekani had spoken of. It was, instead, defensive anger directed at Sekani. Kathy: "I am enraged by the messages I heard from today's guest speaker. I found her hostile, condemning and close minded." Denise: "She started spouting off. . . . I felt it was an insult to you. . . . I felt she was laughing to herself, saying, 'those girls don't have a clue.' " Several journal responses express anger at Sekani less directly. Martha: "Right from the start she expressed she was doing us a great favor by giving us inside information . . . I found [her] attitude increasingly hostile." People who pity others and offer them charity may become angry toward "those ungrateful people" if their offers are refused.

The morning following the encounter I began with a debriefing exercise. I asked the students to write responses to eight questions, two of which explicitly directed their attention to their feelings: "How do you feel about Sekani's story of the blond-haired girl?" and "How do you feel about the presentation as a whole?" I also asked, "Should I invite Sekani back and, if so, what should I ask her to change?" This and other questions tapped into their feelings indirectly.

The students' responses to the question "How do you feel about Sekani's story of the blond girl?" revealed, to my surprise, that at least half the class felt no moral anger at the treatment Sekani had received. For some, the reason seemed to be that they did not consider the story to involve racism. They were enmeshed in what has been labeled color/power evasion.[9] Christina (a Latina) wrote, "I felt [the story revealed] that she [Sekani] still has some personal issues to deal with." Martha wrote, "I've seen similar things happen between children of the same race where a teacher doesn't address a problem at hand."

The answers that Carol, Daren, Lois, and Sally wrote to the questions and read aloud revealed some empathy for the little girl Sekani had been ("Even though," wrote Lois, "I could have been that little blond girl.") Their failure, like the others, to express moral anger may reflect some degree of numbness to the suffering of others, and responsiveness to the norm of emotionless expression, as well.

Thinking About Feeling

The feelings engendered by the encounter—pity, and defensive and, for a few, moral anger— had gotten the attention of virtually everyone. Feeling such feelings is, however, only a first step in the process of reevaluating one's emotional responses to racial injustice. Changing one's emotional responses requires *thinking* about what we feel and do not feel and why. Asking students to write answers to my questions required them to think about their feelings.

After I had posed each question, I asked several students to read their responses to it aloud. I simply organized the hour I had allocated to the debriefing to insure that the students would have an opportunity to learn that some of their classmates felt differently than they did about Sekani's visit. My hope was that the students would implicitly compare their classmates' feelings with, and then reevaluate, their own.

Perhaps because the experience of hearing how others felt provoked them to think about their feelings, some of the defensive anger seemed to begin to abate during the debriefing hour. On the previous night Sally had written that she had associated "militant with words like military and war" and implied she felt resentful if not angry at Sekani for feeling hostile to white people. However, during the debriefing, after hearing her classmates' responses to my questions, she wrote, in response to my question about what Sekani meant by "militant," "that children would have pride in themselves and be prepared to defend themselves in the real world." It appeared her anger at Sekani's militancy had diminished. However, the anger Kathy felt toward Sekani continued unabated during the debriefing session.

The journal entries written the evening after the debriefing activity suggest that this simple exercise continued to fuel change in students' views. Jim: "Today's class [the debriefing session] helped me internalize the messages that were hard for me to grasp yesterday. While the role play exercise was in progress . . . it was very hard to look beyond the feelings I was having. . . . I was angered and defensive. . . . Therefore having an evening and a class discussion definitely helped me look at and comprehend the underlying and important message." Jim continued to think about the processing session. In his final journal entry he wrote: "I'm really starting to GET IT. The comment in the class the other day about how others perceive you really hit home."

Kathy: "I feel much better after today's class. I had such a violent reaction on Tuesday night that I was unable to focus on any positive aspect of Sekani's presentation. After I had the experience of hearing other people's perspectives I realized that I had learned and gained more than I thought. I think it was good for me to hear her anger and to examine the deep feelings it brought up for me."

Denise: "I wasn't sure how the class was going to launch into Tuesday's experience. I thought the way you approached tackling our feelings was a successful method. . . . It wasn't until we were talking that it dawned on me that my reaction to Sekani was so complex. In addition to the 'reasons why' that I wrote in my journal, I also know that I tune out when I am in the presence of loud anger."

And Margie: "I'm going to write a bit more about Sekani's visit. . . . I have to admit I'm still processing it. . . . I feel a bit better after listening to the others in the class talk about their impressions. In particular I related to one woman's statement that she felt discouraged and upset when she left class yesterday."

Isaiah also found the processing session illuminating: "I'm really glad you did the [debriefing] exercise so the many emotions of our classmates could be heard . . . I know you would like me to speak more when we have open discussions, but I don't believe our classmates can even hear ME. . . . This is how I FEEL right now. ANGRY. Thanks Professor Berlak. I needed to see how people really see me. . . . This class has been an awakening for me. . . . I hope it awakes my fellow classmates. But my lenses have been opened as well."

Giving *my* opinion on each of the questions may have had some effect on the students' changing views. Sally mentions this explicitly: "In reflecting on today's class I have to say that I appreciated that you, Dr. Berlak, took time out of our busy class 'discussion schedule' to give us your opinion. . . . I feel that when Dr. Berlak gave her opinion she was contributing a lot to her students."

My written comments on the journals seem to have been important at least for Kathy. I had written in response to her journal entry on the night of the encounter: "I think the pain you experienced as a child witness to your father's alcoholic rage can give you the resources to empathize with the pain of others in many of its various forms—including the pain people of color experience as a result of racism. Getting in touch with your pain is, in my view, essential to being able to empathize with the pain of others and thus to operate humanely in the world and in the classroom. The goal is to be able to hear and feel Sekani's rage against racism, and to be able to listen with empathy to an angry parent of one of your students without seeing that parent as your alcoholic father—without taking it personally."[10]

Kathy had responded: "I really appreciated your comments on my last journal entry. There are not many places (especially in the academic world) where I would feel safe enough to express the pain and rage I have experienced this week. Your comments and the class work have helped me process these experiences in a completely non-judgmental way. It is usually quite difficult for me to hear these responses without feeling personally attacked as you may have noticed. . . . I now think that Sekani did not intend to personally attack the white women in the class. I did respond as if she were my father, angrily arguing and crying simultaneously. This experience has been extremely powerful for me on a variety of levels."

Changes in views continued during the last two days of the course, though we did not discuss the encounter again in class. Wong Wan Shan on the evening of the day we had processed the encounter wrote that Sekani had been unprofessional: "As teachers we must never . . . while inside a classroom be carried away by our emotions." However, in his final journal entry he wrote: "The tension grew, the anger exploded, the self image challenged . . . yet the feelings so true. Through pain we learn more about pain. . . . Through argument we see truth and through struggle we see hope."

Margie's final entry contained the following: "I'm still thinking of Sekani's visit. Of course I am. I feel like my insides have been ripped out and have been replaced, and I think it will take some time to heal! So far, this has been my range of emotions: Intimidation, fear, defensive attitude, hopelessness, realization, guilt, confusion, hope, understanding, admiration, respect. And I would say that's just the tip of the iceberg." Other journal entries indicate that others shared Margie's turmoil as the course drew to a close.

I now wish that in the processing session I had directed the conversation more explicitly toward identifying feelings, particularly contradictory and ambivalent ones, and their origins. If we are angry at Sekani but not at the teacher who failed to protect Sekani from the blond-haired girl or at the racism that, we now see, was conveyed through the history courses we were taught, we need to ask why. Denise needs to ask herself what experiences in her life prepared her to view James Baldwin's militancy as legitimate and yet harbor hostility to Sekani's.

Those who "read" Sekani's stories of the racism she experienced—and her views that the actions of most white people reflect their racist conditioning—as evidence of paranoia must ask how they have come to do so. They must ask themselves why Sekani's claims to expertise rather than the mistreatment she has experienced arouse their anger. They must ask themselves if they accept or discount another's anger because of where they and that person are positioned in the hierarchies of power.

I had encouraged students to do some of this reflection during the first week of the course when I asked them to write their racial autobiographies. I see now, though, that until they have had an opportunity to identify their racialized feelings, their ability to investigate the origins of those feelings is inevitably limited.

Expressing Anger in Multiethnic Classrooms

Though the dominance of the prevailing definition of "proper classroom speech" was temporarily destabilized during the encounter, it continued to command allegiance from most of the students. I think it was because Daren feared Jim's anger that he wrote that he would "absolutely not bring up in class" his view that Jim's reaction flowed from his racist and sexist conditioning. Denise makes it clear in her journal that the only reason she expressed her feelings by breaking into tears was that she was unable not to do so. According to Denise, Margie had told her that she (Denise) and Kathy shed tears "for" many others who were able to restrain themselves. At the end of the course Lois still seemed to continue to feel antipathy toward expressions of anger in classrooms: "The blond-haired girl story might alienate people and Sekani should anticipate that and avoid it if her goal was to get through the 'lesson.' "

There were others who seemed to value the in-class violation of the prohibition against anger. Margie wrote that though she felt intimidated, she was glad the "heated debate" happened in class, and Jim wrote that he considered the experience "*worthwhile.*" As we have seen, Wong Wan Shan also changed his mind about the value of expressing anger.

As I stood back and began to recognize the depths of anger that had been let loose inside the room—indicated by Jim's red face, the loud intense exchanges between him and Sekani, Kathy's explosive retort that Sekani couldn't know much about alcoholism and violence in white middle-class homes—and as I felt the shock of it ricochet among the students, I had no inclination to quell the storm.

Though I flashed momentarily upon the final course evaluations and the possible disapproval of the chairperson were she to hear the shouting from the hall, the main feeling I recall is satisfaction that as a class we were at last nearing bedrock, going beyond where I had been with any class before, and that we were going in the right direction. I recall at this moment my own fear when—before I met Inuka, knowing her reputation as a woman who named racism when she saw it in or outside the classroom—I saw her name on my class list at the beginning of the semester so many years ago.

Only in retrospect do I understand that it was Sekani's use of passionate speech—a socially unacceptable classroom speech genre—that conveyed the primary lesson that was being taught and learned by many, though surely not by all: that racism can evoke justified, deeply experienced (moral) anger (at least) in those who are targeted by it, and that acknowledging and expressing that anger can evoke in white people and in people of color (Wong Wan Shan, for example, and Julia) both denial that the moral anger is justified and defensive anger directed at the people who express it.

Tim's views on the effects of passionate expression parallel my own:

> I think the lesson was great for it has combined the video [*The Color of Fear*] and real life drama. It proves and confirms that the emotion and pain experienced by individuals of minority group[s] in racist society are

concrete and real. At this moment you can also see it on the face of our white folk who felt they are on the receiving end of it. The emotion and pain from the minorities and Blacks on video is one more time vividly experienced by the white folk in our actual classroom. . . .

It is never the intention to do this to our white folk. But if you design a course to fight [for] social justice it is inevitable [this] would be the scenario. . . . I don't know if the white folk have got the message or not since they are busily defending their position. . . . If all of us listen hard enough, we would know that we have to prepare ourselves well by developing sensitivity towards Blacks and minority kids in the inner city. After all, this is the main thing this course is supposed to teach. . . . There are a lot of insights for our white teachers in our room. . . . She [Sekani] is an asset and blessing for the Black because Black teachers are so much under-represented in the schools.

Neither Sekani nor I had anticipated the eruption of such deeply felt emotions—variously referred to in the journals as "intense discussion," "the dynamic between Jim and Sekani," "the debate between Jim and Sekani," "the heated debate," and "the heated argument." Neither did we anticipate that Sekani's expression of her feelings would call up meanings and valuations of civility, respect, politeness, anger, and pain that were profoundly racialized.

As we have seen, confrontation with an other or others who speak a passionate but stigmatized form of the language with confidence and skill may be traumatic for those who have been taught that expression of intense feeling is inappropriate. It is therefore not to be taken lightly. Those of us who are "better" socialized, either through our ethnic culture of origin, or by popularized notions of psychology and psychoanalysis, to express feelings publicly may have to invent ways of expressing feelings that do not so strongly jar the sensibilities of those who are not. We all need to become more bicultural regarding public expression of feeling.

However, a transformation of understanding of racism by members of both dominant and nondominant groups may *require* teachers to expand their views of the array of acceptable speech genres beyond those set by their particular ethnic cultures and by the dominant culture as well. People whose ethnic culture teaches privacy and public reticence may need to adapt to a more expressive public culture, as Wong Wan Shan, who had asked himself on the plane to the United States, "How much are you going to change?" seemed to be doing right before our eyes. He will interact with African American children as their teacher and perhaps with African American adults as an administrator. His ability to listen with respect to passionately expressed sentiments may at some future time stand him in good stead.

As a result of the encounter, I have come to believe that there are some people who may be unable to grasp the degree of damage racism wreaks upon people of color (and upon white people) unless they engage *face to face* with expressions of anger and pain, and are then helped to understand or "process" their responses. Such struggles to understand the effects upon themselves of passionate engagement require that the conversants have some reason to remain engaged in the conversation. Denise, who "tunes out" in the presence of anger, though she left the class early on the day of Sekani's visit, returned in part because we had established a safe space, but also because she wants to become a teacher and she must pass my course to do so.

Perhaps all we can say about Jim, Denise, Kathy, and Margie (and all we can hope for) is that as the course drew to a close the clash of social accents was lively in their heads. Denise wrote me, two months after the course was completed, thanking me for the "gift" that was our class. Jim, who wrote on the first day of class that he doesn't know where he comes from, and who told Sekani some of his best friends are rednecks, after "digesting" our debriefing, came to realize—to put it as simply as he does—that "others have feelings and images . . . just as real [as mine]." This *is* a small step, but perhaps too small for someone who will soon be teaching these "others."

Another way to look at it is that Sekani was willing to speak in other than the academic tones of "civility" to convey the devastating insidiousness of racism experienced by children and adults, to illuminate Black anger and "violence" and their origins, to crystallize the issues, by saying what she really thinks and feels and by telling The Blond-Haired Girl and Ms. Crutch Stories. By breaking the rules of "proper speech" and "proper behavior," she brought to the surface some of the conflicts and contradictions of the heteroglossia and fueled some motors of social change.[11]

Do You Know What You're Saying?

> Every parent knows a little of this dynamic . . . "Why doesn't that lady have any teeth?" comes the child's piping voice. "Why doesn't that gentleman have any hair?" And, "Why is that little boy so Black?" *Ssssshhhh!* Comes the anxious parental remonstrance. The silencing that is passed from the parent to child is not only about the teaching of restraint; it is calculated to circumnavigate the question as though it had never been asked . . . A wall begins to grow around the forbidden gaze; for we all know, and children best of all, when someone wants to change the subject, forever. And so the child is left to the monstrous creativity of ignorance and wild imagination.[12]

As this quotation from Patricia Williams reminds us, what is not spoken of does not simply go away. Instead it is sent underground into those realms of ignorance and wild imagination we call the unconscious. In the moment of the encounter and for several months that followed, I was using the language of critical multiculturalism to think about the encounter. Fundamental to this language, or at least the version of it I was thinking in, was the assumption that if injustice is rationally exposed it will be resisted.[13] Though I, like at least some of the students, had read extensively about, "believed in," and had explored in therapy the power of the unconscious, I, like most of them, had become accustomed to leaving this interpretive lens outside the classroom door.

What unconscious processes of my own could explain how I could be present during the encounter and remain unaware of the multitude of unconscious processes that were surely whirling about the room?[14] How can I understand my failure in that moment to consider the unconscious—what is irrational, unspeakable, forgotten, ignored, and despised, what may be thought of as the invisible third participant in any dialogue?[15]

For example, when Sekani said she was afraid of rednecks and Jim retorted that some of his best friends are rednecks, why did I not bring to consciousness how Jim's warm feelings toward "rednecks" would have been heard by Sekani and Isaiah, and perhaps others. Why did I not recall my own experience with some men whom I had learned to think of as "rednecks": one of the most fearful nights I ever spent, at a remote campground in Missouri next to a tent of drunk white men who were shooting rifles skyward. And why did I not bring to awareness that in the languages I speak, "redneck" demeans white men who do manual labor in the sun. On the afternoon of Sekani's visit, the multitude of nefarious meanings circulating around the term "redneck" were absent from my consciousness.

Fears and Fantasies

I now think my "forgetting" to wonder about the unconscious processes that were operating was motivated in part by my own then unconscious fears, desires, and fantasies that impelled me to actively repress knowledge I couldn't tolerate knowing. Perhaps, rather than wanting to know more about what was going on, I had a passion to not know.[16]

Perhaps I was afraid to face the frightening implications of Sekani's claim that the lesson of the Blond-Haired Girl story was that sometimes (only) violence works against racism. Or perhaps I didn't want to know how powerfully implanted were Jim's fears of and disrespect for Black people, maybe in part because such an awareness would again remind me how deeply I had been implanted with the same. Perhaps I was resisting knowing that my carefully constructed curriculum had left these fears and attitudes untouched, because I wanted to believe that I could change and had in fact changed, in thirty hours, the way my students thought, and I didn't want to face the possibility that I was powerless to do so.[17] Perhaps, I didn't really want to know the hydra-headed shape of racism.

I was not, of course, the only one whose unconscious was active during the encounter. The students' journals provide clues to feelings and thoughts that for the most part remained buried in their unconscious, were at best only briefly acknowledged in journals by a few, and were entirely unexamined in our classroom conversations. One of the most prominent of these was fear. Denise's comments— "Our community was stormed by the militia" and "The discussion became invasive, violent . . . militant"—suggest she feared Sekani. Margie and others acknowledged they felt intimidated and scared.

Denise had written: "I wasn't sure how you were going to launch into Tuesday's [processing] session. . . . My heart rate increased as the questions progressed." Why had having to answer a few questions caused her heartbeat to quicken? What was going on behind the scenes? What was there to fear?

Perhaps these students' fear of Sekani was an instance of a largely unconscious but deeply ingrained suburban (in Jim's case, Simi Valley)[18] fear of encirclement by dark-skinned others. Perhaps they were associating Sekani with the terror they felt at the prospect of teaching a class populated by what they—with the assistance of the mass media and the criminal justice system—had come to see as violence-prone Black children.[19]

Knowledge about racism has been called difficult knowledge because it may threaten a person's entire worldview.[20] Perhaps at least some of the students, though they were unaware of it, were deeply invested in keeping at bay Sekani's view that she and other people of color had been unjustly disempowered because it challenged their understanding of how the rewards and punishments are meted out in a society they had learned to think of as just. Sekani's rendition of the world she lives in may in fact have threatened the students' views of the very nature of the human species.

Threats to belonging resonate in the most vulnerable corners of our psyches.[21] Perhaps Jim feared that if he began to see racism from Sekani's point of view he would be rejected by his "redneck" friends. Or, as Sekani has suggested to me, an (unconscious) attraction to African-American women may have threatened his views of where he belonged in the racial order. Perhaps some students feared Sekani because she threatened their assumption that they would become well-qualified members of the profession they had chosen.

Maybe Jim and others resisted acknowledging Sekani's expertise because they were trying to maintain the floodgates that protected them against a dawning awareness that their positions in the racial hierarchy, which provided important sources of self-esteem, were unearned and undeserved. Perhaps Jim, a white man of working-class origins, who on the first day of class wrote that he didn't really know where he came from, was (unconsciously, of course) engaged in a practice of defining and consolidating his identity through rejection and disavowal of dark-skinned people as embodied by Sekani.[22] Maybe Julia's view that Sekani had a chip on her shoulder flowed from an unconscious attempt to differentiate herself (a relatively light-skinned Filipina) from people darker than she.

Perhaps some of the students feared facing the shameful awareness that they had not noticed, or had not felt outraged or even moved by, the injustices those "beneath" them experience.[23] The white students, and those who, like Julia, reap the benefits of white privilege because of their appearance, may have been afraid to acknowledge what Sekani was saying to them because they didn't want to know that their privilege came at the cost of degradation and exploitation of others.

Their fears may have been intimately connected with profound desires to be, and be recognized as, worthy of their own and others' respect, to be deemed "good" and innocent, not complicit with injustice.[24] Perhaps Jim and some of the others were afraid their self-images would be blown apart if they gave credence to Sekani's experience, for then they would have to face the fact that they are deeply disfigured by the racism that is central in Sekani's universe.[25]

Their need to protect themselves from these largely unconscious fears and desires may have motivated some of the students to deny that Sekani was a person whose views are as legitimate and valuable as theirs, and mobilized their defensive anger at her claims to be an expert who is capable of judging their qualifications to teach Black children. Tim, Carol, and Daren suggested this interpretation. Daren: "The dynamic that I believe was in effect . . . is that James was not prepared to accept that sort of critique from an African-American woman." Tim: "They probably felt more hurt since the comment came from a Black female teacher." Carol: "I found Jim's reaction to her statement before the role play began very male (yes, I said that) because when she stated that he was being set up to fail he asked her if he could try to affect the outcome. He couldn't fail and learn from his failure."

It is likely that I didn't want to bring to consciousness the possibility that our classroom conversations had sent such fears and desires underground by labeling them politically incorrect. Perhaps I was resisting the awareness that this relegation of these fears and desires to the unconscious might have intensified projections of insensitivity, anger, and tendencies to violence onto African Americans—including, of course, Sekani.

Sorrow and Despair

The collision between Sekani's worldview and that of all the others in the class, I think, provoked another set of powerful feelings that were so deeply buried that they were never spoken of. These were feelings of profound loss, grief, sorrow, and despair. During the encounter and its aftermath, these feelings were never identified and remained entirely unexplored. One source of the sorrow flowed, I think, from the immense distrust and disconnectedness the encounter brought to the surface between white people and people of color, and between Latinas and Asian, Filipina, and African Americans, as well.

I catch a glimmer of the profound sadness that underlies Sekani's anger when she sends me an e-mail more than a year after the encounter. In response to having called a white friend on his racism, she had written:

> The pain racism causes stays with you after the damage has been done.
> I weep silently.
> I won't lie.
> I never would have done the right thing if I had known it would hurt this much.
> Even though I knew not doing so would cost me my dignity and my self-respect.
> I'm afraid of the next betrayal.
> Nothing can make up for the persistent fear and emptiness left inside
> From continued denial of the intrinsic value of my existence.
> Get the picture?

The loss and sorrow that are the result of the distance and distrust that has separated me throughout my life from the Black people I have known begins to come into focus only as my connection with Sekani deepens and I begin to see what I have missed.[26] Perhaps we catch a glimpse of the sorrow of disconnection in the tears of the two white women, though I think they would have described their tears as tears of rage.

I could not have encouraged the students to explore these and other unconscious feelings, fears, and fantasies because I was not thinking of these possibilities at the time.

Bringing the Unconscious into Partial Light

I have begun to see many of the white, Asian, and Latina responses to Sekani as unconscious responses to Black anger, as well as to fear of Black violence. I also have come to see them as expressions of desires to maintain precarious identities and connections with others. These fears and desires had, however, in large part, been transformed into something unrecognizable by our conscious selves.[27]

Had I been as attuned to unconscious processes as I am now, I would have realized that students' questions—for example, "What makes her [Sekani] an authority?"—could be clues to unconscious fears and desires. If I had done so, I might have asked the students to consider what their investment might be in denying (or accepting) Sekani's interpretation of the events in the Ms. Crutch and blond-haired girl stories as racially motivated. When Denise characterized Sekani in her journal as "infested with negativity," I might have asked her through her journal to bring to consciousness the fears and desires that were implicit in this choice of words, and the genesis of those fears and desires.

By posing these questions I would have been directing students' attention to themselves and away from their preoccupation with whether or not Sekani's attributions of racism were accurate. Perhaps this would have been the first time most of them had considered that their racial views might be motivated by unconscious desires and fears. I would have been changing the rules of the classroom game by inviting the unconscious into our classroom.

One consequence of this line of questioning might have been to provoke students to consider whether or to what extent they see Sekani as "less than." Next, they might ask themselves what might be the connection between their evaluation of Sekani's expertise and, by extension, her humanity, and the images they had been exposed to in museums, textbooks, films, TV, and magazines they had encountered throughout their lifetimes.[28]

Despite my determination to grapple with some of these unconscious processes next time, I am aware that, because they are infinite in number and always in flux, we can never bring to light all the unconscious dynamics implicit in classroom conversations. Thus, though we could certainly have engaged in deeper conversations than the ones we had, there will always be more going on than we can ever know.

Trauma, Anxiety, Resistance, and Mourning

The encounter sparked a trauma that presented us with an unanticipated opportunity for insight—for learning from, rather than merely learning about, racism. It provoked us to listen in a way that was for most of us unprecedented inside or outside the classroom. It did so by activating or reactivating anger, fears, and desires at various levels of consciousness without suggesting any way to adequately respond to them.[29]

If we had excavated, named, and explored some of the more deeply buried fears, desires, and sorrows that were sparked by the encounter, we would have had to confront a reality for which there is no consolation. We would have been required to recognize that we are relatively powerless to address the suffering racism causes daily and absolutely powerless to reverse the centuries of suffering that white people as well as people of color have experienced as a result of it. And we would have been called to choose between responding with despair and taking the initiative to address racism with full awareness of the immensity of the commitment addressing it requires.

I have come to think of antiracist teaching as woven in a variety of patterns from trauma, anxiety, resistance, and mourning.[30] The trauma of the encounter was sparked by Sekani's call to us to become witnesses to racism. Her call activated feelings of fear, and socially prohibited anger, and intimations of the risks involved in bringing to awareness sorrow deeply buried in those on all sides of the racial divide. These feelings aroused anxiety—a generalized feeling of dread. The most common initial response to the anxiety was denial and resistance in the guises of defensive anger and numbness.

But anxiety can also set the stage for a moment of creative change in those who have the spirit to face resistance and denial and go beyond them. In fact, trauma, anxiety, and resistance can be seen as essential precursors to the complex dynamic involved in mourning.[31] Mourning is a process of naming and confronting our own or others' suffering.[32] It is set in motion when one resists experiencing the trauma and then witnesses oneself denying the feelings the trauma has provoked: witnesses oneself resisting. A number of students engaged in this form of self-reflection when they later acknowledged the defensiveness they had felt during and immediately following the encounter. (Jim: "While the role play exercise was in progress . . . I was angered and defensive . . . .")

Going forward through potentially debilitating anxiety to confront the painful realities of racism by recognizing and coming to terms both with one's fear and with the reality of loss can result in a decision to take responsibility for one's own fate and the fate of others with whom we feel intimately connected. This can engender a deep sense of vitality. I know now that this is what I want my students to experience. But I also know the process cannot be evoked according to plan. A student must freely choose it in response to a compelling invitation.

How is it possible to mourn one's own and others' racism and the suffering it causes, given the complex psychological and cultural dynamics that work against acknowledging suffering in general and the suffering racism causes in particular? It cannot happen without the help of a listener. The listener must have processed enough of her or his own painful experience to be able to listen (as much as possible) without an agenda, to listen with and convey appropriate empathy.

These listeners must be willing and able to look, with those who have the potential to mourn, at their insensitivity to the suffering of others or to injustices that were perpetrated upon themselves. They must help potential mourners look at those despicable parts of the self relegated to the unconscious that they may wish fervently to disavow.[33] People who assist in the process of mourning can help potential mourners understand that their insensitivity is an effect of their prior experience and has been, therefore, for the most part, beyond their conscious control.[34]

Seeing resistance to or denial of their own or others' suffering as unsolicited and at least to some degree previously unavoidable can mitigate the shame and guilt that often stand in the way of confronting anxiety and beginning to mourn. The process of mourning frees those who experience it to participate energetically in unraveling the institutional structures that keep racism in place. Fellow students as well as teachers can become listeners who help to move the process forward.[35]

Elizabeth Ellsworth's thoughts on mode of address suggest another way to look at the part the unconscious played in the encounter. Ellsworth writes that students can only hear teachers if we speak to who the students think they are or who they want to be and could possibly become. Students often perceive any challenge to their racial views as addressing them as racists, an identity most do not think they are and no one wants. Thus, it's not surprising that they don't hear or answer from that position. When Sekani made her presentation, she addressed the class as people who have internalized racist messages and enacted them. In doing so she provoked resistance.

However, when Sekani provoked resistance, I could then speak and listen to the students with empathy, both in the processing session and in the journals. I could recognize their resistance as an effort to grapple with difficult knowledge, and I could appreciate their impulses to be good and just. They could only grapple, however, because Sekani had aroused their resistance. And they could hear me because it was not I who had provoked their trauma. I think that the students' abilities to hear me and to answer from somewhere near where I addressed them in their journals and in the processing session is what Ellsworth would call a "hit." The "who" I was addressing offered students the opportunity to imagine themselves being moved from a place they didn't want to occupy anymore, though they likely had not even brought this to consciousness, to an antiracist place they wanted to occupy.[36]

Before Sekani's visit I had felt intuitively (though I could not have articulated it) that it was important to provoke the fears and defensive anger that I now think must be mobilized if students are to achieve the state of mind both Jim and Isaiah called "getting it." The most effective way that I had found to mobilize students' fantasies and feelings had been to show them the video *The Color of Fear,* which has as its most compelling moment Victor's expression of anger ("I'm so goddam sick and tired of hearing that."). As powerful as that scene is, however, it never activated the students' fantasies and feelings as powerfully as the face-to-face encounter with Sekani. It is for this reason that, until Sekani's presentation, I had not had the opportunity to engage with students who had been as traumatized by a newly cultivated confrontation with some of the realities of racism as the students in this summer class had been.

The process of mourning does not inevitably and simply follow trauma and resistance in the presence of a good listener. The potential mourner, when confronted with difficult knowledge, will vacillate, sometimes violently, sometimes passively, sometimes imperceptibly, between resistance and mourning. Acknowledging the reality of a cruel humanity and of one's own collaboration with and ignorance about it is not something anyone does easily. We see evidence of vacillation between resistance and awareness in a number of the journals. The skillful empathetic listener can help potential mourners balance awareness and hope, and numbness and feeling.[37] This is what I might have been doing the semester a student wrote, "Thank you for controlling the pace at which you let it all seep in."[38]

There is no pattern or sequence for the dawning awareness of how racism works, and for the process of mourning that may follow the awareness. The work we had done in class before Sekani's arrival (and the work some had done before the course began) had perhaps prepared some to begin to recognize and mourn the losses incurred by racism. For others, the mobilization of the fears, desires, anxiety, and resistance that are the prerequisites to mourning had barely, if at all, begun on the day Sekani entered our classroom.

7 Sekani: The Love Letter

Toward the end of the final week of the course, I asked Ann to distribute copies of a letter I had written to the class. I had written the letter because students had posed in writing a number of questions to me during the last five minutes of the class on the day of the encounter, and I had not had time to answer them. When passing out the letter, Ann referred to it as "Sekani's love letter." The love letter that follows is not that love letter. Since my presentation to the summer school class, I have made presentations to several more of Ann's diversity courses, and the original love letter has been revised in response to oral and written questions students in subsequent classes posed during and after the presentations.

* * *

Dear fellow teachers,

I read your journal entries about my presentation and the questions you wrote to me that I didn't have time to answer, and I decided to write responses to some of the questions and confusions some of you seemed to share. But first I want to thank you for your support. I felt most of you were listening, even if we didn't agree. That is the first step to building trust. Because most of you are receptive to thinking about *how* you can work in Black schools, I am ready to take this next step.

Your questions—my answers

A student wrote, *"I have discovered people have so many different ideas about what racism means. What do you mean by racism? If people are using a definition of racism that is in common usage and only well-educated people understand institutionalized racism, won't discussions of racism hit a dead-end?"*

Racism comes in many constantly changing forms and guises. And there are many different forms at any one time in history. Some people talk about "racisms," rather than racism. One reason racism is difficult to talk about is that people simply assume when we talk about it that we all mean the same thing. If you want to discuss it, I recommend you begin *all* conversations by asking the people you're talking to what they mean by it. Many people confuse racism with bigotry and often have not thought about what "reverse racism," "internalized racism," and "institutional racism" mean. They have not been introduced to the idea of reserving the term "racism" to designate *institutionalized* and *systematic* oppression directed at people because of their race, or a *system* of advantages and disadvantages that are exerted in the United States by institutions dominated by white people, usually white men. They don't see that racism involves systematic power.

"Institutional racism" is easier to define than to identify or prove. The term refers to institutional policies or norms that dictate the status of individuals based upon their race, whether or not the individual carrying out the rule or norm is aware of the racist implications. What is difficult is that no institution explicitly states its racist policies. Yet, people of color experience the effects of the unspoken policies many times every day.

A perfect example is Burlington Coat Factory. Burlington had and still has a policy of not hiring Black people into positions of management, but the only evidence was that there were no Black managers. It was a white woman who worked at Burlington and was informed of the unwritten policy who blew the whistle. (They didn't know her husband was Black until he showed up to pick her up and they saw him.) She quit and went to see an attorney with other former Black employees and provided the evidence that had been common knowledge to many Black people in San Francisco for some time.

Now a school where the student body and faculty are 90 percent Black or Chinese or Latino might appear to be a place where institutional racism could not operate. But who controls the resources that flow (or do not flow) into that school? Who sets the parameters of the curriculum by writing the State Frameworks and choosing the standardized tests that specify what knowledge is of worth? I am often followed around a store because I am seen as a potential shoplifter. The store may even have given some "racial sensitivity" training, but if it fails to enforce race blindness by store detectives, institutional racism is still operating.

If I resist, or try to confront, institutional or personal racism I risk getting in big trouble. If the people who are allocating the rewards an institution has to offer—a "not guilty" verdict, a grade of A, an expensive but vital medical test—choose not to acknowledge that the consequences of their behavior target me and other people of color, I usually *have* to tolerate it for my physical safety or economic survival. I and most people of color most often do not have the economic resources to bring the injustice we have experienced into the courtroom. Fortunately there are some exceptions.

If I address the matter through proper almost always white channels or wait until I feel safe to confront white people's racism, they will almost always deny that race was involved. I know it is likely that if I ignore my own safety and confront the racism at the time, they may call the police and claim they were afraid for their safety, or file a complaint against me because of my "attitude." The issue then becomes how *I* reacted, not how they provoked me with comments and behavior that originated in *their* racism. Can't win, can we? Now, how's that for powerlessness? I may have to continue to work with this individual. In most cases, if it gets this far, white people stick together and suddenly my work reviews turn bad and it's time to quit. I'm fired if I fight and abused if I say nothing.

I know that Ann introduced you to the concept of white privilege, and that the White Privilege Exercise was a turning point for many of you. Most white people are completely surprised when their privileges are revealed to them. Some resist acknowledging white privilege, even after doing the exercise. Many people do not see that privileging one group disadvantages others. The idea of white privilege helped many of you finally understand why some people of color are so angry.

There isn't one African American child who did not at first expect to be welcomed by white people. However, even before kindergarten many of us learned that white people see us as "less than," and treat us differently because of it. We learn very early whose hair and skin are assumed to be superior and inferior, though we may be unable to verbalize any or all of this. As we get older we learn one fundamental truth: trusting a white person is dangerous. That is why most Black people develop a healthy form of "paranoia." I hear white folks say, "I didn't do anything to Black people; it's not my fault," or "My ancestors didn't own slaves." The way Black people respond to you may have nothing to do with what you or your ancestors did (though it is likely to be, at least in part, a response to your expressing your racist conditioning that you may not be aware of).

Can you see how white privilege damages white people? Though it's not their fault they were born white, they do pay a price for their whiteness. They will inherit a legacy of distrust and contempt from people of color. They will find interracial relationships confusing and fraught with difficulties. And white privilege will distort their reality. It will give them the understanding that the color of their skin had nothing to do with their achievements. As James Baldwin wrote, "If I'm not who you think I am then you're not who you think you are either."

One of you wrote, *"You told us that racism is a disorder that afflicts European Americans and does not include the racism people of color may have towards other people of color. There are people of Chinese, Filipino, Japanese, Latino and other descents who may be racist. Why didn't you include them in the racist group?"*

I define racism in the United States as an affliction of European Americans because I define racism as a *system* of advantage based on race. Anyone can be prejudiced but only one racial/ethnic group in U.S. society has institutionalized and systematic power. European Americans own almost all of the land and wealth in the United States, and hold nearly all of the positions of power in corporations and politics. (And most of these are men.) Just watch the evening news.

People of color can and do mistreat each other based upon race. They have breathed in the smog of racist images and misinformation like everyone else in the United States. They have internalized racism. I reserve the term "internalized racism" for the negative beliefs, attitudes, and mistreatment people of color have come to accept as deserved and normal, that they direct both toward themselves and their own racial/ethnic group and toward other groups of people of color, because they do not have the physical characteristics and cultural attributes of members of the dominant group. While the mistreatment of people of color by other people of color may look the same to white people as white mistreatment of them, what is happening has very different origins and consequences.

There are at least two devastating consequence of internalized racism. First, the belief that the negative attributions are deserved profoundly affects children of color's success in school. Second, it divides peoples of color from one another, preventing the construction of a unified fight against racism. You will see the effects of internalized racism in classroom behavior, and in the high drop-out and suspension rates and low test scores of poor Asian immigrants, Latinos, Native Americans, and African Americans.

"If I used the definition of racism we used in our class would the rest of the world outside of class understand what I'm talking about?"

Nope, not likely. I believe that if you're a teacher, a true educator, your teaching cannot be limited to the classroom. It is not a job—it's a calling. If you come to understand racism and its importance, you will accept the difficult responsibility of educating those in your life about it, and open opportunities for dialogue. Yes, you risk antagonizing people. But, again, teaching is never risk free.

"Are all white people infected with racism? Are all of us (white Americans) racist?"

Yes.

Now should we argue about it?

You want me to apologize for saying it?

Should you grab a razor and pick a vein?

The effects on white people can vary from inheriting fears, guilt, shame, and misinformation to projecting their worst fears onto people of color and attempting to exploit, punish, and sometimes destroy individuals of the particular racial group they come upon (often in the work place) in various ways—humiliation and intimidation, threats, abuse of authority, and scapegoating.

"Are you saying that because I'm white I can't work in Black schools?"

If I said, "Yes," would that stop you? The question itself falls under the heading of "silly/dangerous white-people questions." A few people were clearly concerned with the implication they took from the presentation, that white people can't work in Black schools because they are racist. Although I never actually said that, it was interesting to see these people jump to defend their right to teach in a Black school.

I think you know there have been, for a long time, some Black educators who have argued that white people should not teach Black children. Now, look around the room. Clearly, their opinions have made no big impact on you and other prospective teachers, since most teachers of children of color are still white, and the ratio of white teachers to children of color is increasing.

One of the luxuries of white privilege is that, when people of color disapprove of white intrusion or conduct in our community, all we can do for the most part is state our objections. White people are going to do what they damn well please. So, when you act as if you actually need or want my permission to teach children of color, I find you irritating. I am sure there must be words to describe when someone more powerful asks for permission to do something they have already decided to do. Or, when powerful people ask for permission and, if refused, guilt trip or abuse you because they only asked in order to give you the opportunity to stroke and pacify them. If you say, "Yes, you're welcome," they come in. If you say, "No," they may come in anyway and verbally chastise you for being rude. If you say, "No," and they don't come in, they say, "See, that's why those people have all those problems. They won't let us help."

It doesn't matter what I think about white people teaching Black children. It's a moot issue now. There certainly aren't enough Black teachers, so I clearly can't afford to say white people shouldn't teach Black children—even if I believed it. If all it takes for you to avoid Black schools is for me to say, "No, don't go!" you have already decided and were just looking for an excuse so you could hide your own fears of Black people. If ever asked, "Why won't you work in Bayview or Western Addition," you can always say, "Well, I wanted to but Sekani said I wouldn't be welcome because I had white skin and I would be abused. So there!! Proof that *I'm* not a racist." That's what I love about the racist pathology. It's such a flawless trap for people of color. It's always our fault, our loss, and you always come out looking so noble.

The fact that all white people are infected by racism doesn't mean they cannot teach Black children, but it does mean that you should consider yourself unqualified when you start out, and understand it is quite likely you have been given a job teaching children of color because there are not enough teachers of color to go around. You are not inherently presumed "right for the job" of teaching children of color because you have a CLAD credential.[1] African American educators like me have continually had to clean up after the damage "licensed" but unqualified whites have done. You are held suspect until you are seen capable of effectively managing the job and can take adult responsibility for your own feelings about people of color and racism. People who have truly dealt with their own racism aren't offended or surprised by these comments. I have to point out again that some people in this class showed that they have the kind of qualities that would be effective and an asset in our community.

"How can I know if my thoughts are racist?"

If you find yourself questioning my credibility or sanity and wonder if I'm hallucinating, you might take this as a clue.

One of you wrote, *"I'm not saying I don't think Sekani was telling the truth. Of course she was but she was only giving us her perspective, which means the reasons she gave for the conflict between herself and Ms. Crutch were really just interpretations. It is hard for me to express exactly how I feel."*

Oh, honey, I think you expressed your feelings quite well. "Perspective" used the way you used it is usually a euphemism for "irrational." In other words, there is what really happened, and then there is what Sekani thinks happened. Not that I am incapable of distorted thinking— all on my own without anyone's help. I am just curious why, in this case, this person questions my interpretation of the events. Why would I not be presumed to be an expert on recognizing racism?

Let me guess—tick-tick-tick . . . I got it. This person is accusing me of "race baiting." That means that instead of me being able to deal with the normal human experience of rejection, or not getting my way, or being corrected when I make a mistake, what I do instead is to blame everything on racism. Yeah, that's right. If I blame ALL my life's problems on racism, that will make my life easier to manage. So, I get it: Racism is really a form of Black denial—right? It doesn't really exist. Unless a CEO of a major corporation walks up to me at my job, calls me a nigger, spits on me and personally throws me from the top of a four-story building and gets away with it, racism just doesn't happen. Good, I feel so much better. The answer to past and current oppression is—just in my head. You know, like menstrual cramps.

The person who questioned whether my perspective was distorted doesn't realize that people do not function in a vacuum and we all do not think like he or she does. Eurocentricism by its very nature assumes that the right answer is the one Eurocentrics come up with. In reality most people of color are much more aware than most whites of the complexities of race and "diversity" and know when racism is operating. Of course, there are people of color, Clarence Thomas being a prime example, who are as Eurocentric in their thinking as many white people. But it is safe to assume that any ethical, sane man or woman of color of normal intelligence will be able to know, most of the time, when they are being mistreated because of the color of their skin, just like women can usually tell when they are mistreated because of their appearance, and men can usually tell when it's because of their height. (Unless, of course, they have internalized so much of the sexism, racism, or sizism from the society that they believe their mistreatment stems from personal failings that have nothing to do with social norms.)

Someone else wrote, *"I can't say that the situations you de-scribed, like the story of Ms. Crutch, were definitely race-related. I don't have enough information. Isn't there a possibility there were conflicts purely from disagreements in how to teach?"*

Can't get away from this, can I? I'm curious. How many years and what kind of training do you think a person of color should have before she can tell the difference between a professional disagreement and racist behavior? I mean, pick a number. What classes should I take? What license should I get?

One clue to discovering your racism is how much credibility you give me and other people of color. I love how white people struggle with the issue of my credibility. I'm a Black woman, I was a Black child, I teach in a Black/Chinese school. I've been dealing with and reading about racism all my life, and yet some people try to get me to prove that I am qualified to have opinions on this subject, or challenge the accuracy of the data I provide. Not that you shouldn't challenge any authority. But examine the criteria you use to evaluate my credibility. For example, do I lack credibility because I make mistakes in grammar or have too many typos? Believing standard language usage is an index of credibility is a good example of elitist thinking.

Another frequent challenge to my credibility has been my "style" of communication. Some of you described me as "overbearing," "hostile," "insensitive to the feelings of others." ("Others" is usually a euphemism for "white people" or "me—personally.") The intent is to challenge *my* ability to identify racism when it occurs. What do you mean by "insensitive" here? That my perceptions are warped? That I refuse to curb what I say to protect your feelings? Yeah! I am and always will be angry around the issue of racism.

One problem with white people making their feelings central is that doing so diverts their attention from the actions and effects of the deeply disturbed racists. Try to put yourself in my situation. I'm walking down the street on a hot day. Two white men drive by in, yes, a pickup truck. I'm drinking my orange juice as I hear, "I'll bet she can take it down the throat! Yeah, they good at that! Ain't ya' girl?" Can you imagine how exhausting it is to be forever concerning myself with not hurting white people's feelings?

I obviously can't tell by looking at you who suffers in greater degree from the disease of racism. If I or anyone could tell just by looking at the color of your skin, I'd be safer all the way around. Unfortunately, dangerous people don't wear labels!! Just fucks it up for all of us, doesn't it? (Remember, *I'm* the one who gets attacked regularly because of my color. If you get attacked, it's probably all in your head—right?)

I am angry and suspicious because the price of trusting white people is too damned high!! Trusting that a white person won't abuse their inherited and socially protected white privilege can cost me my career, my freedom (prison), my life . . . and you want *me* to worry about *your* feelings? Those of you who don't even give me the right to be *suspicious* fall into the "*I don't get it!*" group and have bigger problems than "us angry colored folks."

Some people questioned my credibility because of my suspicious nature regarding "white skin." You're right!! I do find "white-skinned people" dangerous. This is a rational fear. One Black psychological term is "healthy paranoia." I have never been fired by an Asian person, a Latino person, or anyone of color because of my "attitude problem." I have never been fired by any member of one of these groups because I did not do my job. But I have had the food taken from my table by white-skinned women and men who didn't like my "attitude." One said it clearly: "You would do better in this job if you did something about your Black attitude."

It was not I and other people of color who made skin color an issue. White-skinned people did. Don't get mad at me because your own people make you look bad. Talk to them. You think I don't get pissed at some of those violent Black adolescents on the bus? They scare me too. And *they* make *my* life harder. As for gang-bangers, the only thing Black about them *is* their skin. How about men? I have heard "man" and "rapist" used interchangeably by women who fear rape. Must piss real men off. But, guys, don't get mad at the victims of sexual violence who malign you. Don't blame the victims. Turn around and challenge the perpetrators, your buddies who refer to their girlfriends as bitches, for example.

Questioning the integrity and competence of a person of color is another clue that racist assumptions may be involved. One of you wrote: "How did she let the situation with LaTipha escalate? If the situation escalated to the seventh step then it is Sekani's fault. Incidents tend to escalate due to how the teacher handles (or, for that matter, does not, handle) them! If the teacher starts to become frustrated and expresses it, the situation will definitely get out of hand."

I'm packing and moving to her world where teachers are so powerful the mere expression of their feelings alters years of abuse and neglect, and all the children behave when I just "say it right." I'm letting parents know. I'm sure they'll buy a ticket, too. See, this is what happens when you listen to politicians, and sitcoms and professors who don't know much about the world in which children in some of our schools live.

And why do some people assume that the expression of honest emotions and feelings will automatically result in bad things happening? If you believe this assumption, shouldn't it follow that a calm response should de-escalate anyone's behavior? Do you really believe that if I'm calm, others will be calm, and it is my getting upset that, in and of itself, upsets other people?

Another student wrote, *"Before Ms. Moyenda dismisses a child like LaTipha as a 'lost cause,' she might consider that there are several resources to help these children. There are social workers, psychologists, and how about testing and setting up an Individualized Education Plan? I also wonder how much information she had on this student before the incident occurred."*

No more than one person in each class expressed the condescending belief that we had not bothered to do our best for LaTipha. That's not bad at all. One advantage to getting everyone's feedback after I do a presentation is that I can be optimistic that the problems of racism are not as overwhelming as I might sometimes feel. Before I did these presentations, I thought most white people thought most Black people were this stupid. Now I am learning that there are only a few white people who suffer from such distorted thinking. My guess is this person doesn't trust in the competency and intelligence of anyone, let alone Black folks. Racism may actually be the least of this person's problems. It's just the one Black people have to deal with.

Note how this person doesn't ask if I tried something else but instead assumed that I would immediately attack and discard a child. Where is that coming from, if not from her own unresolved and painful past? The people who assumed we at the school had not tried every way we could think of to help LaTipha will probably go into a classroom one day, experience a Level 4 child, and start talking to all the staff about it as if they (the staff) are stupid.

However, most people got it that we, the staff of Rosa Parks, had tried everything we could think of. They realized that disturbed children, unlike adults, cannot be ignored and that even Black teachers and staff know about psychologists and social services. Most of you seemed to realize that many disturbed children are often so disruptive they eventually do something so severe that we are required by law to respond to it in a way that will preserve the other children's rights to an education. Most of you assumed that the most severely disturbed children already have social workers, have had IEPs done on them, and are deeply entrenched in the social service system.

"What can be done for children like LaTipha? Why did you cut LaTipha loose?"

In my opinion, powerlessness is the worst-case scenario for any teacher. Perhaps for anyone. If any of you are at all like me, when we feel we can't *do* something, we assume the end result will be catastrophic. I want to challenge that feeling. Experience has taught me that powerlessness does not always mean catastrophe. It just may mean it's time to let go and turn the problem over to others who may be better equipped, or better yet, to have faith that other forces will do what must be done to help a child. Powerlessness reminds us of our "humanness." We can't go back and undo the past. As teachers we have to confront this fact.

A Level 4 child represents a series of tragic mistakes made by individuals and political and social institutions that resulted in turning a child into a destructive, deceitful, defiant, and sometimes even violent being. I know what it was like to live with insanity in my life as a child. I knew from watching LaTipha and knowing how social services were unlikely to really help her, that LaTipha, like it or not, was on her own. I saw nothing strange about LaTipha's behavior, given who she had to live with. If, like her, I had to live in a home of a crazed, drug-addled woman (who was not nearly as smart as I was), I would have acted just like her. The behavior LaTipha exhibited in class was necessary for her survival in her home environment. She had no reason to believe the situation at school was any different.

I know there is no perfect solution. If LaTipha is taken from her mother, she is likely to end up in home after home or Juvenile Hall and eventually homeless. Unless placed in a lock-down facility for many years, she is not likely to conform. As long as she stays in her home, she has to deal with her mother. For short periods of time she might find some peace at school. But, when LaTipha doesn't want to be at school—particularly after some drama has played out at home the night before—her problems are too big to set aside in order to think about grammar and spelling. It is ridiculous and arrogant for us to decide for LaTipha that she should be able to stay up until two A.M. fighting with her drunk mother, with the police at the house repeatedly, then come to school and settle down to talk division and addition.

I think what I find most disturbing is that most teachers don't recognize that their pleasant lives are blessings, not permanent states of being. Therefore, they can't understand that no amount of social services (as these are offered in *this* society) will help LaTipha and her mother, that things now have gone too far. I think of LaTipha as a casualty of a racist and economically unjust social system and believe she is unlikely to change if she continues to be raised up in her world. Social workers cannot provide drug rehabilitation services, subsidized housing, job training for real jobs with decent pay and benefits, day care and public transportation, all of which are necessary if poor parents are to be able to create predictable and humane environments for their children.

They can't eliminate the racism and class injustice that support and reinforce LaTipha's state of deprivation. Medication does not always work, not all therapists are good ones, and there are not enough therapists, staff, mentors, and caregivers to serve our LaTiphas. The problem is bigger than her teachers and her social workers.

Violence, immorality, and insanity dominate LaTipha's life, and it will take all of her attention and skill to live to be eighteen. Few teachers who were not brought up in her world are able to grasp the dimensions of such children's problems on the same level that the children *have* to grasp them. If I were to make an overgeneralization about the average middle-class white person (and this applies to many middle-class people of color as well), it is that they are unable to see the "darker" side of life. They are ignorant of the pain and dangers that others may experience and are unaware of their own ignorance. Thus, they are incapable of empathy for children of these oppressed groups and their parents. Such denial can make a situation worse; no one can learn how to deal with problems he or she does not know exist.

When LaTipha was around me, she often acted like she had good sense. At those times she was focused, cooperative, and capable. But, when the shit hit the fan at home, she had to find her own way of dealing with it. That meant being around the people who could provide her with what *she* thought she needed at the moment. As her teacher, I felt an obligation to provide her with what *I* thought she needed.

Since her mother had destroyed LaTipha's ability to trust adults, whether or not I was trustworthy was irrelevant. Renewing her faith in adults would take years of positive experiences, including protection from adults and children who will betray her. Although as teachers we are obliged to try, no teacher can provide her with enough of that unless we are willing to take her into our home for the duration of her childhood and young adulthood. Raise your hand if you're ready to take her home to your house—permanently. I know I wasn't.

If I can't control her in a classroom, imagine what it would take to do so in your home. I cannot transform the kind of life she had. LaTipha needed her mother to stop drinking and be a responsible mother. That wasn't happening. Therefore, all we could offer was a temporary Band-Aid on an open, gaping wound. (We call it Social Services.) So, we have to let her deal with *her* life the best way she can. *My* job as a teacher is to offer LaTipha a choice. It is *LaTipha's* job to choose. She was always welcome in my class, if she followed my rules. She usually couldn't do that. She didn't trust me, and I didn't blame her. I think the only real difference between me and other people who dealt with LaTipha was that I treated her like an adult and was respectful of her distrust of adults and of the dangers she faced in her life. I know she was a child, but she had no choice but to make adult decisions.

I reconcile myself to her harsh reality by remembering Malcolm X. It was in prison that he found himself and came to understand what his life was about and what he wanted to do with it. LaTipha will not find the strength to trust again until she can tell the difference between trustworthy and kind versus charismatic and deceitful. At this point in her life, because she is being raised by a *drug* culture—not her Black culture—the values she is learning are backward and upside down, and are not likely to help her make these distinctions.

Several of you asked, *"What did you mean when you said that in LaTipha's view, trust is a weakness?"*

What did I mean? Well, to healthy individuals who can trust their environment (because the people in their life are trustworthy for the most part), to see trust as weakness is absurd. If you are blessed with such a life, you're perfectly aware that kind people are the safest people in the world and quite frankly make life worth living. But if you've been battered by society and/or abused in your family, faith and trust are the first things to go. You learn to trust in the faulty nature of people. You actually grow to rely on the fact that people will lie to you and that everybody is out for themselves and that the fear of violence is all that motivates people. Fear becomes the driving force in your life. For many children raised by an addict, fear is all they understand.

Like it or not—LaTipha has four very *good* compelling reasons not to trust *anybody*.

1. Her parents have betrayed her. They chose drugs over her.
2. She must live with the consequences of that betrayal by herself.
3. When she goes out into the world, racism will betray her again.
4. She will once again have to deal with the consequences (pain and loss) of that betrayal by herself.

You're right; its not fair that LaTipha mistrusts trustworthy kind teachers, anymore than my distrust of you is fair. I, too, am insulted when someone believes I would maliciously or inadvertently hurt another. But that hurt is nothing compared to the devastating effects upon her if she trusts the wrong person again. It can get her killed or further destroy her soul.

What she has to lose if we screw up and make a promise we can't keep is far greater than what she has to gain if a teacher actually comes through for her. If you want to be a teacher, your job is to provide an opportunity for academic and possibly life-enhancing success and achievement. And to teach everyone how to work for a more just social and political system that would nip LaTipha's problems in the bud.

A primary contribution a teacher can make to LaTipha's education is to give her some models of people who share her race and ethnic culture, people who have overcome some of the odds she herself faces. She must find one source of healing in some part of her ethnic culture. Pride in her Blackness is fundamental to her survival (as appreciation of our ethnicity is vital for us all). LaTipha must learn to distinguish the drug culture she grew up in from her ethnic culture. It is arrogant to assume that her ethnic culture provides her with no answers when in fact African American history has been about the overcoming of impossible odds, about finding renewal and healing of the spirit, and about strategies of dealing with situations in which we are and feel powerless.

There is an unknown future. Others will pass through her life. Time will tell. Years from now, I will hear about LaTipha. The news will be either, "LaTipha's going to college now," OR "I saw LaTipha, she was still hangin' on the street with —," OR "LaTipha died from —." But if she survives, she may well become a powerful and formidable woman. She will be incorruptible. She will be another Angela Davis or Rosa Parks, or someone else who will change the world. I have to focus on this possibility—not the likelihood of her failure.

"How does a teacher deal with students, colleagues or parents who are angry with me because I am white?"

First, take the issue of race out of the equation and ask yourself how you feel about and respond to *any* expression of anger. What did your culture, class, family, and ethnicity teach you about expressing anger? If you do your job well, you're going to piss off quite a few people. A decision to commit to teaching to empower the disempowered is an act of rebellion, and there will be people who will be angry that you have decided to do it. I always think I'm not doing something right if someone isn't mad at me for doing it. Being white may be only one more reason people will be angry with you.

Second, ask yourself if you deserve the anger. Did you screw up somewhere? Did you perform a racist act or make a statement that conveyed to a person of color that you saw him or her as "less than"? Were you, for example, condescending? Was your questioning of their credibility in any way a function of your racist conditioning? Make sure you're on moral high ground before you get righteous about how you're being treated unjustly by a person of color just because you're white. You need to scrutinize your behaviors and your words and consider how a person of color might have felt about them. If you're in the right you should be able to give a convincing argument. If you're wrong, you can afford to admit it, learn from it, make amends, and move on.

One of you asked, *"How can I learn to be an effective teacher in a Black classroom?"*

Another wrote, *"What is your most valuable piece of advice for a white teacher dealing with Black students? (Is there one thing— I know there are probably hundreds—you would have liked your teachers to know when you were young?)"*

I would have to say, be yourself. Now, you need to explore who that is. Allow yourself to be transformed by the experience of working with people of color. If you hang around them enough you may find yourself waking up one morning and asking yourself, "Who am I and why am I here?" If you do that, you're on the right track. Pursue knowledge of your own ethnicity. Seek out what it means to be German, Russian, English, or French or any combination of ethnic heritages. Believe me, I know what it is like to try to deny or ignore my own Black culture. It means walking around with a piece of your self missing. My internalized racism worked this way: "I hate poverty—Black people are poor—if I'm not Black, I won't be poor." As a result of denying my reality, I denied the reality of others and it damaged my relationship with them, Black or otherwise, and my ability to function competently.

Since you will exercise your right to work anywhere you please, you have a responsibility not to abuse your white privilege. You do that by learning to be good at teaching children of color. An absolute prerequisite is to become aware of, and begin the lifelong project of, unlearning your racist conditioning. Learn from people of color who have dealt with their own internalized racism and can recognize when racism is guiding the behavior of others, particularly teachers of color, and writers such as Lisa Delpit, Gloria Ladson-Billings, Janice Hale-Benson, and Beverly Tatum. If, after you have done this, you still fail, then we all have failed together. I don't intend to fail. I know what's at stake.

If you're listening with your heart—not your fear—you're one step closer to being a good teacher. I know what it takes to be there and what it will cost if you fail us and yourself. I do think it's possible for white people and people of color to teach children of ethnic/racial groups that differ from their own successfully. But if you are to be one of these, it must be a calling you were born to. Something in your soul says, "I am a teacher. It isn't what I *do*—it is what I am."

As a Black woman, being a teacher of children of color runs even deeper. I am a part of this place, this neighborhood. I leave, a piece of me stays. I am bigger than myself when I teach here. I am home. I am loved and appreciated here. That is why I can put up with so much shit and the exhaustion that becomes routine. But for some white teachers who come here, that light doesn't shine;

they can't do well because they come for the wrong reasons. Racism inhibits their ability to find clarity and to find their place here. And as they struggle, stumble, and fail, they wreak havoc and make already difficult situations worse for us—and themselves. It's because they don't listen, and they don't listen because they don't respect us.

If you're a teacher and this is where you should be, nothing I say will deter you, and maybe, just maybe, you're meant to be one of the few who does well here. However, a couple of you need to let go of the idea of teaching children of color, at least for now. In the comments I made to some of you in response to your written questions, I recommended things you can do to address some specific concerns that arose from the presentation. I addressed the issues honestly. I started doing these presentations because some of you are going to, or already do, teach children of color, so I might as well get to you early and teach you something that may be helpful to my community. I have to do something to minimize the damage some of you are likely to cause once you come to our schools. And maybe, if you listen to me and actually learn something, you will do more good than harm.

"What can you do as a teacher if the students will not stop calling each other names even after you have them do time-out and separate them into different corners of the room?"

There is no one way. There is only the way that will work for you. Discipline is a dance, and you have to choreograph it to suit your nature. There are so many right answers. A lot of them will work for you and many will not. Some will work with one child but not with another.

Someone wanted to know what I do in such situations. "Verbal whoopins"—my personal strength teaching Black children is my voice and language. I know how to make a point verbally and I can get louder and more intense than a child. As any brother will tell you, you cannot win an argument with a Black woman. This is especially true for a child. I pull out my sermon on respect and dignity and express myself with righteous indignation. I pile it on thick. I preach on many ethical issues and challenge these children with their past mistakes regarding issues of "fairness" that at worst stops 'em cold; at best it will not only stop the behavior in the long run, but give their classmates a chance to learn from the misbehaving child's mistakes.[2]

That way I have reinforced a "life skill" to the entire class. If the child doesn't stop, I will have at least addressed the issues, so that *other* children are less likely to think I will turn a blind eye to their misbehavior. (It won't work for everyone. Remember LaTipha.)

After that, *then* I kick their cute little butts out of my class, give them the usual loss of recess, detention, or a call home. Worst-case scenario, I remind them that it is their parents who send them for an education, but if they feel they don't need one, they can call home and explain that to their parents, who will come pick them up and take them home. This is for my hardheads.

Some still won't modify their behavior until I have a conference with the parents, clarify my position about discipline and education, get the parents' support and trust, and in front of their parents force the child to acknowledge his or her responsibility. I have to know the parent well enough to be sure that if I get them involved they won't turn around and abuse their children because of misbehavior at school. This is rarely a problem, though; if the parents of these children are alcoholics or are immersed in the drug culture, they are more likely to simply not pay attention. If the behavior is *really* bad I sometimes ask the student to apologize to me in front of the class for humiliating me (yes, they learn words like this) and disrupting and interfering in the educational opportunities of their community.

It is important to note that "verbal whoopins" only work if you're fair, just, careful, and clear about the lesson you want preach. For example, I have been known to use misbehaviors as an opportunity to discuss the word "contempt," and why I and their classmates don't deserve theirs. Because they don't have the vocabulary yet, I have to teach them that contempt is the opposite of respect.

I do this because many children don't respond to kindness. I have had many discussions with my children about my "two sides." I have my evil side that terrifies, and I tell them I will show it if that's what it will take to get their cooperation in the classroom. Then I have my kind side. I tell them that how they react when I ask them to do something nicely teaches me how they want to be treated. In time, discipline improves because I go back to the question, "How are you teaching me to treat you today?" This works because I am very good at being scary and because I always know how to keep controlling and manipulative children off balance with questions like this. Obviously, they have not thought about such issues before.

I also have the ability to shut off anger and turn on charm immediately in the classroom. I model feelings and, more importantly, model the control of them. I let the children know that I will holler at the one being "bad" and talk sweetly to the one being respectful. If you can't manage your feelings in this way—aren't able to let go of a bad feeling or choose when and to whom to express good feelings—I don't recommend this style. But it works for me. It does tend to scare the fuck out of non-Black teachers and some Black ones as well.

"What can I as a small female Chinese American do if African American or white students get out of hand?"

I think some people may have misunderstood me when I described how I managed children. I use what works for me. As a large Black woman, I can physically restrain a child. I don't recommend it for you. My advice is to do what Mrs. Tagumi did with me. I always remember Mrs. Tagumi because she taught me division.

As you might guess, I was not an easy child to manage in class. I wasn't a Level 3 all the time, but I did have my moments. Growing up I had only one teacher who was Asian, Mrs. Tagumi. To my nine-year-old mind, Mrs. Tagumi understood me better than most adults because she was almost as small as I was. Mrs. Tagumi's greatest power over us was her persistent faith in us. I understood addition, subtraction, and multiplication, but division just made no sense. I would try my long division and would get it wrong somewhere along the line. (This of course was when I was working and not being the class clown.) Every time I tried, I messed it up. Every time I messed it up, she said the same thing: "You'll get it, try again." After a while, I didn't believe her. I actually started to suspect *she* was crazy and *I* was stupid. But she always said the same thing. "You'll get it, try again." She would show me where I went wrong or give me a clue and send me back. Damned if she wasn't right. I did eventually get it—after much frustration and hair pulling.

I remember Mrs. Tagumi because I got in trouble in her class a lot. A part of me feels bad that I gave her so much trouble. I did it because I trusted her. She gave me the space I needed to be myself. I am sure that, compared to traditional Asian students, especially in those days, I was a terror. But of all the teachers I had, she was the most patient and kind. Most importantly, she believed in me and my capacity to learn. I often wonder if she thought I was as much of a terror as I think I was—or if she was just amused. Admittedly, positive reinforcement worked on me. I hope she didn't think she was a bad teacher because she couldn't be harsh. Because my life was so hard, I had to blow off steam. Because she was so patient and tolerant, I blew off in her class. She did her job, anyway: She taught me something I didn't think I could learn. This had a powerful effect on me years later. As a student, a part of me always believed . . . "You can do it—just try again." As a teacher, it's one of my favorite lines.

So my advice—be *you*—don't be me. But believe in the potential of all your students. And make sure you're safe. Does that answer your question?

Criticisms

I got some very good criticisms and suggestions. But the one I want to address is, *"Why didn't you give more attention to people of color other than African Americans?"*

I usually try to stick to what I know. Unfortunately, it becomes painfully clear and obvious to other people of color that I don't know enough about Asian and Latino culture. My genuine apologies to the Latinos and Asians in the class. Many people assumed that I lump other people of color into the same category as whites. I do not. First of all, other people of color, including new Americans, are in no position to be racist. They do not have the power.

Second, I have never personally experienced from them, as a Black child or as an educator, the abuse that whites have heaped upon me and my people. This doesn't mean that prejudice and fear don't exist—in truth, it is very clear to me that many people of Asian descent are afraid of us—only that I seem able to resolve conflicts with them much more easily and with much less hassle. Latinos, Africans, and Middle Eastern people who can be as dark or darker than the average African American, while they may have biases and prejudices, don't seem to go out of their way to be cruel or vindictive. And, of course, it is not they who set the rules that keep people of color competing with one another for scarce jobs, and scapegoating one another. There is a (dare I use the word and risk losing credibility?) conspiracy to insure that other people of color do not form alliances with African Americans.

I do highly recommend that other people of color learn the true history of African Americans. The hype that white America spreads about African Americans abroad as well as at home is devastatingly inaccurate, and many immigrants arrive already having experienced this racist conditioning. What's more, we can be scary if your culture does not believe in open displays of emotion as we do. Find out for yourself who we really are—read about us, go out and have a good time with us. More important, work with us. Your experiences will be far more accurate and enlightening than anything most white people will tell you about us or you will read or learn from the media. Seeing what they have done to us, and how, will help you recognize what they are doing to *your* people. Learn from our experience, and use the wisdom of your culture and your knowledge of your own histories of resistance to resist racism directed at all disempowered people.

I frequently misperceive Latinos as Black. There have been a great many Latinos in my life, and even though some have light skin, they have shared a lot of Blacks' experience with both personal and institutional racism. Many Asians and Latinos have to deal with (for lack of a better way of putting it) the institutional racism that underlies the reverence that so many Americans of European descent have for the English language. I have watched white America beat Asians and Latinas with the "Speak English" stick for as long as I can remember. In reality, Americans are blessed to have second-language speakers in our lives. Yet, native English speakers are often upset because we are afraid our language will no longer insure our "English language privilege."

Conclusion

You will inevitably exercise poor judgment in critical situations in your classroom; everyone does. If you let the effects of racist conditioning cloud your judgment, you will only compound your errors. You will make it worse for yourself, your peers, and, of course, the students. Some guidelines if you choose to work among educators, parents, and children of color (or even if you choose to work in white communities) are:

1. Do your own emotional work to unlearn your racism if you're white and your internalized racism if you're a person of color. Accept the reality that by doing so you will be forever altered by the experience.

2. Commit yourself to additional and extensive education in the ethnic cultures of people whose backgrounds differ from your own. This will enhance your competence when you make academic choices about how and what you teach each day. Be clear on why you teach, and who you are teaching. Know what each community really wants for its children. Don't fall for the "parents don't care" nonsense. Have some clear vision of what the children will need to know when they leave your classroom and enter their communities as well as the dominant culture.

3. Remember, limit setting is different from discipline. The purpose of limit setting and consequences is not to achieve instant behavior modification, but to help children learn how to manage the (we hope) temporary moments of powerlessness in their lives. The goal of discipline is to promote in children a commitment to speak out against injustice, even when you or another teacher may be the perpetrator, and to help them learn the "three Rs," what Lisa Delpit calls the language of power, as well. Discipline is a skill the children themselves must internalize in order to succeed throughout their lives. Setting limits is often required in order to teach discipline. Understand that when you set limits and apply consequences, the children may have no idea why you're doing it; they may not "get it" until they are grown, and maybe not even then. If you can't face such realities, it's not too late to become a secretary. But if you can overcome your fears—then you can change the world because you taught a child.

4. Become informed by scholars and other people of color on these four subjects:
  • Child development, cultural differences, and learning.
  • Racism and its effects on people of European descent and people of color.
  • Views on violence and morality, how these differ within and among racial/ethnic groups.
  • How to teach children to resist and eradicate the violence of racism, and all the other "isms."

I recommend Marcus Bookstore on Filmore and Post Street for learning more about African Americans. There is a rapidly growing literature on Asian and Latino children in U.S. schools and their various ethnic cultures. Avoid white writers because they are often wrong, or they ripped the ideas off someone of color and translated them to be more palatable for "white" sensibilities (which is what makes them inaccurate most of the time). Go directly to the source and build up the courage and strength you need to be able to hear and learn.

5. Follow the lead of teachers, children, and parents of color. Especially the older ones. They teach me a lot! Take the leap of faith. If their viewpoints can't harm you, what's the problem in doing it our way? Beware—you may be transformed. You may no longer be the person you *think* you are—or want to become the person you now think you want to be.

6. Find a diversity group that talks about racism. Find any valid venue to talk about this issue. This is a great way to get specific regarding everyday problems that will crop up. For example, how are you going to respond when or if a Black child calls you a racist? Be prepared. You will hear the views of people of color who range from those who believe white people can become good allies to people of color to those who believe there is nothing white people can do for them, and *you* happen to look just like their most recent perpetrator. The gooood part is you get to talk about your issues. You won't find answers—but you may find greater clarity.

7. If I offended you, and, after reading this, you feel anger, distress, powerlessness, and fear, hold off teaching children of color until you can understand and manage these feelings. Don't go to a Black, Latino, or Asian school until you're in therapy. If you're a substance abuser, stay away.

8. Think about your reasons for working in a community of color. Make sure these reasons are healthy—not based upon neurotic or exploitative impulses. Don't fall for the hype that you want to "give back" to the community. Exactly what is it you've received that you want to give back? If you believe you have something to offer, be specific. Don't be abstract about it. What do you have that we can use every day? Like any job, you should be able to sell yourself to the parents and staff you wish to work with.

The fact that you can read and write is not sufficient. The fact that a white university gave you a piece of paper that said you had a legal right to work in our school is not sufficient either. Why should we allow you into our community? As someone said of my visit to one of your classes, "You're a guest here; don't come in and insult the host." What specifically can you contribute? How do you know we can use it? What's in it for you beside a paycheck? Can you work anywhere else? If not, why would *we* want you? If so, why choose this place when you can make more money and be treated better elsewhere? If we take these gifts you offer, what do you expect to get in exchange? What's the price we pay for them? Why should we trust you? Answer these questions for yourself. As you answer, pretend you're talking to someone like me.

9. One last thing!! Ask yourself, *What of true value do Black and other people of color have that draws you to us and makes you want to teach, learn, and suffer with us?* Note that I didn't ask you what you liked about us. I asked what we have that is valuable as human beings that would enrich your life, soul, and person. What is it that you want so badly, you're willing to endure the challenges in order to get it? *Bet that will keep some of you up tonight.*

Sincerely,

Sekani

8 Conclusion

Ann: Does What We Do Here Matter?

Taking It Personally

Kathy wrote in her journal: "I am upset and enraged by the messages I heard from today's speaker. . . . I got upset and I was overcome with tears of rage." I responded in writing: "The goal is to be able to hear and feel Sekani's rage against racism and to be able to listen with empathy to an angry parent of one of your Black students . . . without seeing either Sekani or that parent as your alcoholic father . . . without taking it personally."

Yet in response to Denise's claim that the information Sekani gave was "personal, not educational," I had written, "I think the educational is personal; I don't distinguish them." Now, thinking about my contradiction, I realize I *do* want my students to take what Sekani says personally. But, I ask myself, what do I mean by that?

That summer, as it turned out, I meant that, in the section of the course devoted to racism, I wanted Kathy and others, white students and students of color, to come to see themselves through Sekani's eyes and, more generally, through the eyes of racially conscious people of color. In fact, I wanted the students to see how they (as well as diverse others) are seen by an ever expanding circle of others, including those whose positions in hierarchies of power are different from their own. This, of course, included wanting students who by accident of birth were able to exercise white privilege to learn to see themselves from the perspectives of those whose views are most often discounted and marginalized by the dominant culture. My assumption was that as the students developed their abilities to see from the perspective of others, they would be in a better position to identify racism in themselves and others and to grasp it deeply enough to be moved to interrupt it.[1]

Jim writes in his journal, "What I'm starting to realize is that . . . others have feelings and images that are just as real, and also based on years of experience." This statement suggests he was beginning a process that started with the very basic realization that Sekani, like himself, is a human being who has feelings and images. It also suggests that it was occurring to him, perhaps for the first time, that Sekani had images of him, and that she might see him in ways that until that moment he had not seen himself. His statement could be taken as an expression of his nascent ability to see how he might be seen and heard by others whose views he had been socialized to discount or to not hear at all.

If this is so, perhaps his "discovery" that others have feelings and images that are different from the ones he has is not so trivial as I had at first thought it to be. Perhaps Jim's encounter with Sekani was simply the last of a series of classroom experiences that revealed to him as well as others how he is seen by those whose voices are submerged and relatively inaudible in the dominant national conversations about race.

Isaiah wrote, "Sekani was great for our class." He also wrote, "They [the white students] need to take a look in the mirror." In his view, Sekani gave white students "more in two hours than they will get in any course or class at this University. . . . Our classmates should be grateful." He's "proud this Sista took the time to deliver the message." What does he think the students got more of that they should be grateful for? What message does he have in mind? Perhaps the "more" and the "message" can be understood as a more comprehensive look by white (and Chinese, Latina, and Filipino) students at themselves, an ability to see themselves through an additional set of eyes.

During the three-week period of the course, Isaiah also came to see himself through different eyes. As he began to see himself and the white students through the eyes of James Baldwin, Sekani, Victor, and myself, he also began to see how some of his classmates saw him: "I don't believe our classmates can even hear ME. . . . That may be me trippin'. . . . I needed to know how people really see me. . . . This class has been an awakening for me."

It was his ability to see how he looked to Sekani and to the white students—to recognize that his perception that he was invisible to some of the white students was not simply the result of his "trippin' "—that led him to decide, as he expressed it in his final journal entry, to commit himself to preparing Black children to "become . . . soldier[s] who will fight the injustices of people who are racist, little soldiers who will be smart, real tough (physically and mentally) and educated."[2]

For some, the opportunity to catch a glimpse of how Sekani saw them became the most relevant experience in the teaching credential program. Why would this be so? Perhaps because, by showing them how they looked to her, Sekani was revealing to them aspects of themselves they had been struggling to shut out. The recovery of those denied aspects of themselves may have increased their sense of wholeness and may therefore explain why so many were so enlivened by the encounter and our subsequent discussion of it.

Seeing themselves through Sekani's eyes revealed to them that they were not who they had thought themselves to be.[3] These changes of self-concepts as a result of seeing themselves as they were seen by Sekani are, I have come to understand, what I mean by taking what Sekani was saying personally.

Seeing the white students through Sekani's eyes confirmed for Isaiah that he, like Sekani, had in fact, as he had suspected, been discounted by at least some of his classmates. Thus, Isaiah too began to see himself through Sekani's eyes. He too began to take personally Sekani's views and the views of other militant Black people.

In the Long Run

> There is neither a first word nor a last word. The contexts of dialogue are without limit. They extend into the deepest past and the most distant future. At any present moment of the dialogue there are great masses of forgotten meanings, but these will be recalled again at a given moment in the dialogue's later course when it will be given new life. For nothing is absolutely dead: every meaning will someday have its homecoming festival.[4]

November 18, Year 2. Sekani and I try to figure out what *Taking It Personally* is really about. Sekani thinks that patterns will emerge, and that, particularly if she and I see the same patterns, these are "truths." I counter that we cannot ever tell the true story, no matter how long a book we write; that if we were to look at the experience in five years' time or others were to read the data we selected for inclusion or the journals themselves, these others would tell very different stories; that what we write will never be the "last word." It's not only that we didn't tell the stories of the Filipina (Julia) in much detail and hardly mentioned the two Latinas, the Japanese exchange student whose English was quite limited, and the biracial and other white women.

It's much more than that. Were we to tell theirs and a hundred stories more about the encounter, it would not change the fact that we cannot know how the experiences of anyone who was present will be called up again in future dialogues that may both continue and redirect local and national conversations about race. Our experiences will become the past that—like Inuka, Keith (entering my class in St. Louis with a noose around his neck), the Harlem Globetrotters, Isaiah's mother's words, Denise's alcoholic father, and the blond-haired girl—will in some form or another be present in the years to come. The time we spent together that summer in that classroom will, for each of us, be a thread in the complex weave that is that future.

What Jim and Isaiah "got" when they wrote, "NOW I GET IT" or "I think I'm beginning to get it," will be not only transmitted, but also transformed and contested by future generations, including, perhaps, generations of their students, children, and colleagues. Some (white people and people of color, both) genuinely "crossed over," that is, became able to see from the viewpoints of institutionally more and less powerful others. We do not know for certain who these are. But, in any case, they may crisscross this stream many times in their lifetimes as the balance of their contending internal voices shifts in response to changes in the history of a society and world they will help to shape.

Denise, who had never heard the words "can't afford," may from this point on hear militancy in an antiracist language and may, at some future time, speak of militancy, or of some synonym for it, in terms of action for social justice. She may in years to come think about her experiences and the experiences of others through frameworks other than the same old readymade ones that with rare exceptions channeled her thinking throughout the course. It is within the realm of possibility that Denise will sometime in the future see and speak out against racial discrimination in the allocation of school resources or the disciplining of students.

The heated argument on which Sekani's visit turned occurred between two individuals, Sekani and the tall, blond, and (during the encounter) extremely red-faced Jim. However, the effects of that clash of languages and of the worldviews implicit in them will in some incarnation continue far beyond that time and place. We can think of Sekani's presence as having reactivated particular and partially dormant historically powerful revolutionary languages that will sometime in the future have their homecoming festivals, though changed in their new contexts and perhaps barely recognizable. The new readings of the racial world sparked by the encounter and the continuing conversations that directly or remotely descend from them are culture in the making.[5]

It is unlikely the people in our class will converse again with others who speak the variety of "languages" that make up the national language— including, most importantly, its stigmatized forms—in a space where dialogues on race and culture are the business of the day. They are unlikely to be provoked again in such a context to question the ways they accent words like "militancy," "Blackness," "whiteness," "violence," to participate in the ongoing social struggles over what meanings will become the common wisdom. (It is for this reason that I cringe at the quickly advancing encroachment of distance learning as an alternative to teaching face-to-face.)

Sekani's and my collaboration has not increased my confidence about the mark my teaching will leave upon the future. To the contrary, as I have become increasingly able to see myself and my views as well as Sekani's experience through Sekani's eyes—to take what she says personally—I have become able to see more and more of what had formerly been invisible to me, and my grasp of the power and complexity of the social and historical forces that sustain racism has increased exponentially.

This new understanding has challenged facile assumptions I have made about the contribution that teaching a diversity course can make to a more just and joyful future. I see more clearly that the kind of work that we were doing in the course needs to begin in kindergarten or before and continue through university if it is to provide a dam against the flood of countermessages and counterimages that surround us.[6]

On that day in July when Sekani made her presentation, we were all surprised. We were surprised to discover that, in spite of our best intentions, we had, as a class and as individuals, only begun to explore the depths, dimensions, and significance of racism. Now that I have looked closely with Sekani at the encounter, I better understand why we were surprised. This understanding has changed my teaching. But perhaps the most profound effect for me of writing about the encounter and its aftermath with Sekani is a new awareness of how much can be learned from looking closely at the unforeseen with another whose life history and present circumstances have shaped a set of lenses that are both so like and so different from my own.

Sekani: Would They Rather Be White Than Right? The Last Word

Ann started her conclusion with a question to herself. I will begin mine with a plea: Please, oh please, don't let my mother be right!

I have come full circle writing this book. A major difference between my attitude toward the racism that revealed itself in the cultural diversity class that day and my current dealings with it is I now have a better understanding of its mechanics and execution. As a consequence, I have modified my reaction and response to it and renewed my commitment to the struggle.

In the past, I viewed racist behaviors as irrational and unpredictable. Though I knew that I somehow brought out "white folks' " evil natures, I felt powerless for the most part to do anything about it because I did not know what I did that "activated" their racism. So, no matter how much I modified my behavior, my appearance, or my language, or renewed my faith and grasped at anything positive in my life, the society, or the media to assure me that things were getting better, I would always run into it. I either could see it like a freight train coming right at me and I was tied to the tracks by my own moral imperative, or I didn't see it at all and I was blindsided by the inherent betrayal of it.

It has become pretty much clear to me that, contrary to what many white people think, their judgments about us have nothing to do with who we really are. I find, however, that most people, both white and of color, *want*, sometimes *need*, to believe the explanation provided by the abuser: "It's not your color—it's *you* who bring these judgments upon yourself."

I always use rape as an analogy to racism, because the abusive dynamics are so similar. How long did women blame themselves when they were raped? I heard once (I have no idea if it is true, but it would surprise me if it were not) that attorneys prosecuting rape cases did not want women in the jury because women were far more critical of the rape victim than men were. A woman *needed* to believe the raped woman had been "provocative" and therefore had brought it on herself. I brought the "wrath of white" down upon me because of . . .

> my language—"redneck," "militancy," or was it —?
> my viewpoint—"O.J. didn't kill his wife," or was it —?
> my anger—"I don't really care about your feelings, this isn't about *you.*"

No one, including me, wants to accept the painful reality of racism, since that includes our own collusion and powerlessness in the process.

My credibility, my sanity, my intelligence, and my integrity were all attacked during the presentation because I triggered the racism of some of the students with the truth of how incompetence is practiced in schools and how racism is often the root cause. Then I created through the role play a situation where they were going to fail, and, despite my warning to Jim that this would happen, his racial arrogance made it impossible for him to accept the possibility of failure even in the artificial environment of a college classroom, in a totally artificial role play. Why was that? Why is it so many white people can't deal with failure as the rest of us have to? Why is it a white reflex to pull out their superior competence and smack us on the side of the head with it?

It wasn't until I ended up in a predominately Black/Chinese school that I saw with my own eyes how disabling white privilege can be to white people. Those white people who pull out their white privilege and execute it do so because they have nothing else—no skill, integrity, sanity, critical thought, analysis, theory, belief, or value system. There is no substantive essence to white supremacy. There never was. Many of us just believed it because in any environment where whites are in control, they can hide the secret of their utter incompetence.

Like parasites, they can take credit for other people's work, re-define the meaning of success, and place power in the hands of the snow-blind. These people believe their own propaganda. They don't have a choice. Who would ever suggest otherwise? The Black or Latino maid, gardener, co-worker, nanny?

But what is driving them to come to my neighborhood? Why didn't they stay where their "innate superiority" was constantly affirmed? They came because they didn't realize we had our own reality that differed greatly from their own. So many white people have no concept that there are people in the world who function with an entirely different set of values, needs, and self-concepts.

The "whiter" the teacher, the greater the likelihood of failure in a Black classroom environment. Not just because they can't identify—but because they can't *modify*. Most white people cannot adapt. In the dominant culture, it is *we* who have had to adapt to them. We change our hair, our clothes, our diction, and even our values.

It is only as adults, when we enter the school setting as parents or teachers, that we begin to see the racism that was directed at us when we were children. It is then that we remember how, within the elementary school setting, we learned what we could and could not say to our white teachers and how to lie by omission because it was easier to get what we needed if we told them what they wanted to hear, as opposed to what we really thought.

But in that lies the problem, doesn't it? Racism perpetuates itself because while we walk around not saying anything to piss off white people, many of them are destroying the educational opportunities of our children. It continues because no one wants to come out and say, "You're incompetent, you don't know what the hell you're doing, much less why you're doing it."

If we continue to hold white teachers to white standards, they will continue to fail white children as well as children of color. Not just academically, but socially. Although, while by white standards they may be considered excellent if they successfully induct white children into the racial hierarchy, I think they have failed miserably—but then, I'm a Black educator and have a different set of standards. If they fail to teach children of color how to be successful on their own terms, as well as in terms of the language of power, they may continue to come out looking great, but Tameeka, Jamal, Juan, and Choon will still be without a place where they can reconcile their cultural values with those of the dominant society. The lie—"Give white people what they want, and you will get what you need"—will continue.

Most European Americans are hooked on a drug that is stronger than crack, alcohol, and cigarettes combined. They are hooked on white supremacist ideologies and the beliefs, power, and privilege that come with them, and they don't even know it. They tell us that they are not racists and they sound like they mean it, because they believe it. Then they will turn right around the next day and refuse to let a Black child go on a field trip because the child said, "I don't like white people, and I don't like *you!*" (I saw this happen just a few months ago.) And it will never stop unless parents themselves become conscious and aware and listen to what their children are saying and find out if there is good cause for the child's rage.

When I heard Jim say, "Some of my best friends are rednecks," I kept thinking of the ideal retort. Not what I said, which was quite civil in my opinion, but what I wanted to say. In my fantasies, I pull a white sheet out of my bag and insist Jim put it on. I don't care how white people define "redneck." I don't care if it was a derogatory term used to belittle "good ole *Little House on the Prairie* people." To me and to most other Black people the term refers to those who, while they may have been someone's uncle, grandparent, or cousin, refused to pay my grandfather a decent wage for hard work, accused my mother of theft, and took my sister to jail, leaving me abandoned on the streets. In my language, "redneck" refers not to poor white people who worked in the sun, but to men who raped our women and men, many of whose sons and daughters are still trying to keep me from getting and keeping what I have rightfully earned.

* * *

After I do a presentation and get the feedback, I'm excited because I think, Well, maybe most of the students don't want to be power junkies or buy into racist rhetoric. I want to believe they are listening when I tell them that they need to get back to their own ethnicities and re-examine the contributions, values, and beliefs of their own people;

that they need to examine their Italian, French or German roots and consciously choose what parts of their heritages they will embrace; that they need to decide how they will interact in a world full of diversity; that they need to recognize that their self concepts and sense of worth are not universal templates everyone should live by.

I want to believe that white people can be taught to redefine their value not by how much they can control others, but by how many they can serve well. I want to believe they can understand that as long as they take for granted their white privilege, they can only give me what they have—*not* what I need.

I get excited when white people get together to address their racism and don't want to make doing so my job, when they talk like people in recovery, when they seem to understand that unlearning racism is a process, a long one, that takes humility, the same humility they have, in the past, imposed on others. I feel hopeful when white people acknowledge that they never did have all the answers because they never had the right questions, and they never had the right questions because they weren't listening.

* * *

This semester I'm dealing not only with racism in classrooms, but also with racism districtwide. I am the technology teacher at my school. The white teachers, with one or two exceptions, place me in a position where the only way I can accomplish my goals is to work overtime. No one offers to compensate me for this or acknowledges my commitment or contributions.

Then a white technician at the district level takes it upon herself to remove the passwords I had placed in the server. Her justification? I am not qualified. Why? Because, despite the fact that for the last five years I have worked nights, weekends, holidays, and summers to learn about networking and servers, what I have learned through practical experience is not in my job description. The fact that I can't very well learn how to manage a server if I am locked out of it isn't relevant. The fact that the Information Technology Department is trying to justify its expenditures at my expense is not supposed to be relevant. The fact that the department is selective throughout the school district about which school sites are allowed access to the server and which are not is not supposed to give me reason for concern.

The fact that no one of color except Asians remains in this department because of the verbal and psychological effects of daily degradation and insults that none of these white men and women would use outside the workplace because they would get the worst ass whoopin' of their lives isn't supposed to faze me. The fact that most of these controlling technicians seem totally unwilling to put in writing what *they* are doing on the server, or how they are doing it, is supposed to escape my "nigger" mentality.

So while I want to believe it's getting better, the reality is that I have another battle to fight on Monday morning, and it all stems from the fact that I'm supposed to be too stupid to be a part of the process. So, when one of the few Black technicians gets on the phone to talk to an outrageously blatant racist supervisor and sits there holding back tears and shaking while she barely maintains control of her voice, it only reaffirms my investment in kicking someone's ass today. While white people can console themselves that I'm paranoid, I don't enjoy the luxuries that denial seems to bring to others, white or of color. I, unfortunately perhaps, cannot survive and remain sane denying *my* own reality.

The strategies being implemented in the Information Technology Department are intended for the same purpose as always: to consolidate power and cover up incompetence. Racism, like any other form of oppression, is drawn to the fertile ground of corrupt and deprived environments. The perfect place is a poorly funded, poorly supported school district. No one knows what anyone else is doing. The district attracts the lowest quality staff because no one with better skills in their right mind would stay—short of political or religious conviction.

(Even I never expected to stay. I was like everyone else, just looking for work, and I met the minimal requirements. I had not planned to become addicted to children. Sometimes I come home to my small apartment, start paying my bills, and feel fiscally stupid. But then I remember how poorly I personally thrive in predominately white work environments, and I count my blessings [the children] and my change [enough for a movie]. It's not ideal—but I'm not afraid of poverty anymore. Racism is still worse, even if one begets the other.)

* * *

To overcome racism, white people must understand that evolving their thinking about racism and acting against racism are two different things. Evolution is an internal process that must begin before anyone can effectively make change. If you can't see racism when it's happening right before your eyes or by your own hand, you can't undo racism.

No one can develop an effective strategy or theory in the management of racism or any form of oppression unless he or she incorporates ethics. The issue that resounds and echoes behind my rage is justice. As long as I don't have fair and equal opportunity to get through my workday, shopping day, laundry day, without running into roadblocks that I trigger for no other reason than that I assume my requests and needs are legitimate and fair, we have a problem.

* * *

One of the consequences of writing this book is that I have come to understand my own internalized oppression better. I grew up not thinking I was poor, but I went to college and like a lot of my peers began to define my success by my ability to work in the financial district and have lots of zeros on my paycheck. Even with the migraines, the constant battles with management, and co-worker sabotage, I thought the track I had chosen was the right one. I even ignored the isolation, the silence I kept when I heard my white co-workers' racist comments, and the blinders I put on when I saw how the Black janitor or the "ugly" white woman were treated with such verbal cruelty.

But one day I went by bus to visit Nimat, one of the few Black friends I had had in college, at her home. She lived in East Palo Alto. It was the first time I had been there. As I neared her home, the color of the people on the bus began to change, and I felt my own excitement. I remember it because I didn't understand it. Why the hell was I so excited? Then I looked out the window and saw people talking on the street, people sitting on porches, kids playing double Dutch, and heard Salsa music blaring, and it hit me—hard—that I missed being Black. I missed being around Black.

But my feelings turned from happiness to nausea in seconds as the bus ride continued. I had no idea why. My first thought was that as a cancer survivor, anything that reminds me of my chemotherapy and radiation triggers nausea. Since Stanford Hospital is in Palo Alto and I was riding a bus similar to the one I used to have to take every day to get my radiation treatments, I thought this was the cause. But if that were the reason, the nausea would have been triggered as soon as I got on the bus. So why was I feeling sick?

Then I realized what it was. The community through which the bus was traveling had changed. When I was looking out the window at the middle-class Black community in East Palo Alto, I felt warm and fuzzy. But as the bus entered the desolate and torn-down part of the city, I became ill.

I don't even remember my visit with my friend now. But I do remember the sickness, because I was shocked by the physical effect poverty had on me. I began to pay attention whenever I went to "certain" parts of town. How did it make me feel? Over time, I started understanding why I went to nightclubs that I didn't even like, and why I didn't do well in most Black middle-class/business-oriented organizations. I realized I went to clubs to be around Black people like myself, and I avoided the Black business organizations because they usually were imitating white business culture and working *very* hard to minimize our own. To this day, I think a lot of the young Black businesspeople I knew then had the same problem I did.

I had to separate my fear of poverty from my Black culture, which is predominately poor. I realized that I had to work through my issues regarding poverty if I was ever going to reconnect to *my* people, whom I so desperately needed and missed. That community is the only one to which I feel I truly belong. I want to share this revelation with the people of color who read this book. I never would have been able to work as a Black educator at my school, in my neighborhood, without understanding my own—until very recently—unconscious pain around poverty.

* * *

The reward for us personally of examining racism is not to get racism out of the society (this is impossible) but to get it out of ourselves, our families, and the classrooms we teach in. Writing this book allowed me to address the real issues. Not the ones white people want to misrepresent as the issues. Not the safe issues. But some of the most fundamental ones.

Every day I see white people as loaded guns. I'm frightened of when they will take something from me I have rightfully earned or deny me something I legitimately need. To protect myself I need to understand racism. I need to know what causes these guns to go off and how to dodge the bullets. Then I have to understand, when I get shot—and I will eventually get shot again—how do I get the bullet out and clean and heal the wound before the next one hits? And as a teacher, a Black teacher, how can I protect my students from the same fate? I can't, can I? I have to admit it, and this, most of all, breaks my heart. They will get shot, won't they? All I can do is teach them what I have learned. Teach them how to clean their own wounds.

White people always ask during my presentations, "Why are you so angry?" "Why can't you forget and forgive?" Most white people act as if racism is something that happened in the distant past. They think because I'm big, Black, and strong/scary that it has not happened to me, instead of understanding that if I had not been big and strong/scary, I might not have survived.

Ann (I think) thought that after we had written this book and looked closely at what had happened as a result of the encounter, I would have become energized to continue the fight because I would see how many people were willing to recover from racism. I told her what my mother told me, I don't fight to win, I fight to fight. I couldn't believe that came out my mouth—I hate repeating my mother.

But I looked back at my life to see if I had ever "won" a battle dealing with racism. I could not think of a single instance. Not one. I guess, like a rape victim, I keep recreating the scene in my head, hoping I can change the ending so that it won't result in the violent impact that seems so inevitable. I keep thinking if I say it different, if I'm a better person, or if I'm stronger, or smarter, that I can stop it. But I never seem to be able to do so. There is always another battle around the corner, another attack.

I left the financial district and found racism in social services. I left social services and found it in education. I went to teach in a poor Black and Asian immigrant school. The school was in a district in one of the wealthiest states in the union, yet the people who were responsible for the allocation of resources to education—a predominately white male legislature and a series of white male governors—showed utter disregard for the inferior facilities and the lowest pay for teachers in the most expensive city in the country. They were apparently satisfied that these "colored" children would not get the kind of education that might turn them into CEOs who might actually marry their sons and daughters. (The people making these decisions often send their own children to private schools or manage to get them admitted to the preferred public schools, where wealthy parents can raise thousands of dollars to supplement state allocations.)

How can we heal a wound that continues to be inflicted?

Once when I was director of a women's center, I spoke with women who had survived rape. Each one had done the same as I had done. We tried at the beginning to convince ourselves that we had done something that brought on the attack. Then we tried to understand the social influences that made it happen. Could it be pornography, advertising, and capitalism? Some of us became political, some became frigid. But we all returned to that moment. That inevitable moment when we knew with absolute certainty that we were going to be raped. It didn't matter if we begged, bribed, or even fought, the rape was going to happen because the perpetrator had decided and had picked us that day.

So, what would you do? Knowing the attack is coming, knowing you can't stop it? As long as I am alive, I have to accept that it will happen. Fighting racism because I believe I will win is not a possibility for me. It is almost an oxymoron in my mind. It's a mathematical equation that makes no sense to me. I fight racism because it is my choice and my nature to fight whenever I am racially violated.

Let me leave you with a thought. We call sexual violence "rape." Why is there no word in English language to describe a racist attack? "Hate crime" is much too vague.

So, in the hope that my mother and I are as insane around the issue of racism as most white people want to believe, I leave you with the words to a song she wrote. I don't know if she necessarily wrote it for bigots. I think the song is really for those who betray, but my mother had told me she doesn't believe in betrayal, because she no longer believes in trust.

QUID PRO QUO
Or
SINCE YOU NEVER SCRATCHED MY BACK

Since you never scratched my back
You better not ever itch
Oh you've already struck out
So just "forgit" the pitch
Oh you've lost all your oars
And you can't even row
And if you're ever in trouble
Make sure I'm the last to know

Since you never scratched my back
You better not ever itch
Now you're the helpless familiar
And I'm the switchin' witch
Oh your fortune wheel has turned
And all your bridges burned
And you still have
Some hard lessons to learn

And I remember
When I got in too deep, you wanted to see me drown
When I tried to get up, you always pulled me down

And my rise from the deep was very, very slow
'Cause you were always my undertow

So
Since you never scratched my back
You better not ever itch
Oh you've already struck out
So just "forgit" the pitch
Oh you've lost all your oars
And you can't ever row
And if you ever need help
Make sure I'm the last to know[7]
—Wilcia Smith Moore[7]

So, if someone of color tells you that your behavior is racist and you tell them they're *crazy* ("I'm sure you may believe that but . . ."), *stupid* ("After our investigation we were able to determine that this was not an act of racism because the legal definition clearly states . . ."), or *lying* ("Clearly in the O.J. defense they were playing the race card, because there has been no clear evidence that the Los Angeles Police department is corrupt . . ."), don't act surprised if this is the kind of relationship you will have with "colored" folks like me. Don't expect trust, alliances, or support. Just be satisfied with both our good fortunes that I simply turn and walk away.

Notes

Introduction

1. We have made the decision to capitalize "Black" when referring to African Americans and to write "white" in lower case to refer to Americans of European descent. We have made this decision because people of African descent whose ancestors were brought as slaves to America chose to define themselves as Black in a particular historical context of resistance to oppression. We write "white" in lower case because the vast majority of white Americans, unaware of the historical forces that have over the centuries broadened the designation "white" to include immigrant groups such as Irish, Jews, and other Southern and Eastern Europeans, have come to take this designation and the privileges it entails for granted. See Brodkin 1998 for a concise history of ethnoracial assignment and ethnoracial identity in the United States and Nieto 2000 for a discussion of the complex issues involved in terminology regarding race, culture, and ethnicity.

2. Twenty percent of all new teachers quit within three years, and 50 percent quit within five years (Johnson 2000).

3. In Gloria Ladson-Billings's words: "The pedagogical instruction that many of the teachers of African-American students [were receiving] from their teacher preparation programs . . . [was leading] to intellectual death" (1994a, 15).

4. All names of students and certain distinguishing features have been changed.

5. Nationally, 88 percent of public school teachers and 71 percent of public school children are white (Rojas and Gordon 1999, 10). In California 60 percent of public school students and fewer than 23 percent of teachers are persons of color (Keleher et al. 1999, 10). The vast majority of the nation's teachers are white, and if current trends continue, white teachers will make up 95 percent of the nation's teachers soon after the millennium, while 46 percent of their students will be children of color (Banks 1997, 101).

6. For descriptions of and references to antiracist postsecondary teaching practices, see King 1997; Adams, Bell, and Griffin 1997; Ahlquist 1991;

Notes

Cochran-Smith 1995; Hollins 1990; Zeichner and Hoeft 1996; Maher and Tetreault 1997; Sleeter 1995.

7. As usual, I had prepared for my summer "writing time" by selecting a single book to stimulate my thought. My choice was felicitous. Laurel Richardson's *Fields of Play* (1997) supported and justified my desire not to simply "tell" what I had learned but to "show" through the telling of stories and suggested there were many possible forms (fiction and drama, for example) that the product of Sekani's and my collaboration might take.

8. Hooks addresses the challenges and dangers facing women of color who "talk back" and speak out, sometimes choosing to write in what hooks refers to as a "direct blunt manner" that was the customary mode of discourse in her family (1989,153). Collins (1990) shows how conceptions of theory that dominate the academy frequently exclude Black feminist thought.

9. I was aware that my selection of the segments privileged *my* judgments about what was interesting and important, but Sekani didn't have the time to work on the selection process.

10. Belluck 1999. See also the excellent report from the Oakland Based Applied Research Center (Gordon et al., 2000) and Gay (2000).

The relationship between race/ethnicity and poverty is complex. Because institutional racism over the centuries and into the present has created presently existing racial disparities in income and wealth, there is a strong correlation between race/ethnicity and social class. That is, Blacks, Latinos, Native Americans and some groups of Asian Americans are disproportionately poor, even though 48 percent of poor people are white. (Seventy-seven percent of the students in large city schools in the United States are both nonwhite and poor [Anyon 2000, 85–86].)

Many recent analyses of equality of educational opportunity focus on racial disparities (Gordon et al. 2000; Gay 2001), even though race/ethnicity and poverty each have an independent effect on school success. For example, there is a disparity between the achievement levels of Black children of every social class and their white and Asian counterparts (Steele 1992).

In *Taking it Personally* the focus is on racism, both institutional and personal, as a significant factor in achievement disparities between racial/ethnic groups. This does not mean that we do not consider of equal importance classism: the systematic, institutionalized mistreatment, invalidation, and marginalization of people because of their economic status. We hope our readers will keep in mind the parallels between the two "isms," and that poor people of color experience the effects of both.

It is also important to remember that data on school success is rarely distributed by subcategories. Thus the category "Asian" includes groups that differ widely from one another, and the category "Black" does not distinguish

174

Caribbean and African Blacks from African Americans whose ancestors were enslaved. Therefore all generalizations we and others make about racial/ethnic groups gloss over essential differences. I want especially to call attention to the limitations of the categorical designations "Asian" and "Chinese." These terms homogenize significant differences in economic and academic success both within and between native-born and immigrant populations, and, because of the stereotype of the model minority, perpetuate the notion that Asian Americans do not face racism or have specific social needs. See Lei 1998.

11. Nieto 1999. The ARC report (Gordon et al. 2000) indicates that there is some variation among cities in Latino dropout and suspension rates. According to a report issued by the National Center for Educational Statistics in August 2000, "the average math scores of black 17-year-olds and white 13-year-olds were the same," and in the past ten to twelve years about half of the gains that African American students made between 1970 and 1980 in closing the gap were "wiped out," creating a "depressing reversal of gains made over the previous two decades." In the past ten years the gap by which Latino students' scores trail those of whites generally remained unchanged (Mollison 2000). By age thirteen almost one-half of African American males and one-third of Latinos have repeated a grade at least once (Gay 2001,199). According to Foster (1996), these differential achievement rates are particularly egregious in the State of California.

12. Kreiger 1997.

13. Thirty-two percent of young Black men and 12 percent of young Latino men are either in prison, in jail, or on probation or parole, in comparison to 6.7 percent of young white men (Davis 1997, 266). African American and Latino youth are treated more severely than white teenagers charged with comparable crimes at every step of the juvenile justice system, according to a report sponsored by the U.S. Justice Department and six of the nation's leading foundations. Among young people who have not been sent to juvenile prison before, Blacks are more than six times as likely as whites to be sentenced by juvenile courts to prison (Butterfield 2000).

14. *San Francisco Chronicle*, September 15, 1999.

15. See Rains 1999, Fine 1997, McIntosh 1995, and Kinchloe et al. 1999 for discussions of white privilege.

16. See, for example, a story by Viadero (2000) on the front page of *Education Week*, entitled "Lags in Minority Achievement Defy Traditional Explanations." It is just one of many examples of the failure of reporters to consider racism as an explanation for differential achievement. Noguera and Akom (2000), writing in the *Nation*, name racism as a central factor in differential achievement, though that magazine is hardly mainstream and this article is exceptional even for the *Nation*.

17. Ladson Billings 1994b; Sleeter 1992; Nieto 1999; Zeichner and Hoeft 1996. Zeichner and Hoeft also cite some research that demonstrates the powerful effects of teacher education experiences, at least in the short run.

18. Delpit 1997; Zeichner and Hoeft 1996; Montecinos 1995.

19. See Zeichner and Hoeft (1996) and Ladson-Billings (1994a) for statements of the view that educational failure of disproportionate numbers of ethnic minority children is less a matter of teachers' failure to use "culturally compatible" or "culturally congruent" teaching strategies than it is of teachers' fundamentally negative feelings towards and low expectations for the learning of these students. Zeichner and Hoeft review studies of strategies used by teacher educators to counter these low expectations.

They also examine the literature on strategies used by teacher educators that provide prospective teachers with information about unique characteristics and learning styles of students from nondominant ethnic groups, and the dangers of stereotyping inherent in these strategies. Given the constantly changing nature of all aspects of ethnic culture and the endless variations related to geography as well as to social class and gender, it is indeed dangerous to teach teachers to identify particular learning styles, behavior patterns, values, and attitudes with particular racial or ethnic heritages. See Kumashiro 2000 for an excellent exposition of the issue. This is not to discount in any way the view that effective teachers use cultural and communication patterns that are familiar to their students (Foster 1994). The extent to which these patterns can be learned by teachers of other ethnic backgrounds remains unclear (Foster 1994).

20. Black men with high school diplomas earned $794 for each $1000 that white graduates earned; the ratio was $796 to $1000 for college graduates (Shipler 1997, 17). See also Noguera 2000.

21. Fordham 1996, 42–53. See also Steele 1992, Cose 1999.

22. Cochran-Smith and Lytle (1995) argue that research by teachers is a significant way of generating knowledge about teaching. We see *Taking It Personally* as an example of this systematic, intentional form of inquiry.

Chapter 1. Sekani: How I Got My "Black Attitude" Problem

1. Delpit 1995, 21–22. See also Foster 1997.

Chapter 2. Ann: How I Developed an "Obduracy of Tone"

1. McIntosh 1995, 104.

2. West 1994.

3. See Brodkin 1998 for an excellent account of "how Jews became white folks," that is, began to be granted many institutional privileges of white racial assignment after World War Two.

4. Davis 1998, 190–92.

5. Till was a fourteen-year-old Black Chicago youth who allegedly looked or whistled at a white woman when visiting his relatives in the South. That photo was a formative touchstone in young Muhammad Ali's life, and in the lives of many other Black people (Alexander 1995).

6. At Swarthmore the idea that "race" is a scientifically identified inherited set of homogeneous categories that fix people's identities on the basis of physical characteristics that are related to cognitive and intellectual qualities had gone unchallenged, even though racial categories based primarily upon skin color had, since the early 1900s, been conclusively if not widely challenged (Sanjek 1994).

7. James Baldwin, quoted in Kaye-Kantrowitz 1996, 121.

8. Today, when Jewish and Black communities seem divided by deeply rooted conflicts it's hard to keep in mind that through the sixties Jewish newspapers gave strong support to African American legal, economic and educational rights, and that collaboration with Black causes went far beyond direct or even indirect self interest (Davis, 1999).

9. As my father and I observed from the balcony I did not know of the breadth and depth of anti-Semitism in the world surrounding me. Some forty years later, as I was reading Blanche Cook's biography of Eleanor Roosevelt, I recalled the balcony event and began to imagine how non-Jews must have regarded Jews at the time. Cook reveals that, though Roosevelt worked within her husband's administration on behalf of the poor and Blacks, she held anti-Semitic beliefs that I now recognize were widely shared by the debutantes, their escorts, my classmates and their parents, and my neighbors, campmates, and camp counselors. During my childhood and youth there were many schools, clubs, and hotels to which Jews were not admitted. The parents of my classmates likely had been exposed to Henry Ford's lurid Jew-baiting campaign to convince the public of an international capitalist Jewish conspiracy as set out in "The Protocols of the Elders of Zion," which was reprinted in several languages and quoted extensively by Hitler in *Mein Kampf*. Both Eleanor and Franklin Roosevelt maintained public silence in the face of clear evidence of Hitler's ferocious anti-Semitism long into the Thirties (Cook 1999, 315–21).

10. See Britzman 2000 for an account of how the diary was presented to the public and how this very influential book actually limited awareness of the Holocaust and marginalized the Jewish aspects of Anne's identity.

11. Part of the reason for this silence was that during the immediate postwar years, the near extermination of the Jews was understood to be something of an embarrassment to them, an indication of the passivity and weakness of the Jewish people (Weiner 1999). It was not until the history of the period had been written that the near impossibility of resistance by the European Jews once Hitler came to power became known.

12. See Thandeka 1999 for a detailed analysis of how the white Anglo-Saxon Protestant upper-class standards of beauty and value are shaped by members of one's own immediate community regardless of the social class or ethnicity of that community. I resonate with Brodkin's awareness that her "sense of Jewish difference was formed through aspiring to blond-people whiteness" (1998, 18).

13. Berlak 1989.

14. The Building Alliances Across Differences model I use to organize the course content and construct teaching strategies is what McAllister and Irvine (2000) call a process-oriented model. They review three models used "to structure cross cultural learning." In each of these, stages of racial or ethnic development are central. The Building Alliances model is not a developmental model. The key concepts are the multiplicity, complexity, and fluidity of identity, the institutional nature of oppression, and the potential of individuals and groups to resist and unlearn oppression. Underlying all process-oriented models is an assumption that changing individuals' perceptions and attitudes will affect their behavior.

Chapter 3. Sekani: The Boot Camp Presentation

1. The Little Blond Girl and Ms. Crutch stories that I told the class are part of my autobiography in chapter 1.

Chapter 4. Ann: Picking Up the Pieces

1. The white privilege exercise, which is described in detail in chapter 5, is an activity designed to help students look at how race determines privilege in the United States.

Chapter 5. Ann: What Makes You Think She's Not an Expert?

Epigraph: Lisa Delpit, *Other People's Children: Cultural Conflict in the Classroom* (New York: New Press, 1997), 47.

1. See Cochran-Smith 1995 and 1997, 33, for a review of research on the uses of autobiographical reflection in the development of effective teachers.

2. I define "institutionalized racism" as the *systematic* and *naturalized* (i.e., taken for granted and therefore largely invisible) mistreatment, degradation, and misrepresentation of people of color that is built into and expressed through the "normal" functioning of social, political, and cultural institutions. "Racism" as I use the term points to a *system* of domination and subordination based on the ideology of the superiority of one race over another. It specifies *relationships* among socially constructed groups of people.

3. There were at the time of the encounter one field-based and several bilingual cohort groups that had a good proportion of students of color, but the "normal" programs remained overwhelmingly white.

4. I do not use the term "racism" to refer to condescending and negative racial stereotypes and judgments that people of a nonwhite group direct at members of their own racial group or members of another group of people of color. I reserve the term "racism" for the perpetration of systematic institutionalized and individual mistreatment of people of color by members of the dominant racial group. I think of racialized mistreatment of one nonwhite individual or group by another as an expression of internalized racism because it results from people of color internalizing the racist judgments of the dominant society, which sets up a white, Anglo-European standard against which all other groups are judged. I do not have a good term for what some call "lateral racism." These negative and harmful racial judgments directed at one another by members of nondominant groups are, however, increasingly of serious concern to antiracist teachers, myself included.

5. This activity, based upon McIntosh 1995, always has a startlingly powerful effect upon both white students and students of color. Some white students are "insulted" and angry at me for "forcing" them to confront their privilege, as documented in Berlak 1999, but most report that it was an activity that brought home the ubiquity of racism quite profoundly. Immigrant students of color often report that the activity clarifies experiences they had previously been unable to understand. Other students of color are grateful to have their experiences publicly acknowledged.

6. Dentith 1995, 35–38. This quotation and the others that structure this chapter present elements of the social philosophy of the Russian social theorist M. M. Bakhtin (1895–1975). I have adapted each epigraph from one of two Bakhtin scholars, Holquist (1990) or Dentith (1995). In recent decades Bakhtin's writing has influenced many scholars in the field of education.

7. Baldwin 1963/1988, 11.

8. Multiculturalism also has multiple meanings. There are a number of typologies or ways of categorizing these different meanings. The language or category scheme I use is most consistent with Sleeter 1991, 1992 and Derman-Sparks 1989. In the following discussion I will make a simple distinction between mainstream or liberal multiculturalism and anti-racist or critical multiculturalism. This latter category includes what Derman-Sparks calls anti-bias multiculturalism.

9. Of course, people of color, regardless of their skin tone, differ regarding the degree to which they internalize (accept as legitimate) the racist judgments of the dominant society. See Carter 1995, 40–41, for an analysis of the dangers of assuming that racism necessarily destroys the self-esteem of people of color and motivates them to identify with the oppressors. Some may internalize racism; others may develop appropriate anger in response to it.

10. Holquist 1990, 31.

11. Dentith 1995, 140.

12. Holquist 1990, 69.

13. When referring to people living in the United States, I use the term "ethnicity" to specify those aspects of one's culture that have historical roots in a particular geographical location that, with the exception of Native Americans and some Latinos, is outside the boundaries of the country. This usage frees the concept of culture to refer to the multiple attitudes, values, and worldviews that have their origins in a variety of sources that include one's gender (women's or gay culture), class (working-class culture), history (Sixties culture), and nation (U.S. culture). This distinction between ethnicity and culture is one way to address the claims of many white students that they have no culture. I think what such students mean by this is that they have "lost" what I think of as the ethnic aspects of their culture. (See Carter 1995, Sleeter 1993, Nieto 2000 for various ways that ethnicity and culture have been conceptualized, and the dangers and advantages of the concept of ethnicity.)

14. See Berlak 1999 for a discussion of the pivotal role students willing to bear witness to racism can play in any given class.

15. Holquist 1990, 68–69.

16. Between the Fifties and the Seventies the Civil Rights, Black Power, and Chicano movements waged an assault upon racism. These social movements had been stimulated by a period of postwar prosperity during which a belief in the desirability and possibility of incremental change in race relations began to mount a challenge to the culturally dominant old-fashioned racism, with its assumption of the genetic inferiority of people of color. In the mid-Sixties the focus of the movements shifted from advocating peaceful, nonviolent, and incremental paths to racial justice and persistence and perseverance in the face of racism, to advocating self-determination, cultural and racial consciousness, and political power (Geneva Gay, quoted in Sleeter 1992, 82). There was at the time among many who called themselves militant an implicit or explicit expectation that they would respond to violence with violence. This, of course, distinguished Martin Luther King's nonviolence from the philosophy of Malcolm X and the Black Panthers (Zinn 1995).

17. It was not uncommon for me to have students in my classes who had come of age in the late Sixties and had at that time engaged in some form of social activism, but who had later lost touch with their activist commitments. Those who share this part of their history with me often report that the course rekindled their lost idealism. For a similar observation, see Macedo 1998, 3. Carol was one of those students.

18. Almost as soon the civil rights and equal opportunity policies (busing and affirmative action, for example) that had been won as a result of social movements of the Sixties and early Seventies had begun to threaten and in some

cases topple long-established racial hierarchies, backlash set in. Well-funded conservative groups began financing campaigns to undermine and dismantle the policies, and the values and commitments that had motivated them (Apple 1993).

19. The belief that U.S. society is colorblind entails denying the persistence of racism. Many students entered the class taking for granted the modern racist view that racism has virtually disappeared, that claims of people of color to the contrary are self-indulgent, and that claims of white people that racism is still active are attempts to be politically correct. Continuing racial tension was often portrayed simply as the result of multiculturalists calling attention to racial differences and to racism (Geiger 1997, 27–29).

20. Sleeter 1992, 53. A good example of how the media construct racism as inconsequential is *Newsweek*'s June 7, 1999, eye-catching headline, all in caps: "THE GOOD NEWS ABOUT BLACK AMERICANS." In lower-case, very small print and in parentheses below the headlines were the words: "(And Why Many Blacks Aren't Celebrating)." Only one of the fifteen pages of the cover story acknowledged the sense of despair and hopelessness that characterizes many of the families of the students in Sekani's school.

21. Only five of the twelve most popular high school history texts James Loewen (1995) surveyed even listed race or racism in their indexes. Only one came close to explaining the connection between slavery and racism. According to Loewen, all portrayed slavery as an uncaused tragedy rather than a wrong perpetrated by some people on others. The emotion generated by the descriptions in the text was sadness, not anger, for "there's no one to be angry at"(145). Lowen provides an example of the texts' silence about racism by telling us that there is no mention in any text that the Patrick Henry of "Give me liberty or give me death"fame freed none of the enslaved people he owned before he died (146). Loewen demonstrates how the texts contribute to students' failure to see antiracist figures as role models by showing that, though abolitionist John Brown is usually portrayed in these books not as a man acting out of Christian morality but as an insane fanatic, few saw him that way at the time.

22. McCarthy 1998, 84. The media also generally underrepresented minorities in films and on TV. This recently prompted a boycott of major networks by a coalition of African Americans, Latinos, Native Americans, and Asian Americans (Garcia 1999).

23. See Milloy 1999 for an excellent analysis of the racism implicit in the press's reporting of the Littleton massacre.

24. Acclimatizing the public to images of Black bodies in pain was part of a long history that began with images of slavery and lynching (Alexander 1995, 85). The media's application of the term "wilding" to Black youth engaged in violence, but not to the white youth who attacked Yuseff Hawkins in Benson-

hurst (Giroux 1994, 194), repeats the same pattern. (On August 23, 1989, three Black men walking casually through the streets of the predominately Italian American neighborhood of Bensonhurst, New York, were attacked by a group of whites. One of them was killed.) Our class's encounter with Sekani was played out within a culture of ubiquitous violence, trillions spent on "defense," and the United States repeatedly bombing civilian populations who live across the seas.

25. Poor communities were plunging into even deeper poverty because of cutbacks in welfare programs, education, and federal assistance to cities, even though tax revenues were high. Responding to homelessness by building public housing was not even on the table. Instead, politicians proposed tax cuts. The unchecked pursuit of profits impoverished members of all racial groups, though the most easily discarded in the lust for profit were Black and brown workers (Winant 1998, 96). The ratio of top-executive-to-factory-worker pay had exploded from 42 to 1 in 1980 to 419 to 1 in 1998. Had worker pay risen at the same pace as executive pay, the average production worker would earn more than $110,000 a year today compared with the $29,000 he or she actually makes (Smart 1999).

26. The longer teachers remain in the profession, the wider the salary gap grows. In 1998 teachers between the ages of twenty-two and twenty-eight earned on average $7,874 less than other college graduates of the same age. Teachers aged forty-four to fifty earned an average of $23,655 less (Posnick-Goodwin 2000, 8).

27. Shipler 1997, 280. Shipler reports a National Opinion Research Center poll "devised with nuanced choices" that found that 6.3 percent of Americans believed African Americans were more intelligent than whites, 40.5 percent believed they were equally intelligent, and 53.2 percent believed they were less intelligent. Of the Blacks polled, 30 percent thought Blacks were less intelligent (278).

28. Geiger 1997, 27–28.

29. Lamont 1999, xii.

30. By 1991 the proportion of African American students in intensely segregated schools (where 90–100 percent are students of color) returned to the level that existed in 1971, when the Supreme court issued its first school desegregation bussing decision. Presently, 63 percent of all white students go to schools that are 90–100 percent white (Rojas 1999), 40 percent of public schools in large cities are "intensely segregated," and current racial segregation surpasses that which existed in the year of the Brown decision (Della-Piana 1999).

31. Most of the white students had not paused to consider why there were so few students of color in their college prep courses, or how the pedagogical styles, curriculum content, and teaching materials they experienced differed from those of their schoolmates of color, who rarely appeared in their classes. See Nieto

1999, 29–30, Oakes 1985, and Gay 1990 for more detailed analyses of tracking and its effects. See Zeichner and Hoeft 1996, 526, for references documenting the paucity of direct intercultural experience of U.S. teacher education students.

32. Though multicultural teaching had its origins in Sixties radical and militant activism and the Seventies was a prime time for developing ideas about and materials for multicultural education, multicultural practice remained largely fragmentary, sporadic, and unsystematic (Sleeter 1992); neither curriculum guides, nor state frameworks, nor the state-adopted textbooks the teachers of the students in our class had taught from had mentioned racism. Though some of the younger students in our class may have read from elementary or high school textbooks that featured multicolored faces to which had been added a few paragraphs or even pages about Latino, Asian, and/or African American history, the texts had not been reworked and remained a central site for the preservation of the selective tradition of the dominant culture (McCarthy 1998, 116). The exceptions were students who had majored in La Raza, Asian American, or Black studies at college or university. Very few of these were white.

33. The students in the summer course were at various levels of completion of the certification program. Jim and Denise had completed the program except for the diversity course. Evidently their experiences in the credential program had not challenged their cultural deprivation perspectives. See Deutsch 1963 for a classic and widely read example of the cultural deprivation perspective. Ryan (1971/1976) presents an excellent critique of that perspective in *Blaming the Victim*.

34. See Kozol 1992. Most really had not considered what the effect upon learning might be of attending a school where the roof was falling down and the toilets regularly overflowed.

35. Presently 10 percent of teachers are described as "minority," and this number is expected to decline even further. Preservice education programs are notorious for their homogeneity, which is in part a consequence of screening practices that discriminate against teachers of color in numerous ways. (Nieto 1999, 31). See H. Berlak 1999 for an analysis of how the California Basic Educational Skills Test (CBEST) required of all teachers in California discriminates against teachers of color.

36. Though in the pre-desegregation era segregated schools were appallingly unequal with respect to resources, Black teachers teaching in them often offered their students an empowering education (Nieto 1999; Foster 1993, 1994). Cross (1998, 33–34) writes:

[In pre-desegregation schools] we were taught to think of the development of our minds as essential to the development of a more humane America where we would not be judged by our skin color but by how we lived our lives. . . . Our teachers recognized an oppressive state. They used curriculum to change it and expected us to use our knowledge to do the same. . . . They saw their educational practice as creating free people—freedom for us, them and all people. . . . The mission of my new teachers in desegregated schools was to teach discrete, seemingly objective academic facts. . . . We no longer talked about freedom. . . . The academic no longer coexisted along with the struggle for freedom.

37. Cochran-Smith writes: "The evidence is clear that successful teachers of diverse learners have a strong belief that all their students are capable of learning at high intellectual levels" (1997, 33). The students in our class were unaware of studies that show that the usually subtle but pervasive racism expressed for the most part by well-intentioned teachers is so powerful it grinds down the confidence and ultimately the graduation rate of Black college students who enter college with test scores equal to those of whites. See Steele 1992 for documentation of this process. In an in-depth study of teachers at a Washington, D.C., high school, Fordham (1996) shows that to a considerable extent the African American teachers shared the low expectations and negative attitudes of their white colleagues toward their Black students.

38. See Boykin 1986 and King 1994 for careful analyses of African American attitudes, traditions, and values. These writers avoid the ever-present danger of essentializing or stereotyping (see Cochran-Smith 1997). According to Boykin, the distinctive values and traditions of many African Americans both reflect African roots that have been passed down across the generations and express modes of resistance developed in response to historical and contemporary racism.

39. Fordham 1996, 88. According to Fordham (1996, 59), many African American students respond to dehumanizing and condescending views of them by striving to achieve, in order to prove the racists wrong. However, King (1994) writes that those students who seek to prove they are capable of achieving in the terms set by the dominant culture are often accused by their peers of acting white and of betraying their Black selves by collaborating with a system designed to destroy their African American identity. Nieto (1999) writes that such students are often seen as cultural traitors. She cites studies that have found that racelessness is related to school success and addresses the psychic costs that result from achieving "racelessness."

40. This Black *alienated* oppositional identity has been described as a recent phenomenon that resulted from the hyperconcentration of unemployed and undereducated adults that, since the 1970s, has come to characterize the segregated inner cities (Nieto 1999, 43; Cross 1998). From this perspective, alienation from school is at odds not only with the dominant culture but also

with a long tradition of Black *defensive* oppositional identity that supports the school learning necessary for "making it" in a racist society, even as it critiques that society and is committed to transforming it.

41. On Black and white employment opportunities, see Ladson-Billings 1994a, 136.

42. See critiques by Thomas Cook (1999) and King (1994) of the common-wisdom, "best practices" research of educators such as James Comer whose policies promote students' assimilation. See Foster 1994, Young 1999, O'Conner 1997, and Cochran-Smith 1997 for arguments and evidence that successful teachers of African American students promote not only students' academic success but also their abilities to develop cultural critique, to recognize and maneuver around racial constraints, and eventually to alter fundamentally basic systems of power and resource distribution.

43. As noted earlier, black male high school graduates earned about 80 percent of white graduates' earnings; the same ratio held for college graduates (Shipler 1997, 17).

44. Lisa Delpit (1997) has written cogently about why children who arrive at school without prior understanding of the basics of school knowledge might not prosper in schools that emphasize fluency of writing and other practices to the exclusion of direct instruction in the skills and knowledge that are valued by the dominant culture, and that all children need if they are to succeed in school.

45. Ladson-Billings 1995a.

46. Foster 1993, 376.

Chapter 6. Ann: Fantasy and Feeling in the Classroom

1. Dentith 1995, 38–46.

2. Ibid., 36–39.

3. This norm is fundamental to the currently popular concept of emotional intelligence. A central index of emotional intelligence is the ability to soothe oneself, to shake off anxiety and gloom. An emotionally intelligent person would restrain herself from expressing "negative" emotions such as anger. See Boler 1999, 63.

4. Lorde 1984, 130.

5. See Boykin 1994 and King 1994 for discussions of Afrocultural expression.

6. Boler 1999, 190–91. In the dozen or so sections of the course I have taught since the encounter, only Patricia, an African American student, expressed moral anger in the open forum of the class. Her anger was directed at a classmate's refusal to acknowledge even the possibility that racism presently existed at the university. The classmate who denied the possibility that a professor could express racism, and those students who agreed with her, in turn reacted angrily

both at Patricia and at me for (as they told another faculty member) justifying Patricia's anger and failing to protect them from her attack. I consider Patricia's anger moral anger and that of the other students defensive anger.

7. Britzman reminds us that one can never actually feel the suffering another feels. She writes: "To be receptive to the difficulties of the other is not the same as feeling another's pain, which is, of course, impossible" (2000, 21).

8. Spelman 1997, 71–80.

9. See Frankenberg 1993; Lesko and Bloom 2000.

10. The views I expressed here were heavily influenced by the powerful writings of the Swiss psychoanalyst Alice Miller (1980, 1984).

11. Giroux 1997.

12. Williams 1997, 8–9.

13. Finke 1997, 122. See Lesko and Bloom 2000 for an excellent analysis of the role of the unconscious in antiracist classrooms.

14. There is not, of course, a clear demarcation between the conscious and the unconscious; what is available to consciousness is always in flux, shaped and reshaped endlessly by social experience, including interactions with media, schools, and other social institutions.

15. Ellsworth 1997.

16. Britzman 1998a, 118.

17. Perhaps I was caught up in what Lesko and Bloom (2000) call "the modernist fantasy in which the main character, the teacher, is engaged in a heroic and solitary act" (245).

18. Simi Valley was the scene of the trial of the police officers who beat Rodney King. The jurors acquitted all of the officers.

19. See McCarthy 1998 and chapter 5 here for discussions of how television and film construct these fears.

20. The phrase "difficult knowledge" is from Britzman 1998a, 117. When David, the white man in *The Color of Fear* who provoked Victor's anger by claiming that each man stands on his own ground, was asked toward the end of the film what kept him from believing that what Victor said was true, he replied that he didn't want to believe the world Victor lived in could be so cruel.

21. Simon 1992.

22. McCarthy 1998, 91.

23. See Britzman 1998 and Salverson 2000 for elaboration of these possibilities.

24. Teachers as a group may be particularly attached to the idea that they act out of impartial and selfless service and devotion (Robertson 1997). See also Kumashiro 2000.

25. Ellsworth 1997, 56. Or the new information might simply engender

guilt at past misdeeds, such as having listened without protest to racist jokes. Such shame and guilt and the fears associated with them might be aroused by as small a detail as Sekani's African dress, or the use of the word "militant," if such garb and words have become associated with violence (Britzman 1998b, 10). The fearful person may not recognize this fear and be aware only of a vague anxiety that he or she may be unable to pinpoint, as Denise described when she first saw Sekani enter the classroom. As Lisa Delpit (1995, 46) puts it, "We do not really see through our eyes or hear through our ears, but through our (conscious and unconscious) beliefs."

26. The analysis that follows depends heavily upon Salverson 2000.

27. Ellsworth 1997, 61.

28. What we bring to consciousness is shaped and reshaped not only by social institutions such as schools and the media but also within our individual families. This distinction between social/cultural and personal/familial experiences that shape what we at any given time bring to consciousness does not, however, acknowledge that media and schooling not only shape our views directly, but also shape experiences we have within our families. Nevertheless, it helps clarify the tenuous distinction between the realms of the teacher and the psychotherapist. The teacher's *focus* is the realms of the unconscious that have been shaped by social institutions, not those shaped by experiences within a student's particular family.

29. Britzman 2000, 48. See also Giroux 1997, Britzman 1998a, Kumashiro 2000, and Felman 1992 for discussions of the role of trauma in teaching.

30. Everyone had experienced some part of this pattern before they had entered my class. The patterns did not proceed in any linear direction for any individual or for any group as they continued to be woven in our class.

31. Britzman 1998a, 10.

32. One cannot, of course, represent or name with precision another's suffering (see Salverson 2000).

33. See Felman and Laub 1992 and Berlak 1999 for a closer look at this process.

34. Ellsworth 1997, 199.

35. Students who understand these dynamics are less likely to be judgmental toward others who resist confronting their own and others' racism, and thus they are able to help their classmates confront their racist conditioning. There are usually a few students in every class who want to distance themselves from others who seem insensitive to racism, saying they can't understand how those others can "think like that." I always respond to such statements by saying that I expect them to understand it before the course is over.

36. Ellsworth 1997, 40–41.

37. Britzman 2000, 51.

38. I have more than once, though far less often in recent years, inadvertently provoked resistance by directly challenging white students' perceptions of themselves as non- or antiracist, that is, by taking something of the role Sekani took in the encounter. Once I found myself responding sharply and without empathy to a student who wondered why Mexican immigrants didn't go back where they came from, asking "Whose land is this anyway? How did California become a part of the United States? What is so sacrosanct about the border?" One consequence of my failure to respond with empathy was that both the speaker and others who shared the speaker's views became resistant and remained so for the rest of the course. I have found that once I have challenged a student's image of herself without conveying (and usually without feeling) empathy, immediate or subsequent attempts to respond empathetically to the resulting humiliation my retorts engender have been useless. I have been unable to recoup trust. Only with my present understanding of the trauma this type of confrontation evokes do I see what would have been required to get beyond the resistance.

Chapter 7. Sekani: The Love Letter

1. CLAD stands for Cross Cultural Linguistic and Academic Development. It is a credential mandated by the State of California to certify cross-cultural competence. The diversity course is one of two courses required for this certification, though all other courses in the certification program are expected to promote "cross-cultural" knowledge and competencies.

2. Fordham (1996) presents one of many portraits of Black parenting styles. Both she and Delpit (1997) point particularly to the tendencies of many Black parents to say explicitly and directly what they expect, rather than "suggesting" to children what they might want to do. My style may be seen as a teacherly version of a direct parenting style.

Conclusion

1. Of course, perspective taking is a necessary but not sufficient condition for becoming actively antiracist, as I have argued here earlier. It is also important to note that those who hold lower positions in power hierarchies are more familiar with the perspectives of those above them than the reverse. Knowing how the world is seen by white people can be a matter of survival for African Americans and other people of color.

2. Gloria Ladson-Billings (2000) might say Isaiah was on his way to developing a sociopolitical consciousness.

3. James Baldwin put it: "If I am not what I've been told I am then it means you're not what you thought you were either. And that is the crisis" (1963/1988, 8). Lisa Delpit said it another way: "Those with the most power are

morally obligated to take responsibility for putting their beliefs on hold, ceasing to exist as themselves for a moment, and to see themselves in the unflattering light of another's gaze, giving up their sense of who they are" (1995, 46). Kevin Kumashiro (2000, 45) said it this way: "A student should engage not only in self reflection (in which the student asks how he or she is implicated in the dynamics of oppression) but also in self reflexivity (in which the student brings this knowledge to bear on his or her own sense of self)."

4. Bakhtin, *Esteika,* 373, quoted in Holquist 1990, 39.

5. Ellsworth 1997, 137.

6. All readers should become familiar with the work of Louise Derman-Sparks (1989), whose primary focus has been antibias work in early childhood education.

7. Words and music by Wilcia Smith Moore. © 1994 by Wilcia Smith Moore. Reprinted by kind permission of Wilcia Smith Moore and Blue Wayne Publishing, P.O. Box 2121, Berkeley, CA 94702.

Bibliography

Adams, Maurianne, Lee Ann Bell, and Pat Griffin, eds. 1997. *Teaching for Diversity and Social Justice*. New York: Routledge.

Ahlquist, Roberta. 1991. "Position and Imposition: Power Relations in a Multicultural Foundations Course." *Journal of Negro Education* 60 (2), 158–69.

Alexander, Elizabeth. 1995. "Can You Be Black and Look at This? Reading the Rodney King Videos." In Black Public Sphere Collective, ed., *The Black Public Sphere* . Chicago: University of Chicago Press.

Alterman, Eric. 1999. "The 'Right' Books and Big Ideas." *Nation,* November 22, 16–21.

Anyon, Jean. 2001. "Inner Cities, Affluent Suburbs, and Unequal Educational Opportunities." In James A. Banks and Cherry A. McGee Banks, eds., *Multicultural Education*. New York: Wiley.

Apple, Michael W. 1997. "Consuming the Other: Whiteness, Education, and Cheap Fries." In Michelle Fine, Lois Weis, Linda C. Powell, L. Mun Wong, eds., *Off White: Readings on Race, Power, and Society*. New York: Routledge.

———. 1993. "Constructing the Other: Rightist Reconstructions of Common Sense." In Cameron McCarthy and Warren Crichlow, eds., *Race Identity and Representation in Education*. New York: Routledge.

Baldwin, James. 1963/1988. "A Talk to Teachers." In R. Simonson and S. Walker, eds., *The Graywolf Annual Five: Multicultural Literacy*. St. Paul, Minn.: Greywolf.

Banks, James. 1997. *Educating Citizens in a Multicultural Society.* New York: Teachers' College Press.

———. 1994. *Multiethnic Education.* Boston: Allyn and Bacon.

Behar, Ruth. 1996. *The Vulnerable Observer.* Boston: Beacon Press.

Bartolome, Lilia. 1994. "Beyond the Methods Fetish: Towards a Humanizing Pedagogy." *Harvard Educational Review* 65 (2), 173–93.

Belluck, Pam. 1999. "Reason Is Sought for Lag by Blacks in School Effort." *New York Times,* July 4.

Berlak, Ann. 1999. "Teaching and Testimony: Witnessing and Bearing Witness to Racism in Culturally Diverse Classrooms." *Curriculum Inquiry* 29 (1): 99–129.

———. 1994. "Antiracist Pedagogy in a College Classroom. Mutual Recognition and a Logic of Paradox." In Rebecca A. Martusewicz and William A. Reynolds, eds., *Inside Out*. New York: St. Martin's Press.

———. 1989 "Teaching for Outrage and Empathy in the Liberal Arts." *Educational Foundations* 3 (Summer): 69–95.

Berlak, Harold. 1999. *Adverse Impact: How CBEST Fails the People of California*. Oakland: Applied Research Center. October.

Boler, Megan. 1999. *Feeling Power: Emotions and Education*. New York: Routledge.

Boykin, A. W. 1986. "The Triple Quandary and the Schooling of Afro-American Children." In U. Neisser, ed., *The School Achievement of Minority Children*. Hillsdale, N.J.: Erlbaum.

———. 1994. "Afrocultural Expression and its Implications for Schooling." In Etta Hollins, Joyce Kink, and W. C. Hayman, eds. *Teaching Diverse Populations*. Albany: State University of New York Press.

Britzman, Deborah. 2000. "If the Story Can Not End: Deferred Action, Ambivalence, and Difficult Knowledge." In Roger Simon, Sharon Rosenberg, and Claudia Eppert, eds., *Between Hope and Despair: Pedagogy and the Representation of Historical Trauma*. Totowa, N.J.: Rowman and Littlefield.

———. 1998a. *Lost Subjects, Contested Objects: Toward a Psychoanalytic Inquiry of Learning*. Albany: State University of New York Press.

———. 1998b. "Why Return to Anna Freud? Some Reflections of a Teacher Educator." *Teaching Education Journal* 10 (Fall/Winter): 3–16.

Brodkin, Karen. 1998. *How the Jews Became White Folks*. New Brunswick, N.J.: Rutgers University Press.

Butterfield, Fox. 2000. "Race Bias Cited Throughout Juvenile Justice System." *San Francisco Chronicle*, May 26.

Carter, Robert T. 1997. "Is White a Race? Expressions of White Racial Identity." In Michelle Fine, Lois Weis, Linda C. Powell, and L. Mun Wong, eds., *Off White: Readings on Race, Power, and Society*. New York: Routledge.

———. 1995. *The Influence of Race and Racial Identity in the Psychotherapy Process: Towards a Racially Inclusive Model*. New York: Wiley.

Cochran-Smith, Marilyn. 1997. "Knowledge, Skills, and Experience for Teaching Culturally Diverse Learners: A Perspective for Practicing Teachers." In J. Irvine, ed., *Critical Knowledge for Diverse Learners*. Washington, D.C.: American Association of Colleges for Teacher Education.

———. 1995. "Uncertain Allies: Understanding the boundaries of Race and Teaching." *Harvard Educational Review* 65 (4), 541–70.

Cochran-Smith, Marilyn, and Susan Lytle. 1995. *Inside/Outside: Teacher Research and Knowledge.* New York: Teachers College Press.

Collins, Patricia Hill. 1990. *Black Feminist Thought: Knowledge, Consciousness, and the Politics of Empowerment.* Boston: Unwin Hyman.

Comer, James, ed. 1999. *Child by Child: The Comer Process for Change in Education.* New York: Teachers College Press.

Cook, Blanch Wiesen. 1999. *Eleanor Roosevelt.* Vol. 2. New York: Viking.

Cook, Thomas D., Farah-Naaz Habib, Meredith Phillips, Richard A. Settersten, Shobba C. Shagle, and Serdar M. Degirmencioglu. 1999. "Comer's School Development Program in Prince George's County, Maryland: A Theory Based Evaluation." *American Educational Research Journal* 36 (3), 543–98.

Cose, Ellis. 1999. "The Good News About Black America." *Newsweek,* June 1, 29–41.

Cross, Beverly. 1998. "Problems of Nonengagement and Practices of Engagement." In Rudolfo Chavez-Chavez and James O'Donnell, eds., *Speaking the Unpleasant.* Albany: State University of New York Press.

Davis, Angela. 1998. *The Blues Legacy and Black Feminism.* New York: Vintage Books.

———. 1997. "Black Americans and the Punishment Industry." In Wahneema Lubiano, ed., *The House that Race Built.* New York: Vintage Books.

Davis, David Brion. 1999. "Jews and Blacks in America." *New York Review of Books,* December 2, 57–63.

Della-Piana, Libero. 1999. "Reading, Writing, Race, and Resegregation." *Colorlines* 2 (1), 9–10.

Delpit, L. 1997. *Other People's Children: Cultural Conflict in the Classroom.* New York: New Press.

Dentith, Simon. 1995. *Bakhtinian Thought.* London: Routledge.

Derman-Sparks, Louise. 1989. *Anti-Bias Curriculum.* Washington, D.C.: National Association for the Education of Young Children.

Deutsch, Martin. 1963. "The Disadvantaged Child and the Learning Process." In A. Harry Passow, ed., *Education in Depressed Areas.* New York: Teachers College Press, 1963.

Ellsworth, Elizabeth. 1997. *Teaching Positions.* New York: Teachers College Press.

Ellsworth, Elizabeth, and Janet Miller. 1996. "Working Differences in Education." *Curriculum Inquiry* 26 (3), 245–63.

Felman, Shoshana. 1997. "Psychoanalysis and Education: Teaching the Terminable and Interminable." In Sharon Todd, ed., *Learning Desire: Perspectives on Pedagogy, Culture, and the Unsaid.* New York: Routledge.

Felman, Shoshana, and Dori Laub. 1992. *Testimony: Crises of Witnessing in Literature and Psychoanalysis.* New York: Routledge.

Fine, Michelle. 1997. "Witnessing Whiteness." In Michelle Fine, Lois Weis, Linda Powell, and L. Mun Wong, *Off White: Readings on Race, Power, and Society.* New York: Routledge.

Finke, Laurie. 1997. "Knowledge as Bait." In Sharon Todd, ed., *Learning Desire: Perspectives on Pedagogy, Culture, and the Unsaid.* New York: Routledge.

Fordham, Signithia. 1996. *Blacked Out: Dilemmas of Race, Identity, and Success at Capital High.* Chicago: University of Chicago Press.

Foster, Michele. 1996. "As California Goes, So Goes the Nation." *Journal of Negro Education* 65 (2), 105–11.

———. 1994. "Effective Black Teachers: A Literature Review." In Etta Hollins, Joyce King, and W. C. Hayman, eds., *Teaching Diverse Populations: Formulating a Knowledge Base.* Albany: State University of New York Press.

———. 1993. "Educating for competence in Community and Culture: Exploring the Views of Exemplary African American Teachers." *Urban Education* 27 (4), 370–94.

Frankenberg, Ruth. 1993. *White Women, Race Matters: The Social Construction of Whiteness.* Minneapolis: University of Minnesota Press.

Gans, Herbert. 1999. "The Possibility of a New Racial Hierarchy in the Twenty-first Century United States." In Michele Lamont, ed., *The Cultural Territories of Race.* Chicago: University of Chicago Press.

Garcia, Edwin. 1999. "Boycott Seeks More Minorities in TV Roles." *San Jose Mercury,* September 11.

Gay, Geneva. 2001. "Educational Equality for Students of Color." In James A. Banks and Cherry A. McGee Banks, eds., *Multicultural Education.* New York: Wiley.

Geiger, J. Jack. 1997. "The Real World of Race: A Review of 'A Country of Strangers: Blacks and Whites in America' by David K. Shipler." *Nation,* December 1, 27–29.

Giroux, Henry A. 1994. "Living Dangerously: Identity Politics and the New Cultural Racism." In Henry A. Giroux and Peter McLaren, eds., *Between Borders: Pedagogy and the Politics of Cultural Studies.* New York: Routledge.

———. 1997. "Rewriting the Discourse of Racial Identity: Towards a Pedagogy and Politics of White Identity." *Harvard Educational Review* 67 (2), 285–321.

Goldberg, David Theo. 1990a. Introduction to David Theo Goldberg, ed., *Anatomy of Racism.* Minneapolis: University of Minnesota Press.

———. 1990b. "The Social Formation of Racist Discourse." In David Theo Goldberg, ed., *Anatomy of Racism.* Minneapolis: University of Minnesota Press.

Gordon, Rebecca, Libero Della Piana, and Terry Keleher. 2000. "Facing the

Consequences: An Examination of Racial Discrimination in U.S. Public Schools." Oakland: ERASE Initiative, Applied Research Center. March.

Hall, Stuart. 1998. "Subjects in History: Making Diasporic Identities." In Wahneema Lubiano, ed., *The House that Race Built*. New York: Vintage Books.

Hollins, Etta. 1996. *Transforming Curriculum for a Culturally Diverse Society*. Mahwah, N.J.: Erlbaum.

————. 1990. "Debunking the Myth of a Monolithic White American Culture, or Moving Towards Cultural Inclusion." *American Behavioral Scientist* 34 (2), 201–9.

Holquist, Michael. 1990. *Dialogism: Bakhtin and His World*. London: Routledge.

hooks, bell. 1989. *Talking Back: Thinking Feminist, Thinking Black*. Boston: South End Press.

————. 1984. *Feminist Theory from Margin to Center*. Boston: South End Press.

Irvine, Jacqueline. 1997. *Critical Knowledge for Diverse Teachers*. Washington, D.C.: American Association of Colleges for Teacher Education.

Johnson, Wayne. 2000. "Make No Mistake About It." *California Educator* 4 (April), 3.

Jones, Marvin D. 1997. "Darkness Made Visible: Law, Metaphor, and the Racial Self." In Richard Delgado and Jean Stefancic, eds., *Critical White Studies: Looking Behind the Mirror*. Philadelphia: Temple University Press.

Kaye-Kantrowitz, Melanie. 1996. "Jews in the U.S.: The Rising Cost of Whiteness." In Becky Thompson and Sangeeta Tyagi, eds., *Names We Call Home: Autobiographies on Racial Identity*. New York: Routledge.

Keleher, Terry, Libero Della Piana, and Manijeh Gonzalez Fata. 1999. *Creating Crisis: How California Teaching Policies Aggravate Racial Inequalities in Public Schools*. Oakland: Applied Research Center. August.

Kelley, Ursula. 1997. *Schooling Desire*. New York: Routledge.

Kincheloe, Joel, Shirley R. Steinberg, Nelson M. Rodriguez, and Ronald E. Chennault, eds. 1999. *White Reign: Deploying Whiteness in America*. New York: St. Martin's Press.

King, Joyce. 1997. "Thank You for Opening Our Minds." In Joyce King and Etta Hollins, *Preparing Teachers for Cultural Diversity*. New York: Teachers College.

King, Joyce, and Etta Hollins. 1997. *Preparing Teachers for Cultural Diversity*. New York: Teachers College Press.

King, Joyce. 1994. "The Purpose of Schooling for African American Children: Including Cultural Knowledge." In Etta Hollins, Joyce King, and W. C. Hayman, eds., *Teaching Diverse Populations; Formulating a Knowledge Base*. Albany: State University of New York Press.

Kivel, Paul. 1997. *Uprooting Racism*. Philadelphia: New Society.

Kozol, Jonathan. 1992. *Savage Inequalities*. New York: HarperCollins.

Kreiger, Lisa. 1997. "Black Men Die Sooner." *San Francisco Examiner.* June 17.

Kumashiro, Kevin. 2000. "Towards a Theory of Anti-Oppressive Education." *Review of Educational Research* 70 (1), 25–55.

Ladson-Billings, Gloria. 2000. "Teaching in Dangerous Times." *Rethinking Schools* 14 (4), 1, 18–19.

———. 1995a. "Multicultural Teacher Education: Research Practices and Policy." In James A. Banks and Cherry A. McGee Banks, eds., *Multicultural Education*. New York: Wiley.

———. 1995b. "Towards a Theory of Culturally Relevant Pedagogy." *American Educational Research Journal* 323 (3), 465–92.

———. 1994a. *The Dreamkeepers: Successful Teachers of African American Children*. San Francisco: Jossey-Bass.

———. 1994b. "Who Will Teach Our Children: Preparing Teachers to Successfully Teach African American Students." In Etta Hollins, Joyce King, and W. C. Hayman, eds., *Teaching Diverse Populations*. Albany: State University of New York Press.

Lamont, Michele. 1999. Introduction to *The Cultural Territories of Race: Black and White Boundaries,* ed. Michele Lamont. Chicago: University of Chicago Press.

Lei, Joy L. 1998. "(Op)posing Representations: Disentangling the Model Minority and the Foreigner." Paper presented to the American Educational Research Association, San Diego, April 13–17.

Lesko, Nancy, and Leslie Bloom. 2000. "The Haunting of Multicultural Epistemology and Pedagogy." In Ram Mahalingham and Cameron McCarthy, eds., *Multicultural Curriculum: New Directions for Social Theory, Practice, and Policy*. New York: Routledge.

Lowen, James. 1995. *Lies My Teacher Told Me*. New York: Touchstone.

Lorde, Audre. 1984. *Sister Outsider*. Freedom, Calif.: Crossing Press.

Macedo, Donaldo. 1998. "Tongue-tying Multiculturalism." In Rudolfo Chavez-Chavez and James O'Donnell, eds., *Speaking the Unpleasant*. Albany: State University of New York Press.

Maher, Francis A. and Mary Kay Thompson Tetreault. 1997. "Learning in the Dark: How Assumptions of Whiteness Shape Classroom Knowledge." *Harvard Educational Review* 67 (2), 321–49.

Marable, Manning. "Class Matters: Economic Inequality and Black Politics." *Democratic Left* 27 (3), 12–15.

McAllister, Gretchen, and Jacqueline J. Irvine. 2000. "Crosscultural Competency and Multicultural Teacher Education." *Review of Educational Research* 70 (1), 3–25.

McCarthy, Cameron. 1998. *The Uses of Culture*. New York: Routledge.

McIntosh, Peggy. 1998. "White Privilege and Male Privilege: A Personal Account of Coming to See Correspondences Through Work in Women's Studies." In Margaret Anderson and Patricia Hill Collins, eds., *Race, Class, and Gender*. Belmont, Calif.: Wadsworth.

McLaren, Peter. 1994. "Multiculturalism and the Postmodern Critique: Toward a Pedagogy of Resistance and Transformation." In Henry A. Girous and Peter McLaren, eds., *Between Borders: Pedagogy and the Politics of Cultural Studies*. New York: Routledge.

Miller, Alice. 1984. *Thou Shalt Not Be Aware: Society's Betrayal of the Child*. New York: Meridian.

———. 1980. *For Your Own Good: Hidden Cruelty in Child Rearing and the Roots of Violence*. New York: Farrar and Strauss.

Milloy, Courtland. 1999. "A Look at Tragedy in Black, White." *Washington Post*, May 2.

Mollison, Andrew. 2000. "Test Scores Improving—For Most." *San Francisco Chronicle*, August 25.

Montecinos, Carmen. 1995. "Multicultural Teacher Education for a Culturally Diverse Teaching Force." In Renee Martin, ed., *Practicing What We Teach: Confronting Diversity in Teacher Education*. Albany: State University of New York Press.

Morrison, Toni. 1998. "Home." In Wahneema Lubiano, ed., *The House that Race Built*. New York: Vintage Books.

———. 1993. *Playing in the Dark: Whiteness and the Literary Imagination*. New York: Vintage Books.

Mun Wah, Lee, producer. 1994. *The Color of Fear*. Film. Berkeley: Stir Fry Productions.

Nieto, Sonia. 2000. *The Light in Their Eyes: Creating Multicultural Learning Communities*. New York: Teachers College Press.

———. 1996. *Affirming Diversity*. White Plains, N.Y.: Longman.

Noguera, Pedro, and Antwi Akom. 2000. "Disparities Demystified." *Nation*, June 5, 29–31.

Oakes, Jeannie. 1985. *Keeping Track: How Schools Structure Inequality*. New Haven: Yale University Press.

O'Conner, Carla. 1997. "Dispositions Towards Collective Struggle and Educational Resilience in the Inner City: A Case Analysis of Six African American High School Students." *American Educational Research Journal* 34 (4), 593–629.

Omi, Michael, and Howard Winant. 1993. "On the Theoretical Status of the Concept of Race." In Cameron McCarthy and Warren Crichlow, eds., *Race Identity and Representation in Education*. New York: Routledge.

Orfield, Gary. 1997. *The Growth of Segregation in American Schools: Changing Patterns of Segregation and Poverty Since 1968.* Alexandria, Va.: National Association of School Boards.

Ornstein, Peggy. 1994. *School Girls.* New York: Anchor.

Portes, Pedro. 1999. "Social and Psychological Factors in the Academic Achievement of Children of Immigrants: A Cultural History Puzzle." *American Educational Research Journal* 36 (3), 489–511.

Postnick-Goodwin, Sherry. 2000. "Show Us the Money." *California Educator* 4 (7), 6–18.

Rains, Francis. 1999. "Is the Benign Really Harmless?" In Joe L. Kinchelow, Shirley R. Steinberg, Nelson M. Rodriguez, and Ronald E. Chennault, eds., *White Reign: Deploying Whiteness in America.* New York: St. Martin's Press.

Richardson, Laurel. 1997. *Fields of Play.* New Brunswick, N.J.: Rutgers University Press.

Robertson, Judith P. 1997. "Popular Culture and the Education of the Female Primary-School Teacher." In Sharon Todd, ed., *Learning Desire: Perspectives on Pedagogy, Culture, and the Unsaid.* New York: Routledge.

Rojas, Patrisia, and Rebecca Gordon. 1999. "Just Facts: Racial Resegregation and Inequality in the Public Schools." *Colorlines* 2 (1), 10–11.

Ryan, William. 1971/1976. *Blaming the Victim.* New York: Vintage.

Salverson, Julie. 2000. "Anxiety and Contact in Attending to a Play About Landmines." In Roger Simon, Sharon Rosenberg, and Claudia Eppert, eds., *Between Hope and Despair: Pedagogy and the Representation of Historical Trauma.* Totowa, N.J.: Rowman and Littlefield.

Sanjek, Roger. 1994. "The Enduring Inequalities of Race." In Steven Gregory and Roger Sanjek, eds., *Race.* New Brunswick, N.J.: Rutgers University Press.

Shipler, David K. 1997. *A Country of Strangers: Blacks and Whites in America.* New York: Knopf.

Shuuja, Mwalimu. 1996. *Beyond Desegregation: The Politics of Quality in African American Schooling.* Thousand Oaks, Calif.: Corwin Press.

———. 1994. *Too Much Schooling, Too Little Education: A Paradox of Black Life in White Societies.* Trenton, N.J.: Africa World Press.

Simon, Roger I. 1994. "Forms of Insurgency in the Production of Popular Memories: The Columbus Quincentenary and the Pedagogy of Countercommemoration." In Henry A. Giroux and Peter McLaren, eds., *Between Borders: Pedagogy and the Politics of Cultural Studies.* New York: Routledge.

———. 1992. *Teaching Against the Grain: Texts for a Pedagogy of Possibility.* South Hadley, Mass.: Bergin and Garvy.

Sleeter, Christine. 1995. "Reflections on My Use of Multicultural and Critical

Pedagogy When Students Are White." In Christine E. Sleeter and Peter L. Mclaren, eds. *Multicultural Education, Critical Pedagogy, and the Politics of Difference.* Albany, N.Y.: State University of New York Press.

———. 1993. "How White Teachers Construct Race." In Cameron McCarthy and Warren Crichlow, eds., *Race, Identity, and Representation in Education.* New York: Routledge.

———. 1992. *Keepers of the American Dream: A Study of Staff Development and Multicultural Education.* London: Falmer Press.

———. 1991. *Empowerment Through Multicultural Education.* Albany: State University of New York Press.

Smart, Tim. 1999. "Pay Gap Widens Between Workers, Top Execs." *San Francisco Chronicle,* August 30.

Smith, Lillian. 1949. *Killers of the Dream.* New York: Norton.

Spelman, Elizabeth. 1997. *Fruits of Sorrow: Framing Our Attention to Suffering.* Boston: Beacon Press.

———. 1988. *Inessential Woman.* Boston: Beacon Press.

Steele, Claude. 1992. "Race and the Schooling of Black Americans." *Atlantic Monthly,* April, 68–78.

Tatum, Beverly. 1997. *Why Are All the Black Kids Sitting Together in the Cafeteria?* New York: Basic Books.

Tellez, Kip, and Sharon O'Malley. 1998. "Exploring the Use of History in Multicultural/Multilingual Teacher Education." In Rudolfo Chavez-Chavez and James O'Donnell, eds., *Speaking the Unpleasant.* Albany: State University of New York Press.

Thandeka. 1999. *Learning to Be White.* New York: Continuum.

Todd, Sharon. 1997a. "Desire in Rethinking Pedagogy." In Sharon Todd, ed., *Learning Desire: Perspectives on Pedagogy, Culture, and the Unsaid.* New York: Routledge.

———. 1997b. "Rethinking Differences, Disparity, and Desire." In Sharon Todd, ed., *Learning Desire: Perspectives on Pedagogy, Culture, and the Unsaid.* New York: Routledge.

Viadero, Debra. 2000. "Lags in Minority Achievement Defy Traditional Explanations." *Education Week,* March 22.

Waters, Mary. 1999. "Explaining the Comfort Factor: West Indian Immigrants Confront American Race Relations." In Michele Lamont, ed., *The Cultural Territories of Race: Black and White Boundaries.* Chicago: University of Chicago Press.

Weiner, Jon. 1999. "Holocaust Creationism: A Review of Peter Novick, 'The Holocaust in American Life.'" *Nation,* July 12, 25–30.

West, Cornel. 1998. "Race Matters." In Margaret L. Andersen and Patricia Hill Collins, eds., *Race, Class, and Gender.* New York: Wadsworth.

———. 1994. "Beyond Eurocentrism and Multiculturalism." *Toronto Public Access Collective.* Vol. 10, pp. 11–19.

———. 1993. "The New Cultural Politics of Difference." In Cameron McCarthy and Warren Crichlow, eds., *Race, Identity and Representation in Education.* New York: Routledge.

Williams, Patricia J. 1997. *Seeing a Color-Blind Future: The Paradox of Race.* New York: Noonday Press.

———. 1991. *The Alchemy of Race and Rights: Diary of a Law Professor.* Cambridge: Harvard University Press.

Winant, Howard. 1998. "Racial Dualism at Century's End." In Wahneema Lubiano, ed., *The House that Race Built.* New York: Vintage Books.

———. 1997. "Behind Blue Eyes: Whiteness and Contemporary U.S. Racial Politics." In Michelle Fine, Lois Weis, Linda C. Powell, and L. Mun Wong, eds., *Off White: Readings on Race, Power, and Society.* New York: Routledge.

Woodson, Carter G. 1993. *The Mis-Education of the Negro.* Trenton, N.J.: Africa World Press.

Yamato, Gloria. 1998. "Something About the Subject Makes It Hard to Name." In Margaret L. Andersen and Patricia Hill Collins, eds., *Race, Class, and Gender.* New York: Wadsworth.

Young, Alford A., Jr. 1999. "Navigating Race: Getting Ahead in the Lives of "Rags to Riches" Young Black Men." In Michele Lamont, ed., *The Cultural Territories of Race: Black and White Boundaries.* Chicago: University of Chicago Press.

Zeichner, Ken, and Karen Hoeft. 1996. "Teacher Socialization for Cultural Diversity." In J. Sikula, Thomas Buttery, and Edith Guyton, eds., *Handbook of Research on Teacher Education.* 2d edition. New York: Macmillan.

Zinn, Howard. 1995. *A People's History.* New York: HarperCollins.

Index

ableism, 47
abused children, and understanding, 61
activism, 62, 93, 100n17, 103n32
addiction, 53, 66, 145. *See also* alcoholism; drugs; substance abusers
African Americans: and learning about, 152–54; and perception of Jews, 39; and student underachievement, 5, 12, 102–05, 106; and World War II era, 37. *See also* Black culture; institutional racism; internalized racism; media; prison; racism; slavery
alcoholism, 45, 53, 55–56, 61, 66, 111, 116, 118, 149, 156, 159
anger, and expression/suppression, 78–79, 108, 117–20; and moral vs. defensive, 109–14
anti-Semitism, 40, 42, 47, 48. *See also* Jews
antipathy, 104, 117
anxiety, and learning to listen, 127–30
assimilation, vs. militancy, 104

Baldwin, James, 91, 93, 117, 134
bigotry, 26, 63, 132, 170
Black attitude, 17, 140
Black classrooms, and fear of, 33
Black culture: and confusing with drug culture, 53, 144; and distinctive values/traditions, 104n38; and fear of poverty; and ignoring own, 147
Black Panthers, 52, 99
blond-haired girl story, 18–21, 32, 53, 69, 73, 77–81, 94–95, 113–14, 117–18, 120, 122, 126
Board of Education, Brown v., 37

Boot Camp for Teachers, 2, 51, 63, 95
boundaries. *See* limits, setting
Brown v. Board of Education, 37
bussing, 18, 100n18, 102n30

Chinese Americans, 5n10, 12, 99–100, 107, 112, 150
Civil Rights movement, 38, 39, 41, 46, 52, 99n16, 100
classism, 5n10, 48
color-blindness, 39, 63, 100
color, and first contact, 102
Color of Fear, The (film), 65, 70–73, 76–78, 82, 83, 93, 95–96, 99, 110, 118, 123n20, 129
credibility, and challenging, 138, 140
criminal justice system, 4, 123. *See also* prisons
crisis classrooms, 12–13, 51–55, 60
critical multiculturalism, 92–94, 97, 121
cultural deficit, 103
cultures, and learning about, 153–54

defensive anger, 109–14
Delpit, Lisa, 31, 89, 104, 124n25, 147, 148n2, 153, 158n3
denial, and moral anger, 112
denial of racism, by whites, 133–34
desegregation, 45, 100, 102n30, 103–04
despair, 120n20, 124–25, 127
Diary of Anne Frank, The, 42
discipline, classroom, 2, 5, 29, 32–33, 54–55, 148–49, 153
diversity courses, and teacher training, 3–6, 48, 106, 160
drugs, 53, 55–56, 61, 66, 142, 144–45, 149

dysfunctional homes, 12, 142–46. *See
also* alcoholism; drugs; violence

Ellsworth, Elizabeth, and mode of
address, 129
emotion: and racism, 78–79; in teaching,
77, 83, 108–12
empathy: and family dysfunction, 116;
and moral anger, 111
equal opportunity, 44, 94, 100, 104, 167
ethics, vs. rules, 55
Ethnic Notions (film), 36
Eurocentricism, 9, 53, 103, 134, 138
Evers, Medgar, 46
exploitation: and "giving back," 154; and
teaching to recognize, 3; and violence,
54; and white privilege, 124, 135
Eyes on the Prize (film), 46

fairness, and classroom discipline, 21,
148–49. *See also* blond-haired girl
story; Ms. Crutch story
fear, and dysfunctional homes, 144–45;
and racism, 81, 82, 121–24
Fields of Play (Richardson), 3n7

"giving back," 72, 112–13, 154
Gone with the Wind (film), 35
guilt, 82, 108, 116, 124n25, 128, 135

heteroglossia (multiplicity of languages),
91–92, 107, 120
heterosexism, 47, 48. *See also* sexism
history, and European perspective, 38
home environment. *See also* alcoholism;
drugs; dysfunctional homes; violence
home ethnic culture, and assuming Black
student antipathy, 104–05
hooks, bell, 79, 110

inequality, and teaching to ignore, 38
injustice, and teaching to recognize, 3. *See
also* social injustice
institutional racism, 3, 5–6, 32, 44,
52–53, 90, 94, 112, 132–33, 152,
165–66, 169–70
integration, of schools, 18. *See also*
desegregation; segregation
internalized oppression, 47, 167

internalized racism, 3, 48, 90, 96n9, 132,
134–35, 138, 147, 153

Jews, 37, 39–42, 73

King, Joyce, 3n6, 104nn38,39,42, 109n5
King, Martin Luther, Jr., 46, 84, 99n16
King, Rodney, 84, 101, 123n18

Ladson-Billings, Gloria, 1n3, 6n9,
104n41, 105n45, 147, 158n2
language: and academic, 97, 108;
and antiracist, 95, 159; and body,
62; and English, 90, 92, 152, 170;
and oppression, 47, 77, 91; and
multiculturalism, 91–96, 108; and
national, 107, 160
Latinos, 5, 6, 12, 90, 98n13, 101, 103n32,
105, 125, 134–35, 151–54
learning disabilities, 12
liberal multiculturalism, 94–95
limits, setting, 153
Lorde, Audre, 108

Malcolm X, 99n16, 144
media: and negative Black images, 84; and
portraying demise of racism, 100–01;
and unconscious processes, 126
Mein Kampf (Hitler), 42n9
militancy: and Black Perspective, 46; and
conflicting meanings, 91–94, 99; and
nonviolence, 62; and social justice, 107;
and violence, 72, 75
morality, and learning about, 153
moral anger, 109–14
mourning, and learning to listen, 127–30
Ms. Crutch story, 28–32, 54, 94, 120,
126, 137–38
multiculturalism, critical, 92–94, 97,
121

Nature of Prejudice, The (Allport), 38
Nazi Germany, 42. *See also* anti-Semitism;
Jews; *Mein Kampf*

oppression, 1n1, 47–48, 77, 91, 96n9,
97, 103n36, 132, 138, 158n3, 166, 167
Other People's Children (Delpit), 31, 104,
124n25, 148n2, 153, 158n3

paranoia, 8, 117, 134, 140, 166
parents, and intervention, 22
pedagogy, 1n3, 80, 102n31
personal, vs. educational, 72, 156–58
perspective, vs. irrationality, 137–38
pity, 112–14
Playing in the Dark (Morrison), 35
politeness, and language, 108–09, 119
poverty, 5n10, 10, 37, 47, 53, 100–01,
    103, 105, 147, 166–68
power: and institutionalized oppression,
    92–94; and language of, 97–98, 153
Power Shuffle (alliance-building exercise),
    47–48, 70
pride, and culture, 145–46
prisons, 5, 108, 139, 144
public schools: and ethnic makeup, 2n5,
    102n30; and lack of resources, 12

race baiting, 137
racial autobiographies, 3, 17, 89, 117
racism: compared to rape, 162, 169, 170;
    and defining, 90n2, 131–34; and early
    memories of, 17–24; and effects of, 5,
    10; and explaining to children, 25–27;
    and learning, 35–38; and overcoming,
    167; and teacher to teacher, 28–32,
    33; and teacher training, 8–9; and
    unlearning, 47–48, 147, 152, 165. *See
    also* institutional racism; internalized
    racism; reverse racism
rape: and blaming the victim, 140;
    compared to racism, 162, 169, 170
rednecks, 61, 91, 120, 121–23, 162, 164
resistance: and African Americans,
    104n38; and anti-Semitism, 42; and
    learning to listen, 1n1, 127–30; and
    understanding own cultural history, 17,
    152
reverse racism, 63, 66, 132
riots, 84, 100
role playing (classroom exercise), 8,
    51–60, 64, 67, 70–74, 79, 83, 114,
    124, 128, 162
rules, vs. ethics, 55

sarcasm, 25–26
schools, and integration of, 18. *See also*
    desegregation; segregation

School Girls (book), 83
segregation, 17, 36–38, 102, 103n36, 104
self, as others see us, 156–58
self-defense, vs. violence, 21
self-esteem, 24, 27–28
self-exploration, and understanding
    racism, 17, 48
sexism, 45, 47, 89, 97, 112, 138
Simpson, O. J., 102
skin color, 90
slavery, 1n1, 5n10, 17n1, 40, 101nn21,
    24, 112, 134
Smith, Susan, 102
social class, 5, 6n19, 43n12, 47, 66, 71,
    83, 97
social death, 104
social justice: and commitment to
    teaching, 47, 145; and diversity
    courses, 5, 76, 119; and Judaism,
    42–43; and militancy, 95, 99, 107,
    150
sorrow, 124–25, 127
substance abusers, as teachers, 154

Thomas, Clarence, 138
Till, Emmett, 38
To Kill a Mockingbird (film), 84, 100
trauma, and learning to listen, 127–30
trust: of adults, 139, 143–45; and betrayal
    170

unconscious processes, 9, 36, 48, 76, 98,
    121–26, 128–29, 168
underachievement, and nonwhite
    students, 5

victimization: and indifference to, 3;
    and misplaced blame, 103n33, 140,
    162, 169; vs. oppression, 69; by peers,
    18–21; by teachers, 21–24
violence: as deterrent to exploitation, 54,
    120, 122; and family dysfunction, 55,
    61; and fear of, 126, 145; and media
    portrayal, 101, 123–24; vs. militancy,
    93, 95, 99n16; and resistance to racism,
    153; vs. self-defense, 21; and white
    middle-class culture, 66, 118

West, Cornel, 37

white privilege: classroom exercise, 67,
68n1, 90, 133; and colorblindness,
112; as disabling to whites, 124, 134,
162; and dominance, 5n15, 96, 136,
139, 165; and multiculturalism, 94;
and responsibilities of, 147, 156; and
violence, 54

white supremacy, 10, 37, 38, 46, 63, 93,
162, 164
whiteness, and aspiring to, 42–43
whites, and Black perspective of, 63–64
Williams, Patricia, 17n1, 121
World War II, 37, 99